Happy Bir[thday]
Sherwin

May You Have Many

Frank and Rudi
73

The Wizard of Westwood

The Wizard
of Westwood

Coach John Wooden
and His UCLA Bruins

Dwight Chapin & Jeff Prugh

 Illustrated with Photographs

HOUGHTON MIFFLIN COMPANY BOSTON
1973

ISBN: 0-395-15477-4
Library of Congress Catalog Card Number: 72-6808

Printed in the United States of America

For permission to reprint copyrighted
material the authors are grateful to the
following publishers and copyright proprietors:
Irving Music, Inc., for the lines from
"We've Only Just Begun" on page 41: Copyright
1970, Irving Music, Inc. (BMI). All rights
reserved. Used by Permission. Lyrics: Paul
Williams. Music: Roger Nichols;
"Glory Road": Stonebridge Music for the lines
from "Glory Road" on page 113: "Glory Road"
by Neil Diamond Copyright © 1969
by Stonebridge Music. Used by permission;
"Holy Rolling": Screen Gems–Columbia Music Inc.
and Summerhill Songs, Inc., for the lines from
"Holy Rolling" on page 237: "Holy Rolling
(Weil-Mann) Copyright © 1971 by Screen Gems–
Columbia Music Inc. and Summerhill Songs, Inc.
Used by permission of Screen Gems–Columbia
Music, Inc. All rights reserved.

For Evelyn, Carla, and Adam

ACKNOWLEDGMENTS

To JOHN AND NELL WOODEN, who gave freely of their limited time to a project that wasn't theirs, without questioning why — a trait that has been common to them in the years we've known them.

To all the players, coaches, managers, officials, and rivals, past and present, who talked with remarkable candor and often rare insight about a man not one of them doubts as a coach.

To families and friends, to an employer who often looked the other way when inspiration got in the way of more clearly defined priorities, to scores of helpful journalistic colleagues.

To a society that can accept that life does not begin and endure and end with yet another championship flag — that basketball is not just a winning, twenty-foot shot at the buzzer.

To George Morgan, a perceptive friend from the start. To John Sandbrook, often a critic of UCLA athletics, but an invaluable aid. To Vic Kelley, master of the Manhattan. To Stan Troutman, Norm Schindler, and George Bloodgood, who opened photographic doors. To Leslie Innis, who helped unscramble some of the tapes.

And to Jim Perry, Tim Salinger, Walter Coulter, Chuck Garrity, Jack Simpson, and Marilyn White, who — in different ways — brought light to a night that was frighteningly dark.

It's More Than a Game

SOME NIGHTS you wake up in a cold sweat.

You dream you're in a giant airport and standing on one of those belts that move people from the terminal to the baggage area — where luggage is disgorged onto *another* moving belt.

It's all so efficient and so impersonal and as you ride on that belt and watch the faces coming the *other* way, you hear that voice, beautifully modulated, horribly prefabricated, saying to you in precise, tape-recorded tones: "Please hold handrail and stand to the right. If you wish to pass, you may do so on the left."

You're a sportswriter and your friends always say: "Man, would I like to have *your* job!" But they don't know about the cold breaded veal cutlet in Knoxville with the sauce congealed on the top; the motel room in Houston where the art on the wall is a bowl of fruit, the sink is caked with axle grease, and the linen hasn't been changed since the Truman administration; the cab driver in Seattle who almost runs over you because you forget to give him a tip.

Or a million things — the fight to meet deadlines and make planes . . . to rent cars and sleep when your watch says it's midnight, Eastern Standard Time, and your body says it's 9 P.M., Pacific Standard Time . . . to forget a topcoat when it's ten below in Chicago or take only your warmest wool suit and find out it's ninety-five above in Washington.

On the road . . . gone again . . . stuff the suitcase. Do I

have enough underwear and socks? Have I packed my razor, my toothbrush, my aspirin?

And then you're at the end of the moving belt and you have to remember to step off briskly or you get dumped on your can. Alongside you is a man who could be your father or grandfather — or *anybody's* father or grandfather. He looks the type.

You like him, this strange, little man — half hard, half homespun — who has accomplished wonders that no one else will accomplish and is loved and admired and envied and hated by many but is known intimately by almost no one. You think about the eras he has crossed, the championship flags that hang in his gymnasium, the changes — not all small — he has made, and the values he has kept.

He is a coach. Basketball will be his life until the end and his achievements will remain huge but he seems somehow uneasy through it all, unequipped to handle the incredible pressures that society and success have placed on him — and that he has placed on himself.

You watch him. You write about him. You interpret him, because that's your job.

And you make up your mind that while his world seems constricted in the semiunreality of fun and games, it's much wider than that — not just a simple "who won and who lost" and "who scored how many points" kind of thing.

His story is a story of life in America. Not just one man's life. Everybody's life. A story of young and old, of black and white, of big cities and small towns, of newness and antiquity, of camaraderie and confrontation, of ecstasy and agony, of generation gaps, and of change and unchange.

You, the writer, fit somewhere in the mainstream of these extremes — in age, in life-style, in philosophy. Your profession enables you to be uniquely a part of them, as well as apart from them. You think to yourself that maybe you'll find a way to etch these impressions into a book some day.

And then you're at the baggage area where people — real

people — are waiting. Girls preparing to embrace their boy-friends who play on the team — sometimes two or three girls waiting for the same embarrassed boyfriend. Wives. Grand-children who see the little coach and call him "Papa." People who are elated or depressed or parked in the no parking zone in front of the airport and hoping they won't get a ticket.

Travelers, home, and you a traveling man. You've been there before and you'll be there again, probably with the UCLA bas-ketball team.

It's your life. And it's John Robert Wooden's life.

CONTENTS

ILLUSTRATIONS

Wooden listens intently to the late Dr. Ralph Bunche

Jamming in a two-handed, back-handed stuff shot as a UCLA sophomore, Lew Alcindor unleashes his most spectacular weapon against Stanford

Lew Alcindor, right arm high above basket, blocks a shot against Minnesota

Before UCLA's historic loss to Houston in the Astrodome, Assistant Coach Jerry Norman chats with Athletic Director J. D. Morgan, while Lew Alcindor gazes warily at the record crowd of 55,000 plus and Wooden looks on benignly

Elvin Hayes of Houston soaring high over Lew Alcindor to score in Cougars' upset win over the Bruins

Basket net draped around his neck and finger held aloft to signify "We're number one," Lew Alcindor stands with Wooden after UCLA's third consecutive win of the Alcindor Era, 92–72, over Purdue

UCLA's Sidney Wicks grabs rebound away from Artis (Batman) Gilmore of Jacksonville University during Bruins' 80–69 championship win in 1970

Wooden samples some of his 60th birthday cake in prepractice ceremony at Pauley Pavilion, and Curtis Rowe and Sidney Wicks sample the punch

In a tense moment, Wooden exhorts his team with a clenched fist

John Wooden The Competitor explodes in a rage while calling a time out (Associated Press)

Bill Walton:

  Snares a rebound against Iowa State

  Turns to look for breaking teammates

  And quickly throws "outlet" pass triggering the fast break

The Wooden family group

Unless otherwise noted, all photographs are by Stan Troutman and Norm Schindler and are supplied courtesy of the University of California at Los Angeles.

Man or Superman?

"Your purpose in life is simply
to help on the purpose of the
universe. By higher and higher
organization man must become
superman, and superman
super-superman . . ."

— George Bernard Shaw

CHAPTER 1

Who IS That Masked Man?

GENIUS.
 Dictator.
 Patriarch.
 Little Man from Pepperidge Farm.
 Wizard.
 Hypocrite.
 Which one is the real John Robert Wooden, the most success-
ful coach in college basketball history, and — despite what
backers of Adolph Rupp, Henry Iba, Phog Allen, Clair Bee,
and Nat Holman might think — probably the best, too?

The man is a paradox, a ruler who sometimes doesn't rule
but a leader who almost never loses. No teams have done what
his teams have done. Six straight national championships, eight
in the last nine years. Three perfect seasons in that time and a
251-15 record. And not one defeat over the last half-dozen
seasons in games he *had* to win.

Think of the other great teams in sports history. The New
York Yankees, in their glory time, had Joe DiMaggio in center
field for thirteen seasons, and Mickey Mantle was there for
eighteen. The Boston Celtic dynasty, for a dozen years, was
built around bearded center Bill Russell. The faces at UCLA
have changed at least every three years, except for one face —
John Wooden's.

The Yankees and the Celtics, too, could lose three games out
of seven and still win their championships. And fat paychecks

await even the *losers* in professional basketball, baseball, and football. In college basketball, *one* defeat in tournament play eliminates you, and the "prize" is a return ticket on the 7 A.M. flight out of Provo or Albuquerque or Corvallis. But UCLA has not lost — in thirty-two straight tournament games stretching over almost a decade. That is the statistic that impresses Wooden himself the most.

"One loss and you get knocked out of business," he says. "On certain occasions, teams of mine have had bad nights in the NCAA. And, on other occasions, opponents have had good nights. Either possibility is all it takes to beat you."

Some have said he is an uncomplicated man who deals only in basics and simplicities. He does *his* thing; he dares you to stop it, in the manner of Lombardi and the Packers, if not with the same bombast. Fundamentals, conditioning, and hard work. Put them together, keep them together, and you win. That is John Wooden's outward image — the virtuous achiever. But is that tiny smile of his sincere or sanctimonious?

He wears a saintly, professorial countenance that cuts two ways. He looks like an English teacher (which he was, for eleven years) and talks like a church deacon (which he is, at the Santa Monica First Christian Church). He's a genuinely devoted family man, who in 1964 was named California's Father of the Year, and he is as proud of that award as any he's ever won. He shuns tobacco, strong drink, profanity, and doesn't like modern movies because there's too much sex in them.

"He is," says wife Nell Wooden, "the same man I married forty years ago. He hasn't changed."

But beneath the placid exterior is a fierce competitive spirit — a need to grab the lance and do battle — that has extended through his life since he started shooting at an Indiana hayloft basket with his three brothers, half a century ago.

The competition, more than anything, has shaped him, driven him, and perhaps obscured other values. It has also led to immense success that has exacted a price from him.

His tone of voice, the deliberate pace, the Hoosier twang, and the unvarnished eloquence are often a smoke screen for the raging inferno inside him, for his enormous self-pride:

"You get a good run of players — a dominant player like Alcindor — and people say you're supposed to win three championships, and we did. But Ohio State was supposed to win three with Lucas and Havlicek and that bunch and it won only one. Kansas was supposed to win three with Chamberlain and one year they didn't even win their conference championship. We were supposed to do it and we *did* it.

"For the most part, we've done what we're supposed to do. There's no way you can have consistent success without players. *No one* can win without material. But not everyone can win *with* material . . ."

As he talks, his furrowed, sixty-two-year-old face wears a mostly austere, partly benign expression, set off by a narrow, prominent nose, horn-rimmed glasses, economy-sized ears, and short, brownish hair flecked with gray and always neatly combed. He stands about 5-feet-10½ and weighs 180 pounds — the same dimensions he carried as a fireball of an All-America guard at Purdue University — but the bulk has settled mainly around his midriff. And the Wooden walk consists of brisk, mincing steps with his body slightly bent because of a back injury he suffered while in the navy during World War II.

The conservative appearance — and myriad other plain qualities — camouflage the ferocity in John Wooden.

He comes across, as ex-protégé Lew Alcindor (now Kareem Abdul-Jabbar) wrote in his autobiography, like the "Pepperidge Farm commercial with the old guy driving the buggy." Or, as Alcindor's mother said when he came to recruit Lew, "more like a minister than a coach." Or, as seen on television by millions of people after all the championships, the ever-humble, ever-gracious winner, praising his own team but lauding the opponent, too.

But he is so much more than these flickering impressions.

❋

Here is John Robert Wooden, the picture of contrasts:

Is he invincible?

"A guy asked me how I thought John Wooden could be stopped," said Abe Lemons, the Oklahoma City basketball coach, "and my reply was, 'Wait, and some night when the moon is full and at the stroke of midnight, drive a silver spike in his heart . . . he is unreal.'"

"I've found it difficult to say 'no,'" says John Wooden. "I've accepted more clinics and coaching schools and speaking engagements than I would have liked to.

"When I had that one hospitalization in nineteen sixty-seven, it wasn't from the pressures of winning. I had a *real* bad schedule — I was hopping from plane to plane, speaking here, taking off there, speaking again, and I just missed being on a plane that crashed out of Atlanta. I got run down physically and it all happened on the way back from our anniversary dinner.

"On San Vicente Street things started spinning and I just stopped driving. I felt this must be the way you feel if you get drunk. I thought the cars were jumping out at me but they were only parked along the sides of the street. The only thing is, I had control to pull off and tell Nell, 'Honey, I'm not feeling well; you drive.'

"When we parked out in front of our apartment I walked in and everything was fine — no problem. Then, about three-thirty in the morning, I awakened and I was trying to hold myself on the bed. Everything was going. And my head. Talk about headaches — oh, ho, ho, I had the headache of all headaches. I felt I was having a brain hemorrhage. I could see — a not very pleasant thing — my brains and blood running down the walls where my head is split. I *see* that! I'm not imagining. I could just see it.

"I tried to get out of bed without letting Nell know — crawl out — but I couldn't do it. Nell called an ambulance and I was taken to the hospital. I was hospitalized ten days and then home three weeks. I walked down to the ocean every day with my little walking stick and talked with the other old people [laughter]. I made a lot of friends down there."

Is winning really everything?

"I've never liked to see players *cry* when they lose a game," says John Wooden. "I don't measure all success by winning and losing. There's no way it [winning] should mean that much. I really feel that's true. I want to do well for the peace and satisfaction I get doing well but we've done well when we didn't win."

John Wooden, speaking to his players at a time out during the Washington game at Seattle in 1971, when UCLA trailed and appeared not only on the verge of losing the game but the Pacific 8 title as well:

"It's not your fault but you've given in to a permissive society. You've lost the conference race and a chance at another national championship."

Is he a graceful or graceless loser?

"I've heard people say, 'If there's anything I *don't* like it's a good loser,'" says John Wooden. "Well, I disagree with that. I don't know if it's a question of semantics or not, but I want to be able to feel — for the most part — that if we're beaten, we're beaten. And why harp and bellyache about it?"

A former Indiana State player remembers a different Coach Wooden:

"We were beaten by Evansville — by one point — and he thought the officiating was bad. He didn't give up on it, either. We all went to the locker room afterward but the coach was still hot. All of a sudden, he took off his coat. He was gonna fight one of the officials. We all sorta held him back."

Is he model coach or miscast man?

"John Wooden," says former Bruin Ron Pearson, "is the finest man I ever met."

"When I quit officiating in nineteen sixty-three," says Al Lightner, "John Wooden wrote me the dangdest letter, said I was the best official he ever saw, and wished me luck. He didn't have to do that . . . Our only association was on the floor, him as a coach and me as an official. If all coaches were like him I'd never have had any trouble."

"Never in the field of college athletics," says Dr. Franklin Murphy, ex-UCLA chancellor, "have I known a more honorable and decent human being than John Wooden."

A recent Bruin player sits on an airplane trip home from Chicago, Coach Wooden in the seat in front of him listening to classical stereo music through earplugs, and says: "I can't say anything against him as a coach. But as a man . . . well, he's not sensitive. He doesn't try to understand any of us, the changes in society, the different role of the athlete and the coach."

A former coaching rival says: "Wooden is a completely different person than what he appears when you see him in practice, or when he's talking to the press. And most of the coaches don't like him because he's never really been one of the guys. He doesn't have to be a bad guy like the rest of us, but he doesn't have to remain apart from us, either. It's not a hate deal with me, but it's just that he's not always the same guy that everybody sees. Wooden acts one way sometimes, another way other times. I don't like that. He doesn't smoke, drink, or swear. He just eats candy bars behind garage doors."

Is he a true sportsman?

It's half time of the UCLA–Ohio State game in the 1972 Bruin Classic at Pauley Pavilion. A Buckeye player is at the free-throw line, shooting a foul shot, and the crowd hoots derisively. Wooden stands at midcourt, raising his arms, trying to bring quiet.

Later, after UCLA has won easily and Wooden is receiving the victor's trophy, he speaks into the microphone: "Thanks for your support but just be *for* us. Root hard for our team but don't get on the other team."

Switch reels to an incident in the early 1960s.
A game at Berkeley. Wooden has hurled every verbal weapon but profanity at a Cal player. The player fouls out late in the game and somebody throws a towel at him to wipe his sweaty face. "Better take that towel with you," Wooden yells. "You'll need it, since you've been crying so much." The player screams back, "You goddamned son of a bitch!"

Is it all sweetness and light?

"It's a joy," a letter writer says, "to watch the first five of UCLA get a game into control. They move with grace and elegance, and it is art. Then Wooden sends in his remaining seven, and it becomes all high spirits, rambunctiousness and circus. The team is one of the ornaments of our time. And Wooden is a great man."

"I am sure John has some faults," says Abe Lemons. "There is no way he can be as he seems . . . sitting on the bench with a rolled-up program, gently tapping it on his other hand or his chin, legs crossed, as if he was watching a ballet . . ."

It is the 1971 Western Regionals at Salt Lake City, UCLA is eleven points down to Long Beach State in the second half, playing artlessly, and it appears the dynasty finally has crumbled. A large vein in Wooden's head stands out. He is furious, smashing the program from one hand to the other and telling his team:
"You're nothing but a bunch of All-American woman chasers and hopheads!"

Is he really only one-dimensional?

"Why are you writing a book about John Wooden?" a friend asks. "He seems so bland, so dull, so unexciting. You know, home and hearth, church and family, the original Mr. Goody Two-Shoes."

"John Wooden," wrote Sid Ziff in the Los Angeles *Times*, "is an unexciting intellectual whose teams play wildly exciting basketball."

"Did you ever know anybody who did *not* have strong opinions about Wooden?" says a man close to UCLA players. "One way or the other. He's like anybody else. You can call him a no-good bastard or God or something in between. Whatever you call him, you still have strong opinions about him."

"Wooden is a salesman . . . cunning," says an ex-Bruin reserve. "I remember him recruiting me, telling me that I had a future at UCLA because they *always* had one 'little guard.' He gets you all hyped up to wear that Bruin blue and gold. But it doesn't always pan out; it didn't for me."

Is he virtuous or venomous?

Hollis Johnson, lunch-counter proprietor and long-time friend of John Wooden's:
"I think there are only a few *great* people who come along. There's a lotta good people. But I think you only see one like John Wooden just every now and then. I've met a jillion coaches in my time, I guess, but . . . well, he's a little different. He really is."

A former Bruin: "I wish just once he'd swear at me — use *all* the words. He puts more venom into his 'Goodness gracious sakes alive!' than any Marine drill sergeant or hippie protestor I've ever heard."

Is he a helper of others but not himself?

Eddie Sheldrake was a member of Wooden's first three UCLA teams. Shortly after graduation, his father died. Not long after that, his wife became critically ill with cancer and subsequently died. John and Nell Wooden helped raise $4000 to partially cover Eddie's medical bills.
"They baby-sat with my kids while I visited my wife, too," Sheldrake says. "Visited her themselves, gave me money. And the coach's doctor took over my wife's case and eventually canceled all the bills.

"I might disagree with John sometimes, get angry at him, but I'm indebted to him."

Sheldrake again: "As anyone gets older it gets tougher, and politically and racially things are rougher, too. But John could have made it less rough if he'd spoken out — stuck his neck out more.

"For instance, a few years ago there were some complaints about his bench conduct after some games in Northern California and the conference commissioner wrote John a letter berating him — saying he was a detriment to the game, not an asset.

"John should have fought back but he didn't. So many people look up to him. There are a lot of people on his side and he should speak out, discuss things for them.

"I think in the early years he really enjoyed coaching and in looking at what his players did and became after they got out of school. Now I think he just wants to win — and get the season over with."

Contrasts, then, are perhaps the best clues to his character. But there are others — his dress, his demeanor, his tastes in food and entertainment, his life-style.

His clothes are conservative, generally pinstripes and subdued colors (blue, green, and brown), and he gets them gratis from Gilbert's men's store in South Bend, Indiana, where he used to coach high school basketball, in exchange for making television commercials for the store. Recently, and somewhat reluctantly, he has acquired double-knit suits with wide lapels and slightly flared trousers. And it wasn't until three years ago that he finally wore colored and striped shirts. "This one young coach's wife came up to me," said Nell Wooden, "and said she's so-o-o-o glad he is because her husband used to wear only white shirts because Johnny Wooden wore nothing but white."

If he is nervous or tense, he rarely betrays it. Away from the basketball floor, he moves in a state of dignified, sophisticated calm, although a certain shyness shows through. And he is devoid of any backslapping effervescence or showmanship. He takes walks in the early morning, naps before games, and can't sleep very much after them because, as one former assistant put it, he is so "emotionally caught up" in the heat of the game. "You could set off a bomb or yell 'Fire!' and John would never hear it."

As for his eating habits, a nutritionist might call them "atrocious." "He eats everything," says trainer Ducky Drake. "He might down a bowl of chili and then follow it with a hot-fudge sundae." Nell Wooden calls him a "crazy eater" who has had digestive troubles lately. "His favorite food is baked chicken and dressing," she said. "It used to be Swiss steak . . . but *my* Swiss steak."

Hobbies? Wooden has none except his family, although he enjoys reading, watching movies, playing cards, and poetry. His heroes are Shakespeare, Saint Francis of Assisi, Zane Grey (he has the complete collection), Scott, Byron, Shelley, Tennyson, Poe, Whittier, Whitman, Longfellow.

T. S. Eliot? "No," he says, "I'm not fond of the modern poets." He reads the Bible daily.

He writes poetry, which he confesses "is not very good" and flows coarsely and haltingly like the red Burma Shave signs that repose alongside the highways of rural America. Actually, he prefers others' poetry to his own, and much of it is found on the walls of his office or in a large zipper notebook also containing epigrams and homilies he has savored for years. A sample:

> *Talent is God-given, be humble;*
> *Fame is man-given, be thankful;*
> *Conceit is self-given, be careful.*

For movie entertainment, Wooden has always liked Western shoot-'em-ups, starting with Hoot Gibson, Buck Jones, and Tom Mix and continuing through Gary Cooper, John Wayne, Gregory Peck, and Kirk Douglas.

"He gets them on so loud on television I can't hear *anything*," says Nell Wooden. "The bigger the fights, the better he likes them."

And the "R" and "X"-rated sex and violence films? Wooden has seen some on road trips, but the main message they held for him was "indecent exposure. I don't know if the acting was good in *Straw Dogs* or not. I don't know how somebody is supposed to act while being raped."

The Wooden home is a comfortable, one-bedroom-and-den apartment on a quiet street in Santa Monica, a few miles west of UCLA toward the ocean. The furnishings include Currier and Ives prints ("American Homestead") over the sofa and a small table that contains books but is really a cribbage board. On the bookshelves are Tolstoy's *War and Peace*, Herman Wouk's *The Winds of War*, *The Christmas Carols of Rod Mc-Kuen* (given to Wooden by his grandchildren), and a book called *Prescription for Living*, in which Wooden's definition of success is published along with similar contributions from such diverse personalities as Billy Graham, John Updike, George McGovern, and Mae West. The dozens of record albums reflect subdued musical tastes.

In a small adjoining den are mementos from Wooden's half century in basketball: old photos, trophies, Perma-Plaqued *Sports Illustrated* covers picturing several star UCLA players, sports books, and a small printed letter of which Wooden seems especially proud. It is entitled "Our Coach," signed and presented to him by the 1943 South Bend Central High varsity before he departed for naval service, and it reflects a simpler era, unencumbered by player protests and disciplinary challenges of today:

"To you, Mr. John Wooden, the best friend, coach and advisor any group of boys could ever have. We look to you as our second father, our guiding ideal. We appreciate your ceaseless efforts in our behalf, in school as well as on the athletic field. We feel proud to have served under a man so highly respected as you are.

Yes, to you coach J. Wooden, we give our unexpressible gratitude and thanks. You're really tops. An All-Time All-American and an All-American all the time."

John Wooden, man and coach, a superlative tactician who is often characterized as a neophyte recruiter. "I don't enjoy it — I never have," says Wooden, who has turned loose assistants such as Jerry Norman and Denny Crum to assemble his championship teams. Or maybe he will visit a prospect (or parents) himself, if necessary, as he did when he landed Alcindor and Bill Walton, the biggest and brightest stars of the UCLA dynasty.

Still, UCLA's seemingly self-perpetuating success makes recruiting easier. And John Wooden's saintly demeanor alone makes him a formidable proselytizer in the living rooms of prospects' parents. Says a rival coach: "We thought we had a kid sewed up, but then Jesus Christ walked in. The kids' parents about fell over. How can you recruit against Jesus Christ?"

You learn more about the man, too, by his superstitions, although he doesn't call them that because they imply "fear": the silver crucifix, the "wishing stone," and the lucky penny he carries in his pants' pocket at every game, or the carry-over from his baseball-playing days in which he finds a hairpin and attaches it to the nearest piece of wood. "It meant you'd get a base hit," he says. "Now, I think it means a basket, subconsciously."

Yet for all his unparalleled success, he is remarkably accessible. It is not like him to snub anyone — regardless of position. Wooden says he answers all letters that are signed, and it is not uncommon to find even Mr. Any Basketball Fan visiting the coach's office next door to Pauley Pavilion, home of the Bruins. "You are beholden to these people," he says. "It's the fans who help make you. If it were not for them, the sport would die out." He is also close to many UCLA staff people outside athletics.

Life for John Wooden swirls around family and old-time

religion away from the playing floor, the Sunday afternoon visits to see his seven grandchildren, the search to find a new minister for the church, the speeches at Fellowship of Christian Athletes meetings, the inspirational messages he delivers on his famous "Pyramid of Success."

But the sinew and fiber of Wooden's life is Basketball. That is what has made him famous and wealthy, although friends describe him as "uncomfortable around lots of money" and he says he has no major investments. His UCLA salary is reportedly $25,000, but his yearly income has been estimated as high as $100,000, counting monies from his in-season TV show, lec-

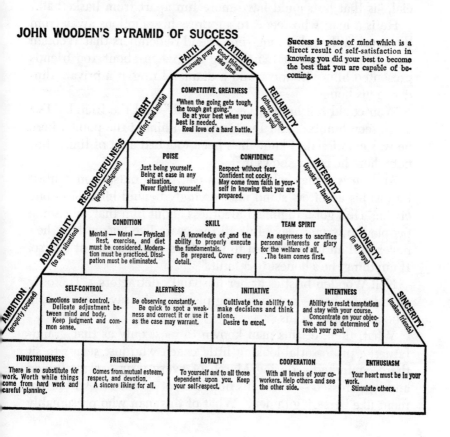

JOHN WOODEN'S PYRAMID OF SUCCESS

Success is peace of mind which is a direct result of self-satisfaction in knowing you did your best to become the best that you are capable of becoming.

tures at clinics, and his lucrative summer basketball camp for youngsters. And basketball has taken him to Spain and New Zealand and Alaska, among other lands, for coaching clinics.

"Basketball is John's life," says a former player and assistant. "We get together socially every now and then. We visit for a while and almost always the entire conversation is basketball. People will turn it that way even if he doesn't. He's almost a dull individual otherwise . . . but he's no dummy. He's very well informed. His life just revolves around basketball and his family."

"The only weakness I know he has," says a retired UCLA official, "is that he should have more fun apart from basketball."

He is a man who seems to suppress his emotions away from the court, although a long-time friend remembers that Wooden was deeply "emotional" not long ago when about 100 friends presented him with a car and a diamond ring at a private dinner in his honor.

"You could tell he was very touched," said the friend. "I've often seen him talk and I've never seen him at the point where he was emotional. I know he's been touched a lot of times, but not where he really shows it."

And he is a man whose critics can be as outspoken against him as his admirers stand unswervingly behind him. Says one critic: "He's got a dignified aloofness about him that rubs some people the wrong way. But all the years I've known him, he's never said an unkind word to me. He's needled me, of course. If anything, he's honest to a fault."

Nell Wooden bristles at her husband's detractors. "The only enemies he has — not including players," she says, "are people who are jealous of his success."

What, then, of this man known to most only as that grandfatherly, professorial-looking little coach who just seems to sit there contentedly during March of every year — arms folded and legs crossed — while his pupils shoot up the NCAA tournament like berserk gunmen? What of this man who presumably

says nothing stronger than "Goodness gracious sakes alive!"?
Or this man who, says one ex-rival player, "is such a perfection-
ist he feels terribly frustrated that he can't leap right off that
bench and try to stop you himself"?

His dry humor, which surfaces only now and then, offers an
insight into the man. Invariably, at dinner speeches for instance, John Wooden will remove a small newspaper clipping
from his wallet — one of those "Twenty-five Years Ago" items
from a town in his native Indiana. Then, in his familiar half-
grin, he will read to the audience:

> Johnny Wooden, South Bend Central's basketball coach, will
> be the featured speaker at Elkhart High's sports banquet, al-
> though they had hoped to line up some prominent coach.

Johnny Wooden likes to poke fun at his obscurity of many
winters ago. But do you also suppose that this is his way of
telling you that it's now John Wooden, All-Time Great Coach,
Basketball Legend Nonpareil?

What it really seems to come down to is: how do you type
him? And which of two basic things is he? The indomitable
Goliath of his profession, steamrollering everything in his way,
or merely a little man from Indiana, still running scared?

CHAPTER 2

A Potpourri

A MAN'S LIFE AND TIMES . . . one woman, the only woman
. . . an image shattered . . . a trip home to adulation . . .
an irascible old rival . . . an overdone roast . . . a small-town
sermon . . . the freaky fans . . . a torrent of letters . . . a
trivia game, a game of competition so typical of him . . . a
search for success . . . a return by the boys of winter.

The sign on a cupboard in Nell Wooden's kitchen:

> This is the Kitchen
> of Nell Wooden
> I Am the BOSS
> If You Don't Believe It,
> Start Something!

She is posing for a photographer outside their Santa Monica
apartment, this small woman with a somewhat scratchy voice
who has been John Wooden's wife, companion, and alter ego
for forty years.

"Should I shoot or dribble?" she asks, and then she and bystanders dissolve into laughter.

But perhaps she could have done either. Back in her grade
school days in Indiana, she once made ten straight free throws
in a basketball shooting contest.

Despite her stature, she has obvious inner strength, too, helping shape her husband's opinions, sharing his successes, fighting
his battles, facing his troubles with him.

"I've been around for years and years," she said, "but I've never given John any advice . . . about basketball."

They met when he was a high school freshman and she was an eighth grader in Martinsville. Their first date was at a carnival. Who asked whom out?

"Well," she says, "we sort of asked each other out. I wasn't too shy — he was. He'd come in my house and say 'How do?' to my parents and hold his head down while he was talking. But my mother adored him — in fact, all her four sons-in-law. They got along beautifully. She always took their part."

She recalls that both she and John felt "uneasy" during their courting days because Wooden's high school coach, Glenn Curtis, lived next to the Rileys (her father dropped the "O" and apostrophe from their name), and Curtis frowned on his players' dating in season.

"The year before we were married," Nell says, "Glenn came up to Purdue to see John play. I was with John and he looked at Glenn and said, 'There isn't a thing you can do about this now, is there, Coach?' "

The Wooden clan, including Nell, sits in the fifth row behind the UCLA bench, alongside press row in Pauley Pavilion. It's often difficult for reporters to work through the ruckus they make.

"We all get keyed up," says Nell, "especially Nan and Jim [their daughter and son] and Stan [Dennis, their son-in-law]. I've had to turn around and tell Stan to shut up. He thinks we *never* commit a foul. But a lot of people's personalities change at basketball games. There's nothing worse than a group of middle-aged rooters."

John, she says, is so calm before games he often comes home and takes naps after pregame meals. Nell's routine usually is to "have a bite" in the Founders' Room at Pauley Pavilion, "but I don't eat much. I should be used to the pressure after all these years but I'm not."

But it was worse back in South Bend. At an important game

Central High played against Elkhart in 1941, Nell fainted and didn't get to see the finish John's team put on to win, 37-35.

And she used to sit right behind the bench at UCLA games until one night when Wooden began substituting earlier than usual. "Too soon! Too soon!" she screamed. And now she's several rows back. "I just can't relax unless we're twenty points ahead," she says.

Before every game, for years, Wooden has gone through a ritual — turning to wink at Nell, patting the knee and shoulder of an assistant coach, tugging at his socks, rolling and pounding his program, tapping the floor, crossing his legs, donning his eyeglasses.

At Notre Dame last season, however, Nell was across the floor from where the UCLA team was sitting. Wooden couldn't find her and she was nearly beside herself. But athletic director J. D. Morgan knew where she had been assigned a seat and waved his large arms like an airport runway crewman. Nell saw him and then the Wooden wave got through.

Nell hasn't missed a UCLA home game in twenty-four years and passes up road trips only occasionally.

But — at least in basketball season — the Woodens' free moments are almost all spent in church work or with their family. Nell points to a recent color portrait of all thirteen of them. Son Jim, a welding supply salesman, and his wife Carleen have four children — Gregory, nine; Johnny, eight; Kim, six; and Michael, three. Daughter Nan and her husband Stan Dennis, who works in the sales department of an aerospace firm, have three daughters — Christy, fifteen; Caryn, thirteen; and Cathleen, eight.

"We sometimes talk," Nell Wooden says, looking again at the picture, "about how we could ever wake up unhappy with their sunny faces there."

Nell and John Wooden differ on some things — his penchant for reading poetry and inspirational sayings for one thing. On a night not long ago he had just finished a particularly dramatic recitation for some visitors, his voice rising and falling as if he were William Jennings Bryan or Clarence Darrow. The visitors were struck by the power and eloquence of his delivery. Nell, across the room, just shook her head back and forth.

"That's the kind of thing he used to do when we were first married," she said. "I'd be out in the kitchen, fixing dinner or washing dishes, and he'd come in and start reading me poetry and things. Shakespeare mostly. I wanted to get away, but he'd lock the door so I couldn't."

But their bond is close.

Displayed prominently in their trophy room is his "Pyramid of Success" — his code — and in one corner of it is the penned inscription: "For my wife, Nellie, who has been 'my life' and without whose patience, faith, understanding and love, I would be lost. As ever and forever, John."

A popular image of John Wooden: A man who practices what he preaches. No drinking, no profanity, no smoking.

There were many years, however, when he committed what a close associate described as "the only vice he had." John Wooden *smoked!*

A one-time assistant coach remembers Wooden smoking "in moderation" during the off season at Indiana State and UCLA. "He used to smoke all year long until the first day of practice," said Ed Powell, "and then he would not touch another cigarette until the season was over. He really prided himself on being able to quit during the season, too. He used this as an example to show he could quit when he wanted to and really put his mind to it."

Powell said Wooden viewed his habit with remorse and finally quit, as did Wooden's wife, several years ago during the "big national health scare about smoking." But, at Indiana State, Wooden often preached to his players about "clean living," particularly no smoking or drinking. His reason: tobacco and alcohol turn basketball teams into losers, not winners.

The theory was put to an intriguing test one night during a

game against Marshall College of Huntington, West Virginia. The Indiana State locker room was adjacent to Marshall's, thus affording a clear view of the opposing team's quarters if the door were open. When the door swung open, there, before the boggled eyes of Wooden's players, was the Marshall team *smoking cigars!*

"They had a good team and beat us badly," said Powell. "Ran right over us and threw in baskets from all over the place. They had a lot of fellows just out of the service too. Older guys. They'd all been around."

When the game was over, the Indiana State players were flabbergasted.

Main Street was suddenly alive and living again in the Age of Aquarius. Beneath the autumn sunshine lay memories of a simpler time, a page fresh out of Norman Rockwell.

Leaves brushed with red and gold. A town square and an ancient courthouse. Batons and balloons and big bassoons. Homespun virtues and plain-folks humor. Nostalgia hanging thickly, like the frost on the pumpkin.

They were four days to remember in October 1969. Days when Johnny Wooden came marching home, five NCAA wristwatches richer.

The world had changed drastically in the four decades since he had departed, books in tow, for college. A Great Depression and a New Deal, a World War and a New Frontier, three assassinations, color TV, seven-foot centers and a walk on the moon. But the town was pretty much the way John and Nell Wooden had left it. Now they were back home in Indiana, where it all began.

The place was Martinsville, deep in the heart of Basketball Country, where the population of 5000 wouldn't even fill the high school gym! The occasion: Morgan County's annual Fall Foliage Festival.

This, however, was a festival different from all the others. The town was also paying tribute to its favorite son by dedicating a new street in his honor. Today, you can find "John R. Wooden Drive" just east of town on the way to Indianapolis. It intersects Sunshine Street in a new residential section where a high school, a junior high school, and a hospital have risen.

People came from farmlands on both sides of the White River, from hamlets like Centerton and Waverly and Hall and Morgantown. They jammed the sidewalks, 65,000 strong, to see the parade. John Wooden was marshal, riding in a white convertible with his wife and two children, Jim and Nan, and happily waving to the crowds.

He was keynote speaker that morning at the Mayor's Breakfast. He was inducted as a "life-time member" of the new YMCA. The mayor gave him a gift from the city, an old oaken bucket now on display over the kitchen sink of the Woodens' apartment in Santa Monica. And friends sent John and Nell an enormous scrapbook brimming with memories of the occasion — newspaper clippings, snapshots, souvenir disks called "Wooden nickels," a photo with a billboard inscribed with "Home of John R. Wooden," and an advertisement by radio station WCBK headlined "Welcome Home, Johnny Wooden."

One story in a Martinsville newspaper on the eve of the festival tells you how the townspeople felt about John Wooden:

> Local people swell up like prideful toads at the mere mention of his name — and the greater the friendship, the bigger the swell.

There were bottles of medicine stacked on the hotel room dresser. Adolph Rupp, the Baron of the Bluegrass, excused himself from an interview to grab one and put a solution in his eye.

"Infection I had fifteen years ago," he explained. "It flared up 'bout six weeks ago."

The Baron was just days away from forced retirement as the University of Kentucky's head basketball coach, after forty-two years. He was at the 1972 coaches convention at the Biltmore Hotel and getting ready to watch UCLA win its sixth straight national championship.

He talked about what might have been: "Sure wish my team were playing Johnny Wooden's Saturday in the NCAA final. Wouldn't that be a great confrontation? Two old boys in against each other."

They were never consistently direct rivals, although Rupp's Wildcats beat Wooden's Bruins each of the three times they met. But it was a rivalry just the same. Rupp clearly chafed when Wooden deposed him as the king of college basketball. Rupp has four national titles. Wooden has eight.

Rupp's conversation on this spring day was a mixture of bluegrass platitudes, back pats, and vituperation.

On the record, he would say things like, "Wooden is a helluva coach and as far as I know we're the best of friends. I have nothing but the greatest admiration for him and I wish you'd print that. He's one of the outstanding coaches the nation has produced. Hell, the nation didn't produce him. He produced himself!

"Johnny has some system going for him. What I can't figure out is how he keeps everyone happy."

Off the record, Rupp would intone, "Put ya pencil down." Then he would question the eligibility of most of the Texas Western players who beat Kentucky for the national championship in 1966, wonder what "special favors" Lew Alcindor got at UCLA, imply that *every* coach in America was cheating — except him.

"Kentucky basketball has been my very life," he said, on the record again. "They can leave me with the team or they may as well take me out to Lexington cemetery."

A week later, the university retired him. His "cemetery" was a job as president of the Memphis Tams of the American Basketball Association.

It had been said over the years that John Wooden secretly

envied Adolph Rupp while he publicly admired him. They were tactically compatible. They taught fast-tempo basketball and abhorred ball-control strategy. During the Great Stall Controversy of 1967, when Wooden said stalling was "bad for basketball" in the wake of Lew Alcindor and Company's harrowing overtime win over a USC team that sat on the ball, ex-California coach Pete Newell disagreed with the UCLA coach.

"It's obvious that the less time the ball goes up, the less chance the ball is going to be played around the boards — that's Alcindor's game. This is what makes college basketball great, the tactical angle."

At a luncheon the next day, Wooden needled a writer for quoting only Newell on the subject of stalling. "Why," he said, "didn't you ask Mr. Rupp of Kentucky what *he* thought, too?"

The specter of the Baron's records, intimates say, haunted Wooden for years though. By the end of Wooden's third season at UCLA, Rupp already had won three NCAA crowns (1948, 1949, and 1951), and John Wooden sat in his office at Westwood with a friend and pondered things like the Kentucky dynasty and coaches' salaries.

"Well," he sighed, "I guess Adolph got a new contract — maybe a salary increase and another Hereford for his cattle ranch."

Their teams met for the first time in the 1951-1952 season, at Lexington. The Bruins had a couple of black players who weren't welcome to stay at any of Lexington's all-white inns, so Wooden found housing for the full squad in Cincinnati — a three-hour bus ride each way from the University of Kentucky.

"We agreed with the coach's decision," said Don Bragg, then a Bruin freshman. "We all thought he did the right thing."

UCLA shot only 24.3 percent from the field (eighteen for seventy-four) and Kentucky, led by Cliff Hagan (thirty-four points), Frank Ramsey, and Lou Tsiropoulos, waltzed, 84-53.

The next two games were in Los Angeles — in 1959 and

1961 — and much closer. But UCLA still lost, 68-66 and 77-76. "This is the first time in three years Kentucky has played before an empty seat," Rupp said. "We lost thirty thousand dollars by coming here. If we'd played at Lexington we'd have had twelve thousand, five hundred in the seats and two thousand standees. That's double the crowd you folks have."

He sat there on the stage at the Friars Club, smiling but dour — obviously very uncomfortable — as comedian Dave Barry, a veteran of the Las Vegas lounges, raced through a seemingly endless collection of dirty stories that made the all-male crowd of 400 roar and wince. They were there to toast John Wooden, UCLA basketball coach. John Wooden there at the Friars was like seeing Joe Namath at a monastery.

Embarrassing but not all bad. Several ex-players lauded Wooden. So did emcee Sam Balter, a UCLA man who once was a strong Wooden critic. "He has perpetrated the greatest criminal achievement in sports by robbing all the other coaches," said Balter. "His genius will die with him." And then there were the remarks by Tommy Prothro, at the time UCLA's head football coach.

"Nobody is better qualified to work with the youth of America than Coach Wooden," said Prothro. "I wish you could work with more students than the basketball team to offset some of the other things they learn in other classes at the school."

And Wooden received gifts, one of the most prominent a Kawasaki motorbike that most of the Wooden clan — including the coach himself — later took turns riding.

But through it all, as Wooden suffered the off-color gags without blushing, you couldn't help but think: "What's a nice little Hoosier like you doing in a place like this?"

His voice rose and ebbed like that of a backwoods preacher, the words tumbling out eloquently, emotionally.

"I don't like to hear coaches blame officials or officials blame coaches," said John Wooden, answering a question from the audience about violence in college basketball games. "I don't like to see coaches and administrators blaming each other. What the administration permits, coaches are apt to do. What coaches permit, players are apt to do."

The coach was in hostile territory — Pullman, Washington, a wisp of a college town in the heart of the Northwest's wheat country, half a continent away from Middle Indiana.

But you got the impression one winter day in 1972 that they really weren't so very far apart after all.

Wooden was there on his annual visit, trying to mastermind his young basketball team through the asylum of horrors known as Bohler Gymnasium, home of the underdog Washington State Cougars. It's a matchbox of a place, where the fans yell, "Feed 'em to Butch! Feed 'em to Butch!" (the school's live cougar mascot who lives in a cage outside the gym) and where they hold the noise level to the blast of a Boeing 747.

But now, a few hours before the tip-off, he was in a more palatable setting. It was a tiny banquet room overflowing with WSU fans, members of a booster group called the Cougar Club, and they were infinitely friendlier now than they would be that evening when the twenty-foot jump shots rang out.

They all had gathered at a weekly luncheon to hear John Wooden speak. Middle-aged men in business suits, their ladies smartly dressed, and wide-eyed kids out of school because it was Washington's Birthday.

There were student yell leaders from WSU, clad in scarlet and gray, and well-scrubbed pompon girls who led the crowd in a cheer: "W! . . . O! . . . O! . . . D! . . . E! . . . N!" And there was the Cougar coach, who good-naturedly presented Wooden with a pair of red earmuffs "to keep out all the noise in Bohler Gym."

They laughed and John Wooden smiled a little and occasionally adjusted his bifocals. His sermon was short, plainfolks, and impassioned. It touched on the traditionals: the 1964 full-court press, Lew Alcindor, Bill Walton, the "pressures" of being on top, virtues that sounded as if they were right out of his "Pyramid of Success."

He fielded questions from the audience. Someone asked about the American Basketball Association's raids on undergraduate players, and Wooden responded: "Greed devours itself. That's what it'll do in the case of the ABA. It's bad for everyone — for that league, for the colleges, for all of us in the game of basketball. I cannot say that the rare individual player does not profit. Of course, he does."

Somebody wondered how the NCAA tournament would be affected now that Marquette's Jim Chones had turned professional. The coach deadpanned. "I guess they'll go ahead and have it anyway," he said. More laughter. "It'll be a fine tournament with sellout crowds," he added. "I wouldn't mind being there myself."

Inevitably, an elderly man raised his hand and asked, "What about all the turmoil among the youth of today?"

The coach's voice crescendoed. "The principal turmoil among youngsters is not the fault of the youngsters but of those who have sired them," he said. "We have examples of the permissiveness of the coaches and we have examples of the permissiveness of parents. As coaches, how can we preach self-control, one of the great values of basketball, and then act like maniacs ourselves at times?"

He paused and grinned. "Gracious sakes," he said, "we've had similar problems all through history. I guess I really haven't answered you, have I? But I did beat around the bush pretty well."

You see them lining up outside Pauley Pavilion at 8 A.M. and sometimes two or three nights in advance.

They are college kids — guys wearing jeweled headbands to keep their shoulder-length hair in place, girls clad in trousers perfect for greasing cars, some very obviously wearing no bras. They sprawl across the pavement in sleeping bags and blankets, poring over books on Western Civ. and Hero's Hymns or writing everything from doctoral dissertations to telegrams asking Dad for more money — all against a backdrop of Frisbee games and rock music piped in from the campus radio station.

These are UCLA's Basketball Freaks, the student insurgents who stomp and shriek for the Good Guys, who heckle the men in the dark jerseys and the striped shirts, and who worship the little man in bifocals sitting there in row one with arms folded, legs crossed, and rolled-up souvenir program clenched in his fist.

And this is Basketball: Westwood, U.S.A. Call it an obsession, a carnival, a fashion promenade, a social phenomenon. Certainly it's more than a game.

"It's all kindred to a religious experience," said a graduate student named Sherman Gordon, twenty-three, who sees all the road games too. Which may explain why rival teams are often regarded as symbols of irreverence, if not downright transgression. There are handmade banners (some unprintable) and hooting and chants of "Pour it on!" (even when the home team is leading by sixty points) and, lamentably, the not-very-tender sonnets yelled at rival coaches, notably Bob Boyd of arch-rival USC.

"The students get personal with Boyd because he is USC and an advocate of the stall — a direct affront to 'Saint John,'" said John Sandbrook, former *Daily Bruin* sports editor. "They feel they have to protect their religion, their saint, the sacred traditions — the NCAA titles."

Here come those UCLA song girls, leggy blondes and brunettes who are wriggling and dancing in hot pants to "Jesus Christ Superstar," "Lucretia McEvil," and "American Pie."

There is a standing ovation for the band's rendition of Tchaikovsky's *1812 Overture*, and cheers for the male undergraduate who performs a striptease while the band plays "Let Me Entertain You."

There are short tempers in the rooting section when ushers seize two-dozen phony student ID cards used by rooters to sneak their dates past the door. And there are angry words near courtside from two families, including seven immaculately groomed youngsters, shrieking, "Gracious sakes, ref! Open yer eyes!" It is the family of John Wooden.

Such is life in Pauley Pavilion, the "sacred temple," the sparkling, antiseptic, $5 million arena where eating and smoking are prohibited on the main floor — and where it seems that the visiting team is prohibited from winning (UCLA has lost only twice there — both times to USC — in seven years).

It's a world of sellout crowds, fans leaving behind their season tickets in wills and divorce settlements, a handful of students driving 11,000 miles to every road game in rental cars, a quick postgame snack at Monty's or the Chatam — then home to watch the replay on television.

To the students, it's a "social experience," one of the very few left at UCLA now that homecoming and dances have been scrapped. It's also a unifying force among faculty, alumni, and students. "It gives the students a bond they wouldn't ordinarily have," observed Sandbrook. "It isn't just because the team is a winner. It is Wooden, the model man, a father image the students are all proud of. It is UCLA as a school — the only time a commuter school of twenty-seven thousand with myriad interests can have a common experience. That's the key."

Basketball: Westwood, U.S.A. It's a world John Wooden didn't build in seven days or seven years. It's a madness that has mushroomed from B.O. Barn, the old men's gym, to chants of "We're Number One!"

Outside the pavilion, a graduate student named Ron Kendiss, one of the masses huddled in the overnight chill waiting for the doors to open, looks up at an interviewer and sighs: "This is Camelot! When Wooden retires, it will set basketball back ten or twenty years."

Letters, he gets letters . . . stacks and stacks of letters. And John Wooden answers every one of them, even the nasty ones, and often in his own bold, neat handwriting. Once in a while, he will even compose a poem in reply.

One of the correspondents who wrote Wooden a particularly vituperative message must have been stunned by the coach's reply. The last four lines:

> But we'll accept what's
> happened, that is past
> and done.
> If the Bruins can win, in
> spite of you, in 1971.

Wooden says that his greatest volume of mail comes after defeats, such as the loss to Cincinnati in the NCAA semifinals in 1962, to Houston at the Astrodome in 1968, and to Notre Dame at South Bend in 1970. "It has a lot to do with human nature," he says. "When you lose, there are always people who feel for you."

Wooden's secretary, Jean Dunne, says that he comes back into his office each night, even when at his summer basketball camp in Thousand Oaks, to answer his mail. "I don't look on it as a chore," he says. "I believe that if people are kind enough to write, I owe them the courtesy of a reply."

The attention — along with the success — has paid off in name identification. According to *Sports Illustrated*, a ninth-grade English class at Princeton Junior High School in Cincinnati is occasionally given quizzes by teacher Noel Johnston to test the youngsters' awareness of the world around them.

One of the questions in a recent quiz asked what the letters UCLA stood for. To Johnston's amazement, thirty-seven of the forty students correctly answered "University of California at Los Angeles." One thought the letters meant University of Cincinnati, conveniently ignoring the LA, and another came up with United Citizens Law Association. But the fortieth answer, ah, that was the one.

It said simply, "Basketball."

*

The scene: the Santa Monica apartment of John and Nell Wooden. More a museum, a repository of memorabilia, than a dwelling, but it suits them. As the championships grow, so do the treasures — the trophies and newspaper clippings and letters from Presidents.

"We may have to move to find room for all this stuff," says Nell Wooden.

The night is warm but tinged by a beach breeze. An occasional car screeches around a corner outside. The clock creeps past 1 A.M. John Wooden has been talking for hours — first at a Wilshire Boulevard steakhouse and then at his apartment — about his motivation, his methods, the reasons for his success.

Now one of his interrogators brings up a baseball trivia question. Wooden the baseball fan (he has said it's his favorite sport), Wooden the competitor responds quickly with the answer. Then, warming to the game, he asks one himself:

"Who holds the major league record for runs batted in?"

"Hack Wilson," comes the answer.

"What year?"

"Nineteen thirty."

"How many?"

"One hundred ninety-six."

Wooden says nothing, just nods.

Then he is asked, "Who pinch-ran for Eddie Gaedel, the midget Bill Veeck had go to bat for the St. Louis Browns?"

Wooden doesn't know — and doesn't want to say so. He takes the offensive — much in the manner his teams fast break.

"I think it was one-ninety," he says.

"One-ninety what?"

"Hack Wilson — one-ninety runs batted in, not one ninety-six." (He was right.)

He attacks again.

"Who was the shortest man ever to play in the majors?" he asks.

"Come on" is the response. "Trick question. It's Eddie Gaedel."

Wooden smiles, pleased at his deception, and goes right on. "Think it's possible for a one-armed man to play in the big leagues?" he says.

"You're doing it again," a listener says. "Pete Gray. Outfielder. St. Louis Browns. Nineteen forty-five."

The talk turns to teams. Wooden goes down the roster of the 1930 Cubs — Hack Wilson's Cubs — flawlessly. One of his questioners mentions he has been a lifelong Cardinal fan.

"OK," says Wooden. "How about the Gashouse Gang?"

For a while it's easy. Frankie Frisch, Leo Durocher, Pepper Martin, Ducky Medwick, the Dean brothers, Wild Bill Hallahan. Even Bill DeLancey, the young catcher, and outfielder Ernie Orsatti don't cause much trouble. But who's the other outfielder — and how about the first baseman? Should be simple, but it isn't.

Wooden admits he doesn't know this time but goes to his library. For the next hour, he shuts out everything else and pores over his sports books. Lots of material turns up on the Gashouse Gang but nothing on the two missing players.

"I won't sleep tonight," says the guy Wooden has been questioning.

"Neither will I," says Wooden.

The next night a phone rings.

"I called the newspaper to get your number," a voice says. The caller obviously is John Wooden. "I believe it was Rip Collins at first and Terry Moore in the outfield. Had to tell you."

Collins was right; Moore was wrong (it was Jack Rothrock).

But the 1934 St. Louis Cardinals obviously had been on John Wooden's mind all night — and all day.

A few days later . . .

The scene was the same, but the game was different.

This time Wooden left a conversation and came back holding a copy of a magazine. The visitors could not see the cover — and he didn't tell them what it was. He merely started reading.

His first selection was Paul Harvey's "The Amazing American," which said, in part:

> . . . He would not steal money from his neighbor, but he'll pay tax collectors to collect it for him.
>
> He irrigates deserts to make farmland, then puts the extra acres in a soil bank.
>
> He spent $280 million last year on tranquilizers — and an equal sum on pep pills.
>
> He tosses beer cans out the car window, drops gum wrappers in the gutter, plants auto graveyards along the highways, hides a mountain or meadow with a billboard selling laxatives, then stands up at his civic club meeting, and, with a lump in his throat, sings "America the Beautiful."
>
> Yet, for all of that, the Amazing American is still a pretty nice guy.
>
> Despite all that he is not — because of all that he is — calling anybody "a real American" is still the highest compliment you can pay.

Then, while wife Nell endured, he plunged on. This time it was a poem by "author unknown" called "Lord, Forgive Me When I Whine." It told of a girl with one leg who used a crutch, a blind boy who sold candy, a child with eyes of blue who did not answer a question because he could not hear.

Voice rising strongly now, Wooden delivered the last verse:

> With feet to take me where I'd go, with eyes to see the sunsets glow, with ears to hear what I would know . . . Oh, God forgive me when I whine. I'm blessed, indeed. The world is mine.

His listeners wondered what Wooden was quoting from. He told them it was the August issue of a rather symbolic magazine, *Success Unlimited*. But he said nothing more.

A few days and dozens of futile trips to newsstands later, there it was, big as life, on a bottom shelf of a stand in Hollywood. *The Magazine!* And what was on the cover and in the centerfold?

John Wooden's "Pyramid of Success."

They were like *objets d'art* that had been polished, precision-built, and proudly exhibited for all the connoisseurs to see.

The towering fellow wearing skull cap and African-style smock was 7-foot-1-and-whatever-he-is Kareem Abdul-Jabbar, striding into the arena to a standing ovation from the people who used to cheer him when he was Lew Alcindor. He had narrowly made plane connections on a transcontinental flight from Harvard University, where his summer classes in Arabic had just ended. And he had come this night — as he had promised — to play basketball voluntarily for a charity in which he believed.

In a moment, he would be joined by his former compatriots — Sidney Wicks, Lucius Allen, Curtis Rowe, Steve Patterson, John Vallely, and Terry Schofield — and by heroes of older, and more recent, vintage, Gail Goodrich, Abdul Rahman (nee Walt Hazzard), Fred Slaughter, Henry Bibby, and Kenny Booker. The boys of winter were back again for a midsummer night's dream, young men from all seasons.

Pompon girls pranced, bandsmen played, and 10,000 voices thrilled to every "slam dunk" and behind-the-back assist as the UCLA Alumni All-Stars, returning to the scene of their earlier glories, battled the Elgin Baylor Pro Stars, a team of assorted professional players and rookies-to-be. The game benefited a scholarship fund in honor of the late Nobel Peace Prize winner, Dr. Ralph Bunche, himself a former UCLA player back in the days when a nation worshiped Charles Lindbergh and Babe Ruth.

But the charity — and even the score — were transcended on this August evening by a nostalgia that was as spellbindingly alive as the tradition it symbolized.

There, gathered on the floor of Pauley Pavilion, were many of the legends, the joys, the sorrows, the moments to remember and forget that spanned all eight championship teams of the John Wooden dynasty. In the courtside bleachers were other former Wooden pupils, Johnny Moore, Willie Naulls, Bill Ellis, and Denny Miller of the 1950s, Mike Warren and Bill Sweek of the 1960s, and Andy Hill of the 1970s, not to mention a rival player, formerly of USC. His name was Don Crenshaw, home on leave from army duty at West Point, and he would say what Abdul-Jabbar and Wicks and Rowe and Bibby could not say: "I never lost on this floor."

Of course, Goodrich and Rahman and Slaughter could echo those words, for they had never played on this floor. Their college basketball memories harked back to pre-Pauley days — to a downtown arena, a junior-college gym, and a facility that often housed sailboat and auto exhibits.

They all were individually introduced now, clad in powder-blue uniforms specially ordered for the occasion but looking as if they had been borrowed from a North Hollywood church league. The starting line-up would have been as formidable as any NBA team's — Abdul-Jabbar at center, Wicks and Rahman at forwards, Goodrich and Allen at guards.

The Good Guys controlled the opening tip — to the delight of the near-capacity crowd — and suddenly the place was a kaleidoscope of Abdul-Jabbar hooks, Goodrich jumpers, Super Sidney blocks, Lucius lay-ups, and sleight-of-hand Rahman passes that elicited "Ohhhhs!" and "Ahhhhs!" from all corners of the pavilion.

"Did you see that pass by Hazzard? — er, I mean Rahman?" said a shaggy-haired young man, sitting in the bleachers behind one basket. "God, he's outta sight! I used to watch him on TV when I was playing high school ball — he was my idol in those days!"

The Rahman-worshiper was Bill Sweek, the scrambling, gambling swingman on the Alcindor teams. He sat with his wife, Debbie, and friends while home for a month's vacation from Tunisia, where he had taught school and coached the Olympic basketball team while on assignment for the Peace Corps.

For him, this was a night to reminisce about seasons past. During the pregame warm-ups, he stood at courtside, garbed in an embroidered smock worn by natives in Senegal, warmly slapping hands and chatting with ex-teammates Abdul-Jabbar and Allen. And now, amid the roar of a crowd that wildly cheered every UCLA Alumni basket, he talked openly of the man with whom he had bitterly clashed during his college years.

"Yeah, we yelled at each other," said Sweek, rehashing his relationship with John Wooden. "But it was different then. It was like a father-son thing. We didn't always see eye-to-eye. But now, I look back and feel differently about him. The other day, I spent two hours in his office with him and we talked about coaching and problems of discipline. I was seeing him in a different way now, man to man instead of player to coach. I can see now that he did change and try to adjust with the times. . . . When you're playing for him, he seems like another person. I always thought he was the same and would never change . . . Now, I look at him as a man who's still a lot different than I am, but still a man I respect . . ."

Meanwhile, out on the floor, Gail Goodrich threw in a baseline jumper, twisting loose from two defenders who nearly arm-wrestled him — NBA style — to the floor.

"Everybody's been telling me," said Sweek, "what a fantastic year Goodrich had with the Lakers. I knew he'd be good . . . but *that* good too?"

Suddenly Curtis Rowe knifed past a defender, went airborne, and rammed in an acrobatic "slam dunk" that brought down the house. Sweek's eyes brightened. "That," he said, "had to be the shot of the night!"

The stroll down memory lane moved on. Bill Sweek, the

nonstop kid from Pasadena who used to crash-land into the tenth row to save out-of-bounds passes, the guy who broke up the USC stall game and whose last-ditch shot beat Purdue, sat there spellbound. He was captivated — as was everyone else — by this return to yesteryear, especially from a new home half a world away.

The past became reality again and again. Sidney Wicks and Gail Goodrich and Henry Bibby and Curtis Rowe worked a perfect play that looked as if it were right out of John Wooden's textbook. The crowd loved it.

"See that?" said Sweek. "They're running the old high-post offense now! Remember, before the game, how we thought they might just run and shoot and use *no* offense? Well, that high-post stuff has to tell you more than anything about how the players feel about Coach Wooden, more than any single word ever could."

Then came a "Walt Hazzard special," a full-court bounce pass — bull's-eye! — to Sidney Wicks, who soared up, up, up toward the basket, then cleverly dumped the ball to an open man, Gail Goodrich, storming in for a lay-up. More cheers. A clenched-fist gesture of "thanks" from Goodrich to Wicks. And more memories.

It remained for the script to end on a believable, familiar note, just like it did on those late, late show televised replays over Channel 5. As if it were decreed, the UCLA Alumni triumphed and that 7-foot-1-and-whatever-he-is fellow was the game's premier scorer — even though his body wearily told him it was now 2 A.M., Eastern Daylight Time.

Outside the locker room, Mahdi Abdul-Rahman signed autographs for admirers who remember him as Walt Hazzard, the kid who passed and dribbled and shot a team into stardom and triggered a dynasty.

"This is a great thrill for me, one of the highlights of my career," he said. "This is the greatest sports tradition ever in the country. Sure, Bill Russell won championships eleven out of thirteen years, but nobody can match what has happened here. Look at the turnover! First, they win it with guards, then a center, then forwards. I'll say this: if we were playing together in the NBA, we'd have the greatest franchise ever assembled."

He talked of John Wooden, the man with whom he, too, often clashed and who now is a friend. "He's a decent man and he's won graciously," he said. "Even though we've had differences, it's still a matter of people respecting each other. And I know one thing: I'm gonna feel sorry for the guy who takes his place . . ."

The boys of winter were leaving now, the midsummer night's dream over.

For John Wooden, who watched proudly from the stands and visited the locker room afterward to say "hello" to the young professionals he used to teach, it must have seemed like springtime again.

PART TWO

The Longest Days

===

"Before the rising sun
We fly
So many roads to choose
We start out walking and learn to run
And yes we've just begun . . ."

— From "We've Only Just Begun,"
    by Paul Williams and Roger Nichols (BMI)

CHAPTER 3

Hot-Shooting Hoosier

HIS FRIENDS AT UCLA have said it again and again. Sports-
writers have written it. John Wooden reaffirmed it when he arrived at Westwood. And everybody has pretty much accepted
it as gospel.

"John Wooden, as a high school and college coach, has
never had a losing season."

It is glittering testimony to a man whose very livelihood for
three and a half decades has hinged on whether he wins more
games than he loses.

But it isn't true.

John Wooden did have one losing season. His very first. The
record was six wins, eleven losses, at the high school in tiny
Dayton, Kentucky, a tough, swashbuckling river town where
just about everybody worked for either the Wadsworth Watch-
case Company or the Perry and Derrick paint factory and
where, as one of his players recalled, "The folks who lived up
on the hilltop looked down on us city kids."

His players remember him as a "strict disciplinarian" who
paddled them for loafing or missing cheap baskets and as a
coach who "treated us all like buddies" by transporting them
on weekend trips to Indianapolis so they could watch him
play pro basketball with the Kautsky Grocers for fifty dollars a
game.

Even then he was a picture of contrasts. A tranquil, affable
young man outwardly, he also had a temper that sometimes exploded like a runaway rocket.

One night during his rookie season, Wooden nearly got into a brawl with an opposing coach. It happened immediately after a game with bitter rival Newport High. The Newport coach, Lou Foster, stalked angrily into the Dayton dressing room and accused Wooden of coaching "dirty basketball."

An eyewitness said Wooden went into a wild-eyed rage and lunged at Foster, but he was forcibly restrained by Dayton players and other bystanders. One was the Dayton chief of police, who smiled and barked: "Aw, turn him loose."

But the chief's orders were disobeyed. Peace prevailed across the locker room — fortunately for Lou Foster.

"Johnny was so furious," says the witness, "that it would have been the wrong thing to turn him loose. Foster would have been no match for him. He was about the same size, but Johnny was better built. He was muscular and really in shape And he was so upset that I bet he coulda taken on Goliath right there and won!"

Then there was the afternoon when Wooden blew up at the whole team at a practice:

"All right, you guys!" he roared. "I'm gonna show you how bad you are!"

Johnny Wooden, the reigning Big Ten scoring champ, challenged the whole Dayton starting line-up to a "five-on-one" battle. "Do anything you want to try to stop me!" he yelled.

The Dayton starters put up a stubborn, if not seamless, defense. Wooden dribbled, darted, and dodged through everybody and scored.

"He didn't pull any punches and he wanted us to rough him up," said one player. "But if you got near him, you wound up on the floor. And we were all pretty good-sized guys too."

But while he battled, Wooden also taught. Significantly, he is remembered as a tactician who was far ahead of his time.

"As I look back on those years today," said team captain Bill Smith, an engineer now living in Erlander, Kentucky, "he was trying to teach the type of basketball that wouldn't be popular for thirty years. That's why we didn't win very many games. We just couldn't grasp his fast-breaking style and all the other things he was trying to teach us. We couldn't do things the way he wanted them done."

A nation lay in semiparalysis. The years were 1933 and 1934. Depression years.

John Wooden was fresh out of college, a three-time All-American and honors English graduate from Purdue University, newly married to his high school sweetheart, Nellie Riley.

At age twenty-two, he was barely older than his players, at least one of whom was twenty, the maximum age under Kentucky high school eligibility rules. So there was no such thing as a "generation gap" in those days. Even so, the rookie coach ran the Dayton High Greendevils with whip-cracking authority.

"We had some real loafers on our team," said Bill Smith. "He wanted us to go full blast up and down the court. He'd stand there with a paddle and speed 'em up."

The Wooden paddle left an even larger imprint in the memories of two other players. "He'd whip guys up one side of the bleachers and down the other," said one. "He really meant business." Said 6-foot-2 forward Charles Carmichael: "If you missed an easy lay-up, he'd be right there to crack ya. And while he was doing it, the other guys would be standing there, laughing at the guy getting paddled."

Carmichael said Wooden asserted himself only on matters pertaining to on-the-court discipline. "He didn't intrude into your private life," he said, "but he had that sixth sense in knowing whether a guy didn't get seven or eight hours' sleep the night before. He could always tell. And he'd let you know about it too."

Why did the Greendevils win only six of seventeen games in their first year under Wooden?

For one thing, Dayton was a small school (enrollment 300) and used mostly football players on the basketball team. For another, the Wooden way was a drastic change from the old system of Willard Bass, who was unceremoniously demoted to coaching the girls' basketball team.

"His tremendous drive and stress of fundamentals still stand out in my mind," says Carmichael, now a retired IBM engineer living in nearby Fort Thomas. "We had to change our whole way of playing. We had been a slow-breaking team and very deliberate under Coach Bass and then, suddenly, Coach Wooden wanted us to speed it up more. We had difficulties at first making the switch, and we ended up with a not-so-hot record. But he was the kind of man who gave you confidence, winning or losing."

The biggest difficulties, said Smith, were learning the fast break, beating a man one-on-one, and setting screens. "He tried to teach us the pick-and-roll," he said, "and nobody had ever seen that before. Even the referees couldn't get used to it. They kept calling us for blocking."

It was the age of the center-jump rule, which required a jump ball at midcourt after every basket. Even though the rule wasn't scrapped until a few years later, in 1937, it didn't cramp Wooden's up-tempo style for long. Interestingly, the Dayton Greendevils were 15-3 in his second year as coach. Their only defeats were to arch-rival Bellevue, 15-11 (a loss avenged in a rematch), to Cincinnati city champion Purcell, 25-20, and later in the first round of the district tournament.

But John Wooden had won respect, if not championships. His players were captivated by his basketball skills. Everybody remembered him as a spirited, aggressive guard who would have smashed through a brick wall, if necessary, to make a lay-up.

"Fastest dribbler I've ever seen, bar none," said Bill Smith. "Nobody could beat him to the basket. He'd scrimmage with us a lot too. He'd take two subs, and the three of them would take on the whole team — and beat us! And as small as he was [about 5-10½], he could really jump! One time I saw him jump so high that he put his whole hand above the rim!"

And he was respected as a man who maintained a close rapport with his players off the court. A familiar tableau at Dayton High each morning before classes was John Wooden, sitting in his small office in the corner of the gymnasium, informally holding "bull sessions" with groups of players.

"I remember he really took you to heart," said Carmichael. "He was a very considerate man, and he used to take some of the team members home to dinner with him at times. He'd treat you like a real person. In fact, he was such a good Christian man. He had a tremendous influence on our lives. I really think he would have been a successful minister."

Of weekend trips to Indianapolis for Sunday pro games, Carmichael said: "He would take us kids with him and even put us up in a hotel overnight. That was a lot of fun. He treated us all like buddies."

As a college senior in 1932, John Wooden pondered a career in teaching or coaching, or possibly one with a publishing firm, editing textbooks.

He also strongly considered remaining at Purdue to work as a postgraduate assistant in the English Department — that is, until a man named Olin W. Davis, who was superintendent of schools in Dayton, talked him into coaching the high school basketball team.

Naturally, the hiring of Wooden irritated Willard Bass, the man he replaced. "Willard figured we were going to have such a promising team," said an ex-Dayton player, Jack DeMoss, now living across the river in Cincinnati. "And I know he wasn't very happy about having to coach the girls' team."

Two years later, when Wooden departed, Willard Bass was coaching the boys' varsity again. It was obvious to everybody that Bass had profited enormously from two winters of observing the Wooden way.

"It certainly made him a better coach," said DeMoss. "In fact, we were runners-up in the state tournament my junior year. Willard Bass had become one of the outstanding coaches of Kentucky."

John Wooden made lasting impressions in many ways his first year of coaching.

There was Wooden, the Fiery Competitor, who cleverly deployed only seven players per game and promptly benched and chewed out the ones who committed foolish errors — a technique he uses today.

"I remember he was usually pretty calm on the bench," recalled Charles Carmichael. "But one game we were playing Newport High and there wasn't gonna be much difference between winning and losing. We were in a fast break in the last minute and the Newport coach suddenly called 'time out,' which was illegal for a coach to do in those days. Well, it killed our whole momentum — and we lost the game.

"As soon as the game was over, Coach Wooden really told this man off! He gave him a real tongue-lashing! He wasn't gonna hit him, but you had the feeling he might have done it."

There was Wooden, the Good Example:

"We all lived pretty much the way he did," said Carmichael. "I realize the kids today are different, but that's because the mores are different. In our day, we didn't have the freedom of life-styles that the kids have today. We didn't mind trying to live up to the life that John Wooden followed."

And there was Wooden, the Man Who Sought the Extra Edge:

"He talked about staying at Dayton one more year," said Bill Smith. "He knew we'd have a good team if everybody could have stayed. Three of us were seniors, but we were gonna fail our classes intentionally so we could stay around and play for him another year. Because of the Depression, there weren't any jobs for us anyway. So we figured there was nothing else to do but play ball. They put in a rule that limited the number of years that guys could play, though."

"Did Coach Wooden," he was asked, "give this idea of intentional failure his blessing?"

"Well, yes," said Smith, "he did."

But the next year, John Wooden was headed for Central High School in South Bend.

Indiana was where it began, on October 14, 1910. John Wooden was and is a product of white mid-America, conservative mid-America. Town squares and town halls. Pickup trucks and produce. Ice cream parlors and Sunday drives. The Bible for prayer and the belt for discipline.

Centerton, Indiana, where he was born, was a community with little more than a blacksmith, a grain elevator, and fifty people. Wooden was third in a Scotch-Irish family of six children. The family raised stock — cows, pigs, chickens — and crops — wheat, alfalfa, corn, tomatoes, watermelons.

Father Joshua Hugh Wooden was a baseball pitcher of some skill and had carved a diamond out of the family's farmland. But there was a hoop nailed up in the hayloft, and John and his older brother, Maurice (Cat) Wooden, either played there or at a dirt court outside the grade school.

"Our first problem on that makeshift basket on the farm was getting the hay out of the way," Wooden says. "We would use an old tomato basket for a net. I don't think we ever had a real basketball. We'd usually make one out of rags and round it out as best we could and then our mother would sew it up with old cotton hose she'd gotten runners in. On special occasions, like Christmas, we might get a rubber ball from the ten-cent store. It wasn't the size of a basketball, but it served our purpose."

The Wooden brothers went to the same three-room school

and were on the basketball team, but there was little indication then that Johnny Wooden would become the scourge of the sport in Indiana.

"We were always competing," says Maurice Wooden, "but we really didn't think about things much then. It was all too far in the future."

But Johnny's athletic promise was discovered early, by his first coach, Earl W. Warriner, who was also his grade school principal and teacher.

Wooden found out about Warriner's discipline the hard way. He was the team's high scorer, but Warriner once set him down for an entire, losing game because he had challenged the coach.

"After it was over," says Wooden, "he put an arm on my shoulder and said, 'Johnny, we could have won with you in there but winning just isn't that important.'"

Wooden said thank-you many years later. UCLA was scheduled to play at Chicago Stadium and Warriner wrote John for tickets, sending a blank check. The tickets — and the check — came back, with the notation: "Friendship far too valuable to be measured in dollars."

The other major figure in Wooden's early life was his father. An austere man, Joshua Hugh Wooden wore the sort of rimless wire-frame glasses that are popular today. He gave son John his large ears — and his motivation.

Inside John Wooden's wallet is a crumpled piece of paper, inscribed with this message from his father: "Be true to thyself [Polonius to Laertes in *Hamlet*], make each day a masterpiece, help others, drink deeply from good books, make friendship a fine art, and build a shelter against a rainy day."

"My father," Wooden says, "would not speak an unkind word of another person. He was far more interested in character than in reputation. In my opinion, he came as close to living the philosophy of the Golden Rule as any person I have ever known."

But some bad investments and crop failure robbed Joshua Wooden of his farm and he moved the family the eight miles into Martinsville in 1924, about the same time the red brick high school gymnasium went up on South Main Street.

The Martinsville population was 5200. The gym held 5520. John Wooden turned to basketball in high school after a process of elimination: Martinsville didn't have baseball or football teams.

He came under the guidance of Glenn Curtis, who Tony Hinkle, the former Butler University coach and a long-time observer of Indiana basketball, says was "a great fundamental coach."

Wooden calls Curtis "one of the four most important men in my life," and adds: "He was a brilliant psychologist and handler of young men. He had a tremendous talent for inspiring individuals and teams to rise to great heights. He demanded perfection in the execution of fundamentals and was a master strategist."

Off the court in those days, John Wooden was something of a Hoosier hotshot. When he went into the Candy Kitchen — where the action was in Martinsville — he usually had a toothpick in his mouth and was wearing his letterman's sweater and a green hat Maurice had brought home from Franklin College.

On the court, he began to develop the moves of a master. He was a starter as a sophomore, and Martinsville reached the state finals before losing to Marion, 30-23. The next year, Wooden was the high scorer with ten points as his team beat Muncie for the state title, 26-23. The same two teams reached the final game in 1928. Martinsville lost, 13-12, but it took "the greatest basketball shot" Wooden has ever witnessed to do it.

"On a center jump," he says, "Muncie's center, Charlie Secrist, tipped the ball back to himself. In those days it was legal. He pivoted and let loose an underhand scoop shot that was the highest arched shot I have ever seen. The ball seemed to disappear in the rafters. It came straight down through the hoop, not even touching the net."

Time remained for two easy shots by Martinsville but both of them missed.

"Maybe that's why I get philosophical about winning and losing," he says.

There were three main things in John Wooden's life now: basketball, baseball, and Nellie Riley. Nell played trumpet in the school band and, as a sophomore, John began to wink at her before every game. He's still doing it, but the romance had to survive the serious roadblock of Coach Curtis and his strict "no dating" rule for his players. "That," admitted Wooden, "made it kinda tough."

On the baseball field, Wooden was a promising shortstop — a good hitter with an exceptional arm — but his career in that sport came to an abrupt end one summer night.

"I lost a pitch in the lights," he said. "The ball hit me on the shoulder and richocheted right to my head. It didn't damage my hard noggin much but it ruined my arm. I just couldn't throw well after that."

Kansas and most of the Big Ten schools sought Wooden as a basketball player. Purdue got him because of its engineering school and the influence of Coach Ward (Piggie) Lambert.

Wooden moved purposefully from high school to college, apparently without any of the self-doubt common to many students today. "My father had instilled in all four of his sons that if you worked hard at the beginning it would pay off," Wooden says. "This was not true for him but he got the idea across. Financially, he was not able to help any of his sons get a college education. But all of us did — and they didn't give athletic scholarships in those days. Two of us competed in college and got part-time jobs but they weren't 'false' jobs. If you worked a half-hour, you got a half-hour's pay — fifteen cents. If you worked an hour, you got thirty cents. I never questioned this, never considered it adversity, just as I had never considered my family poor. We made the most of what we had."

As a freshman, Wooden played halfback on the Purdue football team, but he injured a knee. Finally, he was a one-sport man. Basketball. The sport. The one that was to make the Martinsville Chamber of Commerce put up a sign years later that read: "Home of John Wooden."

The portrait is of a three-time, All-Big Ten, All-American guard, and Helms Player of the Year in 1932. His hair is slightly tousled and loosely parted in the middle. His eyes are steely, resolute. His calves bulge, his left arm is extended, his right hand dribbles a leather basketball that looks as big and unwieldy as a dirigible.

This is John Wooden of Purdue, the complete competitor, 5 feet 10½ inches and 183 pounds of slashing, daring fury, one of the premier "floor guards" of his time — and, until Oscar Robertson came along, generally rated the greatest player ever produced in Indiana.

Most of the old-timers of the sport probably couldn't make it big in the sport today. But don't bet Wooden couldn't. He was not only talented, he was resourceful.

Against Indiana, he was belted to the floor near the free-throw line. Before he could get up a shot was missed, the rebound landed in his hands, and he put it in from a sitting position. It won the game.

He bounced off the floor so much he got a nickname: "The India Rubber Man." It was said that during his Purdue career he ran full-bore into every wall in the Middle West. Was there any end to his talents?

"He had a way of stalling the game by fantastic dribbling," says a teammate, Dutch Fehring, who later coached at Stanford. "He would dribble from backcourt to forecourt, all around, and nobody could get that ball away."

Former football star Tom Harmon was a Gary, Indiana, schoolboy when Wooden played at Purdue, and he remembers going to Lafayette to watch him. "In my era," he says, "Wooden was to kids what Wilt Chamberlain or Kareem Jabbar are today. He was king, the idol of any kid who had a basketball. In Indiana, that was *every* kid."

But, apparently, the king's crown stayed on pretty straight. Says Charles (Stretch) Murphy, another teammate:

"Even then he was a team man. It was teamwork all the way, just like it is today. He was a great dribbler — even with those basketballs, which had laces and were lumpy — but not to the extent where he ruined team play. Everything he did was for a purpose — and he knew what the purpose was."

Murphy, now retired executive director of the Tampa (Florida) Boys Clubs, played against Wooden one season in high school, with him one season at Purdue, and several seasons with the professional Kautsky Grocers, for whom Wooden once sank 134 straight free throws.

Murphy was the big man ("I was six-foot-six-and-three-quarters," he says, "a real freak in those days"); Wooden was the little man. They worked out a routine.

"The two of us had a combination defense going," Murphy says. "Johnny would be out in front, harassing the ball handler. I'd fall back in the hole in sort of a one-man zone. Johnny would force the pass and I'd nab it and fire it to him running back up the court. We made it pretty rough on a lot of those boys in those days."

But Murphy knew when to get out of Johnny Wooden's way himself: "There wasn't much variety in offense then. If you tried anything but a two-handed set or a drive, you'd get a ticket to the bench. But Johnny could really drive."

Johnny, however, often had trouble stopping. If unchecked, he might fly ten rows into the bleachers after making lay-ins. Fraternity brothers — and friends — would station themselves at the end of the court to catch him and keep him from hurting himself.

"After a while," says Murphy, "the fans knew what would happen too. Either you were a friend of Johnny Wooden's —

and stood under the basket to stop him — or you wouldn't go there in the first place. You'd find someplace else to watch the game."

It is not recorded that Wooden lost any arguments with the bleacher seats.

But he *did* spend every Christmas while he was at Purdue in the hospital. As a freshman, he had scarlet fever. His leg was injured as a sophomore. His junior year, while practicing the day before Christmas, he stepped on a loose board and suffered a serious leg cut. And, as a senior, he had his tonsils out.

Wooden, despite his skills, was anything but a pampered athlete. He had no free ride. He waited on table for his meals. When he was late because of practice he had to eat and then scrub out the fraternity kitchen. The work didn't end there. Wooden was adept at finding other means to raise funds in a lean time.

One was called "walking to Chicago." Wooden purchased the rights to all concessions on the annual train ride from Lafayette to Chicago for the Purdue-Chicago football game at Soldier Field. He sold everything from doughnuts, apples, and cigarettes to handmade black-and-gold Boilermaker lapel buttons. But sandwiches were the big seller.

"Using a letter of introduction from Coach Lambert," he says, "I'd get donations of ham, cheese, bread, and other things from various Lafayette merchants. The night before, I'd make up the sandwiches. The next day I'd hustle up and down the aisles of the train all during the trip, selling them. It was all profit."

He taped football players' ankles for thirty-five cents an hour and, during the home basketball season, he produced a mimeographed program. The cost: a dime.

"Since I was playing," he says, "I'd arrange for some trustworthy students to sell them. Right after the game, I'd check them out and we'd split the proceeds."

He was as large a success educationally (he won the coveted

Big Ten medal for scholastic achievement in 1932) as he was athletically and economically. He developed a fondness for poetry, notably Whitman and Longfellow and the works of Shakespeare, Scott, and Byron.

And he formed lasting associations, such as that with the Ward Lamberts.

"I'd say Johnny was Ward's favorite player," says Grayce Lambert. She could never forget one incident: "The team was going to a game in Wisconsin, I remember, and I walked into the train depot. Ward's face was just ashen. He said Johnny had not been on the team bus because he had tried to hop onto the back end of a truck and hurt his knee. I've never forgotten Ward's words. He said, 'Grayce, Johnny is ruined forever.'"

Lambert, of course, was wrong. His widow now says she thinks he has forgiven Johnny Wooden. She herself asked Wooden for an autographed picture to hang next to her husband's in her living room.

"Thanks to Grayce," he wrote, "for considering me worthy of being placed beside Ward. He was the best, in every way."

Lambert was a little man — just 5-foot-6 — but it took two student managers stationed alongside him to hold him in his seat in tense moments. Even that didn't always work.

Lambert was a shouter, a screamer, a cajoler — and, if need be, he cussed his players out as they raced by him too. He was as much a show as the run-and-shoot style of ball his teams played.

Once Wooden hurt his leg in the first half. The game wasn't close, so Lambert told John to shower and dress at half time, which he did. Then, in the second half, the opponent began making a run at Purdue.

"Get into the game, Wooden!" Lambert roared.

"But, Coach, I'm dressed in street clothes," Wooden said.

"Who in the hell told you to get dressed?" Lambert demanded.

Wooden adapted Lambert's theories on fast-breaking, free-wheeling basketball, as opposed to a wait-and-shoot style.

As a player at Purdue, Wooden started making a coaching notebook. "It was just for my own interest," he said. "I didn't know I was going to coach at the time."

He talked to the big names of the day — George Keogan of Notre Dame, who won 77 percent of his games and created the "shifting man-to-man" defense, Doc Carlson of Pittsburgh, who invented the "figure-8" offense and won national titles in 1928 and 1930, Walter Meanwell of Wisconsin, who won four Big Ten championships, Tony Hinkle of Butler, dean of Indiana coaches and a national titlist in 1929. All are now Hall of Famers.

"By the time I finished talking to them," said Wooden, "I had a pretty fine notebook."

But the Piggie Lambert influence has remained at the core of Wooden's coaching philosophy through the years.

There is a touch of Lambert in the Wooden psychology too.

"If you knew him the way I did," said Wooden, "you'd find him to be a warm human being. Of course, he did things a certain way that upset many people. But he had a reason for doing them that way."

Lambert, like Wooden, had a single-minded dedication to basketball. Mrs. Lambert recalls: "We were on a long train trip east to play in Madison Square Garden. Ward never could sleep. He would just pace the corridors of the train, back and forth, all night. The train stalled, in subzero, snowy weather, and I got very cold. I woke up and Ward had stolen one of my blankets. When I asked him why, he said, 'Use your coat for a blanket. Johnny Wooden is cold and I gave him your blanket. He's got to play tomorrow night; all you're going to do is sit and cheer.'"

Despite the hard times of 1932, Wooden had saved $909 and a nickel by the time he was graduated from Purdue. But two days before he was to marry Nellie Riley, the bank where he had his savings shut down — and its directors went to prison. Wooden had to borrow $200 to pay for the wedding and a one-day honeymoon — in Indianapolis.

But he had nothing left to buy a car. Relatives drove the newly-weds to Dayton, Kentucky.

Wooden was a high school coach for more than a decade. In addition to basketball, he also coached baseball and tennis at South Bend Central, taught English, and served as athletic director and comptroller.

"I really liked high school teaching," he says. "If it hadn't been for World War Two, I probably would still be back there in South Bend."

Walt Kindy and John Wooden came to South Bend Central at the same time. Kindy assisted Wooden in almost all of his jobs and observed him very closely. In a voice that has the same flat twang as Wooden's, Kindy says: "South Bend Central was a big school — nearly three thousand students. But before Wooden came it was sort of a joke in basketball. In a couple of years, Wooden made 'em contenders, put winning spirit in their blood. South Bend Central was on the map."

But the ultimate success — the Indiana state high school championship — was to elude Wooden, just as national titles would for so many years at Indiana State and UCLA.

The competitive fires definitely raged within Wooden throughout the South Bend years.

Take the Central versus Mishawaka games. Two traditional rivals from the basketball badlands of northern Indiana. When they clashed it wasn't just acrobatic lay-ins and two-handed push shots, it was sometimes mayhem and hand-to-hand combat. The Battle of Tippecanoe, without Tyler too, in black, high-top sneakers.

John Wooden took his team to Mishawaka one night for a showdown. The crowd was typically hostile, the feelings tense.

"Whenever we traveled to Mishawaka," remembers guard Ed

Powell, "we always got police escorts to and from the bus. Right after the game, you *ran* to the dressing room."

Central High triumphed on this night, and Wooden walked over to exchange a perfunctory handshake with the losing coach. Witnesses remember the Mishawaka coach telling Wooden about how Central "lucked out and played dirty basketball and won because of bad officiating, then took a swing at Johnny. And Johnny swung back."

The Central players, of course, had run to the dressing room as soon as the game ended.

"Somebody told us Coach Wooden and the other coach were fighting," said Powell. "We all rushed back to the gym and helped break it up. Now that was a switch! This time, it was the players who broke apart the coaches."

Powell, who later would be Wooden's assistant at Indiana State and UCLA, played for him in 1937, 1938, and 1939 at South Bend Central.

"Every year we were ranked number one, two, or three in the state but we never got to the finals or won the championship," he says. "At the time, we all thought it was a weakness John had — that he had just one way of coaching. That's it. No more. He would make no adjustments in the tougher tournament games, especially in the last two or three minutes.

"His thought was, 'Why should I change now when we've been doing these same things to get us this far?'

"I remember something about Glenn Curtis, his high school coach, saying to him once, 'John, you'll never win the important games because you're not mean enough.' Well, that's where I believed John learned his lesson. He changed. As a player at Purdue he suddenly had a reputation for scoring winning baskets in the last minute. He raced around the court like he had a motor up his fanny, passing and cutting all the time, while a man tried to guard him, all over the court.

"His idea was that, eventually, his superior conditioning would put him one step ahead at the finish. He truly thought,

'If conditioning made me an All-American for three years, then why can't I apply the same theory to coaching, too?' He thought if he could outplay the other guy on sheer conditioning, then why not condition his teams too? He always had a saying, 'We'll stay with 'em in the first half, and beat 'em in the second half.'

"But conditioning, it turned out, wasn't enough to win the big tournament games. You needed to make changes in strategy and personnel too. He didn't learn that until much later."

Wooden apparently was unshaken by South Bend Central's failure to dominate Indiana basketball, however.

"He was much the way he is now," Kindy says. "He'd already made a lot of decisions about life — very early. His fundamentals were so strong that he wasn't like many other men. He didn't have to think a long time on things. He would just say yes or no — or he'd agree or disagree — right now."

Organization enabled Wooden to pursue three careers — coach, teacher, and player — for the first six years after he graduated from Purdue. He was a player on weekends for Frank Kautsky's Wholesale Grocers and other teams. Often this period involved all-night drives from games at outposts such as Oshkosh or Sheboygan so that Wooden could check in on time at his Dayton or South Bend Central classroom on Monday morning.

It was barnstorming basketball, with Kautsky's often playing against a black team from New York City, the Renaissance Big Five — Rens, for short — a team Wooden still calls "the best I ever saw."

The Rens had succeeded the Original Celtics as rulers of the basketball world. From 1932 to 1936, they took on all comers, traveling in their own bus — Harlem Globetrotter style — on a four-month tour of one-night stands. Usually, they ended up sleeping in the bus because they couldn't get accommodations at hotels.

"The Rens didn't make race an issue," says Wooden. "In those days, things were just accepted."

Kautsky's and the Rens might make an Indiana swing — Muncie to Kokomo to Indianapolis, where they'd play before 15,000 screaming fans at Butler fieldhouse. Or they might play on a dance floor in Chicago's black section, where a band featuring Cab Calloway's sister Blanche would entertain at half time and during time outs. To sell pro basketball in those days, you had to offer dancing and music too.

Which team won the most games? Wooden the Competitor answered:

"Oh, we were about even in games won. Maybe they were better. But almost always the games were close — one or two points. The largest margin of victory was ten or twelve points." He smiled wickedly. "And *we* won those games."

But Wooden's respect for the Rens and players such as Clarence (Fat) Jenkins, who guarded him, Wee Willie Smith, and Bill Yancey remains as strong as it was then. He knows the Rens won 473 games against only forty-nine losses over a four-year period, including eighty-eight in a row.

He cuts into a filet and talks: "Wee Willie Smith was the meanest player I ever saw. He was six-foot-five and two hundred and ten pounds. Whenever he got into a fight, it was over right now. He was one person who'd have had a chance in the ring with Joe Louis. I'm not ashamed to say I was scared of him. We started our games when Wee Willie was ready. But, you know, I saw him at a Hall of Fame dinner recently. He has white hair now. Gentlest man you'd ever want to meet."

He smiles, then thinks about Yancey:

"Along with Bobby McDermott [later player-coach of the Chicago American Gears of the NBL], Bill Yancey was the greatest outside shooter I've ever seen. Even with not too round a ball, he would hit every shot from nine different positions around the perimeter. I saw him do it, moving from one corner to the other and back, eighteen times in a row! Without missing a shot!"

The stories roll now . . .

"When I hit my one-hundredth consecutive free throw, the

game was stopped and Frank Kautsky himself presented me with a hundred-dollar bill . . .

"I was playing with another team once and a teammate and I were delayed by a snowstorm on a car trip from South Bend to Pittsburgh. We got there at the half and our team was trailing. But we managed to win. When we got our pay envelopes, though, half of our pay had been deducted. I immediately went to the owner after the game and said: 'We want our transportation money.' He said, 'No.' So I said, 'All right, we want our full money in advance for the next three games or we're gonna drive back to South Bend right away.' We got the money . . .

"I was driving high and hard on a center jump-tip play and ripped my thigh. My knee and ankle turned black right away. I played the next year, even though my leg wasn't recovered. That was the year the center jump went out. Just to show you what *that* meant to the game, I scored twice as much, even though I wasn't half the player I'd been before."

Pro basketball in the 1930s was a back-alley sport compared to its glitter and gold of the 1970s. It was smothered somewhere beneath all the headlines about the more prestigious college game, particularly the Big Ten. Teams in the National Basketball League, the forerunner to today's NBA, were financed by industrial firms in big cities and rural villages with names like the Whiting (Indiana) All-Americans, the Kankakee (Illinois) Gallaghers, the Akron Goodyear Wingfoots, the South Bend Studebakers, the Battle Creek Kelloggs.

As a professional player, John Wooden is still known as a nonstop dribbler.

Chuck Bloedorn (pronounced BLAY-dorn) had the unpalatable task of guarding Wooden in those days, a task at which he failed more than succeeded. "Johnny was constantly in motion," said Bloedorn, then a backcourt star for the Wingfoots, "and about the only way you could stop him was not to let him dribble, shut him off before he had a chance to. But that wasn't easy. In fact, if you held him to fourteen or sixteen points, you were doing a pretty good job. I'd say the only real chance we had against him was when he got sick. You just had to hope he got a heavy cold or the flu or something."

Wooden's nine-year tenure at South Bend Central was interrupted by navy service (as a lieutenant, his job was to get combat flyers in shape). Because of his three-year tour of duty, Wooden was unable to maintain house payments and lost his home. "I had no personal complaints," he said. "They gave me my job back, but so many things had changed."

He was offered two other high school jobs, plus the head basketball job at Indiana State Teachers College. That's the one he chose. He was replacing a familiar face, a man he highly admired — Glenn Curtis, his old high school coach from Martinsville.

"I thought I might as well change to a college," says Wooden. "I had my eye on coaching in the Big Ten."

Headlines flashed and radios crackled with news from across the oceans:

American troops badly beaten by German tanks and dive bombers at Kasserine Pass in North Africa . . . Allies commanded by General Eisenhower invade Italy . . . U.S. Marines seize the island of Tarawa from the Japanese . . . FDR and Churchill meet Stalin at Teheran . . . General Patton slaps a U.S. soldier.

And from the home front:

"Oklahoma" sets up a beachhead on Broadway . . . Twenty-three persons die and 700 injured in Detroit's bloody race riots . . . Pvt. Joe DiMaggio, pride of the Yankees, patrols the outfield for the Camp Santa Ana (California) team . . . Lt. Johnny Beazley, the Cardinals' hero of the previous World Series, is pitching fastballs at Nashville's Berry Field . . . The line-up at Norfolk Naval Air Station includes Dodgers Pee Wee Reese and Hugh

Casey . . . A wounded GI returning to America peers out the window of a hospital train and says, "Even the dump piles here look swell."

It was 1943, a turning point in the World War and a year when John Wooden volunteered for navy preflight as a physical training instructor. He was assigned to Chapel Hill, North Carolina, then Iowa City, where he met fellow instructors Bud Wilkinson and Jim Tatum, who would go on to postwar football glory as head coaches at the Universities of Oklahoma and Maryland.

It was there, too, where Nell Wooden became a "believer in fate."

On what she describes as "the saddest day of my life," her husband received orders to serve aboard the carrier U.S.S. *Franklin* in the South Pacific. But shortly before Wooden was to bid farewell to his family, he was stricken with appendicitis and had to undergo emergency surgery. His orders were abruptly canceled. In his place went Freddie Stalcup, a fraternity brother of John's and a budding Purdue football player, who, says Wooden, "even looked a little like me." Within weeks, while Wooden was convalescing in Iowa, tragic news arrived from the South Pacific: the *Franklin* was blown up by a kamikaze plane. Among the many dead was Freddie Stalcup. Fate had cost John Wooden one life, a friend's — and probably preserved another, his own.

Wooden had orders to go to the South Pacific again when the war ended. In 1946, a year later, he was discharged — his only affliction to show from his military service an injured disk in his lower back (which still bothers him today) suffered in a spill onto a cement court while playing basketball.

"When John looks back on those years," said Nell, "he feels now that he'd have been better off staying in coaching. But when John went in, he felt he had a duty. He felt somehow that, if he went, his son would never have to be in a war."

But as Nell Wooden spoke on a scorching afternoon during the summer of 1972, the headlines flashed and radios and TV sets crackled with news not unlike that of three decades before:

South Vietnamese paratroopers capture the battle-scarred Quang Tri Citadel . . . A U.S. pilot is killed when his A-37 fighter-bomber is shot down over An Loc . . . The Soviet navy is reportedly building twice as many nuclear submarines as the United States . . . Thirty terrorist bombings in Buenos Aires gravely injure six persons on the 20th anniversary of the death of Eva Perón, wife of the erstwhile Argentina dictator . . . President Nixon assures Israeli Prime Minister Golda Meir that the United States will continue to work for "a just peace in the Mideast that will protect the integrity of Israel."

CHAPTER 4

Terre Haute and Westwood, Ho!

THE BLOODIEST WAR in the history of mankind was over. A nation and a world struggled back to normalcy. The boys were coming home. So was Lieutenant John Wooden, age thirty-five, to his first college coaching job.

The year was 1946. The place: Terre Haute, Indiana, the "Coal Capital" of the Midwest, a soot-covered town not far from the Illinois border and near a site where General William Henry Harrison built a fort back in 1811.

At Indiana State Teachers College, Wooden held four jobs. He was athletic director, coached basketball and baseball, and taught English. It was a small school (enrollment: 2500), and the six-man coaching staff had to spend considerable time away from the athletic arena, lecturing history classes and supervising chem labs, among other assignments.

At the same time, one of Wooden's protégés from South Bend Central had been discharged from three years in the Marine Corps. Ed Powell had attended Indiana University and played for a championship House of David basketball team before entering the service. Now he was at Indiana State, pursuing his bachelor's degree and trying out for John Wooden's first college varsity.

Make no mistake, this was Basketball Country. Despite the school's small enrollment, Wooden was greeted on the first day of practice by 170 players! The turnout was swelled by dozens of GIs in their early twenties returning to school from battlefields, boot camps, and aircraft carriers. And now came a major problem: how to slash the turnout down to squad size?

That led to his first — and probably severest — crisis at Indiana State.

Eager to rekindle the glory years he had known as a high school coach, Wooden promptly looked to South Bend. Now that the war was over, the coach knew there would be dozens of fellows who had played for him — and against him — fresh out of combat fatigues and searching for a suitable college. Freshmen were eligible for the varsity in those days, so Wooden was anxious to load his roster with young men who were familiar with his "controlled fast-breaking" style. Result: many telephone calls and trips to South Bend later, Wooden took along his trainer and about twenty players.

He knew he could win lots of battles on the basketball court, but John Wooden was confronted by a different kind of battle. The townspeople of Terre Haute were angered by the influx of South Bend players. In sports pages, in barber shops and drugstores, on street corners, Wooden was bitterly criticized for spitting in the eye of tradition. Everybody knew you didn't field a basketball team at Indiana State unless it was stocked mostly with local kids. Why, the nerve of that man! Importing those carpetbaggers all the way from South Bend!

What's more, the team was returning intact! An outstanding team too! The year before Wooden arrived, the Sycamores won twenty-one of twenty-eight games and reached the National Association of Intercollegiate Basketball (now the NAIA) finals against Southern Illinois, only to lose by nine points.

But now, the coach — and the choreography — were different. Glenn Curtis, still recognized as one of Indiana's premier coaches (he had led Martinsville High to four state titles), was headed for pro basketball to coach the Detroit Falcons. He left behind a patterned, slowdown style that just wasn't John Wooden's style.

"The people always had strong feelings that mostly local

players should be used," Ed Powell remembers. "In a way, you almost got the idea that using local kids was more important than what kind of record you had. Well, John was criticized for this more than anything else. And what really upset a lot of people was that a local kid, who'd been a star as a high school senior the year before, barely made the club. But John was interested only in how good you were, not where you came from. He didn't care whether his players came from South Bend or New York, or were black or white."

As it was, the Wooden way prevailed as the *only* way. On Indiana State's 1946-1947 varsity, several holdovers from the previous year's team were cut, much to the dismay of parents who complained to — and won sympathy in print from — local journalists. And two starters named Lenny Reszewski and Dan Dimich, as well as the first handful of substitutes, were freshmen from South Bend.

The scenario was different. Basketball at Indiana State, an independent school, was already riding a prosperity wave when John Wooden arrived. There would be not quite the same echoes of Dayton and South Bend this time.

Wooden inherited a program that under Curtis had enjoyed seven winning seasons in eight years. But the success was perpetuated by the little man from South Bend.

The first season, the Sycamores were 18-7 and qualified to play in the NAIB tournament at Kansas City. But Wooden suddenly had to grapple with his first known confrontation involving racial feelings — a black Indiana State player "they wouldn't let play in the tournament." Wooden met the issue squarely: he pulled his team out.

The player's name: Clarence Walker. "Not a great ball-player," said Wooden, "and not one that's gonna get to play very much. Nevertheless, he was on my traveling squad. I wouldn't take the team and leave him home."

Thus, the Sycamores *all* stayed home that year. "I didn't

make any great issue of it, or try to publicize it," said Wooden, looking back. "When I found out, I just said 'no.'" And he kept the matter so quiet he never told Ed Powell.

The next year — a 27-8 campaign — Wooden took his team (including Walker) to the NAIB. The Sycamores beat Hamline University of Minnesota and former Minneapolis Laker star Vern Mikkelsen in the semifinals, thanks to heroics by All-American Duane Kleuh (pronounced Klee), a skinny forward. In a heart-stopping thriller, Kleuh sank two free throws after time had run out to send the game into overtime, then hit a fifteen-footer to win the game. "We celebrated so much that night," Kleuh recalls, "that we didn't have anything left for the next game. It was sort of an anticlimax."

The following night, in the 1948 championship game, Indiana State put up a valiant fight most of the way, but lost to Louisville, 82-70.

Again, shades of South Bend. John Wooden did not win the Big Game.

"Be on the floor by ten past three!"

Duane Kleuh says he must have heard those words a thousand times. There were afternoons a quarter century ago when John Wooden's daily practice sessions were infinitely more austere, longer, and more punishing physically than they are today.

"We practiced thirty-five to forty percent longer every day than most teams," said Kleuh, "and seldom less than three hours. He'd keep us on the floor until six o'clock, sometimes as late as six-thirty. And even during the season, we'd always scrimmage one hour the night before a game!"

As a tactician and psychologist, Wooden — then as now — rarely, if ever, mentioned the enemy.

"When he talked to us the night before the game, or just prior to the tip-off," said Kleuh, "he was very strong about not talking about the other team. He told us he was always concerned about what *we* do, not what they do. He knew what we should be doing out there, but I often felt that maybe a little scouting of the other teams might have helped."

Today at UCLA, practices are much shorter — generally one and a half to two hours. And there is *no* scrimmaging on the eve of a game. But conditioning is — as it always was — an obsession with John Wooden.

"I remember one of our players asking him how he led the Big Ten in scoring," says Kleuh, "and John sorta stood there, smiling modestly and shaking off the question. When he finally did answer, he told us that in the last five minutes of every game, he was the one player on the court who was in better condition than everybody else. He said he was physically ready to score a lot of points in those last few minutes. I don't know if that was really the truth or not, but that's what he said."

The scene: Downtown Kansas City on a blustery day in March 1948.

John Wooden customarily wore a hat outside in winter, and he was wearing one while strolling the streets with Ed Powell on the eve of an NAIB tournament game.

Suddenly Wooden approached a stranger.

"Excuse me, sir," he said, "can you please tell me what the population of Kansas City is?"

The man shrugged. "Oh, about five hundred thousand, I guess," he said.

"Thank you very much," said Wooden, half smiling and moving on.

Powell was puzzled. "What," he said to his boss, "brought that on?"

Wooden smiled nervously and removed his hat. The brim was dirtied with fresh pigeon droppings.

"I just wanted to know," said Wooden, "what the percentages were of that happening to *me*, out of all these people in Kansas City."

*

They were years of basketball affluence at Indiana State, but not personal affluence for John Wooden. In March 1948 he longed for a more comfortable life-style.

The scene: Downtown Kansas City again. The team had checked into its hotel and sat down to its pregame meal. John Wooden grabbed a fresh apple and left with Ed Powell to walk the streets again. They walked a few blocks, gazing mostly into windows of shops and stores, whereupon Wooden turned to Powell and said: "Do you know that if someone were to offer me a contract at five thousand dollars a year for life, I'd sign it right now!"

Today Powell remembers the remark as if it had happened yesterday. "John and I were laughing about it not too long ago," said Powell, now city manager of Placentia, California. "He was saying, 'Boy, just imagine what bad shape I'd be in today! Still making five thousand dollars!'"

Within a few weeks, in the spring of 1948, the dream of a bigger contract became reality.

Wooden had a chance to realize his goal of coaching in the Big Ten, then perhaps the country's most prestigious basketball conference. The University of Minnesota job was open. So, for less money, was the one at UCLA, where college basketball was like a "B" movie by comparison (as it was up and down the Pacific Coast) and where Wooden was recommended by Bob Kelley, the late Rams' radio announcer, who had known him in South Bend.

Wooden leaned toward Minnesota. But there was a condition. He would have to accept the current Minnesota basketball coach as his assistant. He said he could not do that and wanted to bring along Ed Powell instead. Minnesota officials took the matter to an athletic board.

Fate turned around a Midwestern snowstorm, which temporarily knocked out telephone service between Minnesota and Indiana. Wooden waited by a phone that didn't ring for word from Minnesota. The deadline they had agreed upon had passed. UCLA did call — and Wooden accepted the offer of Athletic Director Wilbur Johns to succeed him as Bruin coach.

An hour later — the telephone service restored — Minnesota reached Wooden. The Gophers wanted him. He could bring along his assistant. But it was too late. The Hoosier was going west.

"I still don't know why UCLA offered me the position," he says today. "But I like to think Dutch Fehring had something to do with it. He'd not only been a teammate of mine at Purdue, he was now football line coach at UCLA. I've never regretted the decision to accept."

But, for an unsettling time, there was doubt.

They call it "The Village," although many say it doesn't look like a village anymore.

High-rise office buildings shoot up all over the place, twenty stories into skies heavy with ocean breezes and clouds of ozone. Sidewalks are jammed with movie goers, mostly college kids, waiting to see any of several first-run flicks in lines that stretch around entire blocks. Parking lots ("That'll be two dollars, Mister, and leave the keys in the car!") and narrow streets intersecting at jagged angles are choked by bumper-to-bumper Rivieras and VWs and Datsuns and LTDs and Pintos, many with rear-window decals that say "UCLA."

This is Westwood Village, Los Angeles, a cluster of cafés and fashionable boutiques and bookshops and theaters bustling in the shadow of a massive university.

The faces, the places, the character are a curious but fascinating blend of quaint and modern, of Establishment and Free Spirit, of festive gaiety and urban crawl, of Mediterranean and Twentieth-Century Steel-and-Glass. Still, the merciless hand of "progress" has not quashed all the storybook charm and "College Town, U.S.A." feeling — the red-tile roofs, the Spanish courts, the brick walls, and exquisite girl-watching that grew out of a vast bean-and-barley acreage four decades ago.

Nearby lies the university. Modern. Sprawling. A mixture of Romanesque and Antiseptic Modern, cloistered amid eucalyptus trees beneath the hills of Bel-Air and alongside Beverly Hills, both just a short T-Bird flight away. The campus writhes with 27,000 students of assorted nationalities, colors, and politics — sort of a United Nations West. And it turns out diplomas almost as fast as all those computerized registration cards and parking tickets.

What's more, it has cultivated a strong reputation in not the three Rs but the three As: academics, activism, and athletics. As a center of higher learning, UCLA ranks among the dozen leading universities nationally. As a seat of student activism, it ranks below Berkeley and Columbia, but above most other campuses — a whirlwind of antiwar rallies, Angela and Che posters, and nudes and four-letter words in the *Daily Bruin*. As a sports power once described by *Life* as "the Athens of Athletics," UCLA has climbed further faster than any other institution (twenty-seven national championships — all since 1956). It has developed famous names in the world of professional and Olympic sport: Jackie Robinson, Bob Waterfield, Rafer Johnson, C. K. Yang, Arthur Ashe, and Kareem Abdul-Jabbar. And ex-Bruin athletes who achieved fame elsewhere: the late Dr. Ralph Bunche, a United Nations undersecretary, and Mike Frankovich, a motion picture producer.

A village and a university. Two worlds of splendor and tumult. Into this cataclysmic setting, a quarter century ago, came John Robert Wooden, age thirty-seven, his wife, and two small children, although things weren't nearly so cataclysmic in those days.

He arrived at a time when whole neighborhoods spent Sunday afternoons cheering Hopalong Cassidy and Buck Rogers and laughing at Milton Berle and Ed Wynn in the living room of the only family on the block with a TV set. Westwood Village was really a village ("You wouldn't believe it! This was the loveliest place I've ever seen in my life!" said one merchant), a place with no high-rise buildings or parking meters, only two movie-houses, and where kids flocked to Tom Crumpler's for his famous milk shakes, chilled in aluminum containers and topped by a generous helping of whipped cream. "Why, everybody," says a long-time villager, "knew who Tom Crumpler was."

Meanwhile, the university had come a long way from the days when it was L.A. State Normal, located on Vermont Avenue between downtown and Hollywood, and when angry Angelenos decried the choice of Westwood's farmlands as the school's new campus in 1929 by saying, "Nobody's ever going to drive to school all the way out there!" But UCLA, even with 15,000 students, was still a place with no medical center or multilevel parking garages or athletic teams as prominent as those of older, arch-rival USC — a smug, private university where football had been king with Howard Jones's famed Thundering Herd and basketball rosters included such names as Ralph Vaughn (an ex-Indiana schoolboy who made the cover of *Life*), Alex Hannum, Tex Winter, and Bill Sharman.

Still, John Wooden was a long way from Indiana in 1948.

One day, he and Nell went to lunch at a fountain and grill on the corner of Westwood and Weyburn. They sat quietly at the counter, transplanted Midwestern strangers who had migrated westward with the masses during the postwar years.

John Wooden turned and asked a waitress: "Hello, is Hollis Johnson here?"

Of course Hollis Johnson was there. Back in the kitchen where he usually was, flipping hotcakes or frying eggs, and peering out of an open window every now and then to see who his customers were.

"I'd never heard of Coach Wooden," says Johnson today. "But right away he wanted to establish himself, get acquainted in the community." He paused and thought a moment. "I'm just a common person," he said. "I guess maybe he wanted to get hold of somebody who's common. Right away, we struck up a friendship."

Perhaps, too, John Wooden was groping for a link to his past somewhere amid all these bright lights and fast convertibles and big-city folks.

Hollis Johnson's Fountain and Grill, open since 1944, might have passed for the Candy Kitchen back home in Martinsville. It's tucked away in back of a corner drugstore, decorated with photos of UCLA basketball players and jammed every lunch hour with shoe salesmen, history profs, and lady shoppers against a backdrop of clattering dishes, rattling trays, and plump, matronly waitresses shouting, "Two eggs over easy!" or "One burger! Hold the O!"

To this day, Wooden remains one of Johnson's most regular customers, sitting there almost every noon hour at the counter over a deviled-egg sandwich and a dish of custard — or sometimes a French dip sandwich. He also is a steadfast friend of Johnson, as is the Los Angeles Lakers' star guard, Jerry West, who stops by frequently to chat about fast breaks and full-court presses and whistle-happy referees.

In Hollis Johnson, a white-haired man with a smooth face and a quick smile, they have an ardent admirer who talks basketball incessantly and outspokenly, the words spewing out like machine-gun fire in an accent as flat as the prairies of his native Texas.

"Sometimes," says Wooden, grinning, "you get the feeling *he's* the coach of my team."

Says Johnson of Wooden: "He's the greatest, smartest man I've ever met. Look at the way he talks to the kids, saying things like 'Be quick! Don't hurry!' And how he writes sayings to his wife like 'As ever, forever.' You know, he's really sharp! And he's criticized me a lotta times too. Sometimes I've done or said things that weren't for my own good. But he's right. I really respect him."

Johnson relaxed over coffee in a corner booth one morning after the breakfast traffic had subsided, reminiscing about the coach and his years in Westwood: "Ya know, when he came here, he never really had any great bonus players to start with. Oh, maybe he had one or two good ones, but all the rest were just average players — and he turned basketball into a real spectator sport here. A lotta people said his teams didn't play much defense, but that's not right. Why, believe me, they'd chase ya and rush ya all over the court!"

His thoughts — and his words — skitter and meander and leapfrog from subject to subject. The games. The thrills. The heartbreaks. The players UCLA recruiters brought into the kitchen to meet him. And many of those same players, notably Lew Alcindor, who ate lunch on an old orange crate — in the privacy of the storage room behind the kitchen.

"And that Kareem Jabbar!" he said. "He was the greatest player I've seen in my life, really and truly! Ya know, UCLA never got, for a long time, the good big man. Not the six-nine or six-ten big man — until Kareem came along . . .'"

The subject quickly changes to the coach.

"Coach Wooden's an aggressive coach too," he said. "A lotta people don't believe that. They think he just sits there and does this and that. Aw, that's a lotta . . ." His voice dies suddenly, then revs up again. "I guess nobody would ever know that about him. He's not that type of man. He was so gentle and kind . . . but that didn't make any difference. Men like that should be destined to become great coaches. He's had so much ability. The players all say, 'He's the greatest coach I ever played for.' If you don't believe it, ask Hazzard. He'll tell you. Ask Goodrich. I bet Jabbar will tell you the same thing. And he's an understanding coach too."

What, then, of the changing times? The placid youth of yesteryear? The restless youth of today? Society then and now? Now Hollis Johnson's sixtyish generation was showing; so were his rural, conservative roots. His words rambled on, and the sentiments could well have been John Wooden's. Or maybe those of any man on the street back in Centerton or Martinsville or South Bend or Terre Haute.

"Look at the movies today!" said Johnson. "What are they

about? Sex! Gosh! People living together when they're not married. Hell, I don't believe in this stuff! And look at that *Penthouse* magazine they sell in the drugstore up front. The way they show women in those pictures. Why, that's horrible! That's pornography! And Coach Wooden believes the way I do. About the kids today too. He feels that if the parents bring 'em up right, they'll go a long way in this world."

He sipped some coffee and sighed. "Maybe ya have to compromise sometimes," he said. "But I guess you could call me a square. Of course, I believe the kids should have every right in the world to do a lotta things. But . . ."

His eyes gazed up at the gallery of photos on the walls. At number thirty-three, Lew Alcindor, who spoke out for black power. At number thirty-two, Bill Walton, who spoke out against the war.

"A lotta people," he said, "come in here and say, 'Why don't you take those pictures down, Hollis?' But I say, 'Well, listen, I feel today just like I did when they first came here and I first got acquainted with 'em.' There's no change. They've never done anything to hurt me. Except I sometimes get upset with 'em about some of these things. I say, 'I hope these kids who demonstrate nowadays will change before it's too late, that's all.' Really, UCLA's never been a bad school like some of those other schools with a lotta trouble . . . It's been pretty peaceful here."

He thought back to a decade ago. Perhaps, he said, that's when the seeds of youthful discontent were sown. "Now this wasn't something that just happened on the UCLA basketball team," he said. "It started happening all over the nation. And it's a funny thing. These kids are very interested in the country. Maybe they haven't worked a day in their life . . . Maybe they got an extra job, but they wanta change the world. There's twenty-five million of 'em who are gonna be eligible to vote now too. Maybe we better stop and listen to some of 'em."

He sighed. "Really, they don't have to get mixed up in this

other stuff now," he said. "Five years from now, they'll look back and realize they'll still have plenty of time to do all they wanta do. I'm sure that's how Coach Wooden feels about these things. He's a man who has a lotta influence on the youth of today, especially those who'll listen to him."

Hollis Johnson got up slowly from the table. It was time to go back to work. Back to the steamy kitchen and the sizzling grill where he has toiled for almost thirty years.

The lunch crowd would soon be pouring in. So, too, would a familiar face in the crowd, a face that wasn't very familiar back in 1948. Hollis Johnson knew he'd better start fixing the deviled-egg sandwiches and dishing up the custard.

L.A. in 1948. Even then, it was a proliferation of suburbs frantically searching for a city that, unlike New York or Chicago, was searching for itself. The City of the Angels was a place nobody ever wrote a ballad about. She had not one personality but several. There were Hollywood and tract homes, shopping centers and hillside mansions, beaches and mountains, a Spanish heritage, and a "melting pot" of new settlers who were astonished, along with those who came before them, to learn that there was such a thing as a "native Californian."

They came from the Midwest and South mostly, riding the tide of the great aircraft boom. They left behind the arctic blasts of Iowa and Nebraska and the dusty flatlands of Oklahoma and Texas to find their place under the California sun in a land virtually devoid of the two monsters they would unwittingly create — freeways and smog.

Once a sleepy pueblo. Now a burgeoning metropolis. This is the L.A. to which John Wooden came in 1948. This is the L.A. that was galaxies away from the Indiana he left behind.

Indeed, the contrast was mind-boggling. Take Martinsville, for instance. It had the traditional accouterments of Midwest Americana — a town square with a courthouse (which has been condemned as unsafe) in the middle, where the folks used to hitch their horses on Saturday nights and now park cars around.

There was Barskin's Department Store and the Candy Kitchen, the latter still there. "John and I went in for a soda when we were back for the day he was honored," said Nell. "No, it's not that much like Hollis Johnson's. Hollis' place is too modern."

There were the thirteen spas and the natural spring water for which the town was famous and the Home Lawn Sanitarium, where they gave baths to rheumatism patients and where Nellie worked as a telephone operator.

And there were the ten-cent movies ("I believe the nickelodeons were gone," said Nell) at the Martinsville Theater, where teen-age sweethearts Johnny and Nellie thrilled to Tom Mix and Rudolph Valentino and Wallace Reid cavorting across the screen. "John couldn't always pay the day we went," recalls Nell, "so he'd run ahead so I wouldn't know it and pay in advance."

Two decades later: It is the spring of 1948, and the newly hired basketball coach at UCLA is off to an unforgettable start in the big city. This was John Wooden's second visit to Los Angeles — to attend the Bruins' basketball awards dinner — and he was staying at the home of trainer Ducky Drake.

Early one morning before sunrise, Wooden got up quietly — so as not to awaken Drake and his wife — to telephone Nell back in Terre Haute. As he carefully picked his way through the darkness to the phone, the quiet was shattered by the sounds of bells — BLANG! CLONG! BLANNNNGGGG! Wooden had walked smack into the doorbell chimes, arousing the Drakes. Even after all these years, Wooden tells the story now and then, perhaps subtle testimony to his uneasiness about offending friends. "He's still embarrassed about it," says Drake today.

But that was only a minor annoyance compared with the arrival of the Woodens a few months later after a leisurely, two-week trip by car across the continent, including stopovers at Carlsbad Caverns, the Grand Canyon, and other sightseeing

wonders that Nell Wooden denounced as "too big — I'd get
lost in those places!"

It all happened so very spectacularly. California, here they
came! The vignette probably has been replayed umpteen
million times: a family of four, aliens from a faraway land,
driving west on Route 66 into the urban jungle, overwhelmed
by all the orange-juice stands and drive-in chili bars and all
these strange inhabitants wearing sunglasses and crazy clothes.

Then the freeway. Or was it really the Indianapolis Speed-
way, where Johnny Wooden once drove a race car just for fun
("I didn't go as fast as they go in a race") as a college kid
working there part-time? Suddenly cars whizzed past them
again and again. Billboards became blurs. Signals and stop
signs were nonexistent. And all these traffic lanes! Doesn't
anybody here ever stop? California, here they were. And
so, it seemed, was everybody else.

"We got on the Pasadena Freeway and it almost scared us to
death," recalls Nell. "We'd never seen a freeway before. I remember John getting all upset and saying to us, 'What are we
doing here, anyway?'"

The Woodens settled in a university-owned home in Culver
City — not far from MGM Studios — but their discomfort,
their alienation would last for several years.

Basketball, for one thing, was merely a seasonal avocation in
Southern California along with body-surfing and boat racing
and mountain climbing — and it was dwarfed by football.
Back in Indiana, basketball was religion.

Nowhere was the comparison more vivid than in high schools,
where Wooden and assistant Ed Powell began reconnoitering
gymnasiums for budding UCLA players. What they saw made
them wince again and again.

"We couldn't believe how low-key it was here," recalls Powell,
"compared with Indiana. Here, they had such small gyms —
nothing like back there. And small crowds. The games were
played in the afternoons — and kids would wander in and

out of the gyms the whole game. It was almost like they didn't know who was playing — or care."

A former player recalls, too, that Wooden was shocked to discover that basketball players in California "went to the beach every day in the summer and played volleyball and drank beer."

But the coach believed the indifference could not last forever.

On a trip a few years later to Kentucky, where Wooden's team was thrashed, 84-53, by Adolph Rupp and Company, he told a friend during a long bus ride from Lexington that someday . . . somehow . . . somewhere . . . a few superstars would emerge from California's high schools.

"He told me most of the boys out there were interested in playing tennis and golf," said Melvin Wuest, who was the Woodens' landlord back in Dayton, Kentucky. "He said the college coaches out there didn't have it easy. The high school players didn't know fundamentals. He said that as soon as he got the players really interested in learning fundamentals, the caliber would pick up. John said he had to sell basketball on the Coast to the high school coaches, and he also told me, 'I'll be back to play Kentucky someday — and I'll have a real good team then.'"

It also is known that Wooden's taciturn presence alongside the bombastic UCLA football coach, the late Henry (Red) Sanders, a hard-drinking, irascible Southerner, was equally distressing.

The trouble was, most athletic monies were being pumped into football — a disproportionate share, Wooden thought — whereupon Sanders' single-wing teams quickly became a national power, while basketball was relegated to orphanhood. "Some strong feelings developed between Wooden and Sanders," wrote Melvin Durslag of the Los Angeles *Herald-Examiner*, "but John suffered in silence and never made a public issue of his grievance."

At the same time, Sanders seemed more appealing to the news media than did Wooden. "Red had come in and captured the town," recalls Vic Kelley, UCLA's sports publicist. "He had great personality, magnetism, and charisma. He and Wooden would be together at many social events and the people would gravitate toward Sanders. This was part of Wooden's uneasiness. People in L.A. were more outgoing than anyone he'd met before. He was shy; I think this is why he's never been an effective recruiter."

Wooden's inhibitions — coupled with back-slapping, gregarious Californians — did not mix socially. A typical scene: coaches and writers, drinks in hand, exchanging boisterous laughter and stories, while John Wooden stood calmly in a corner away from the crowd, sipping a cola. "At parties," recalled Ed Powell, "you knew he was not a big-city fellow. I wondered whether he was happy out here. He'd go to alumni functions at fancy hotels and stand there, with his back against the wall. My job was to introduce him to people and say, 'Have you met our coach?' It just wasn't his nature to take the initiative."

Nor was it Wooden's nature to accept a hard drink when offered — or forced upon him. He tells of an approach by one writer "who later became one of my good boosters" at a preseason gathering.

"He had too many drinks, this writer," said Wooden, "and he came over and said, 'You're gonna drink with me.' I said, 'No, I just don't care to; thank you very much.' He said, 'You're gonna drink with me! You're not too damn good to drink with me.' Sam Barry [USC coach] intervened and he said, 'Now, Johnny doesn't drink. You shouldn't be trying to force him to. He's not criticizing you for drinking. You shouldn't criticize him for not drinking — and trying to force him to.' This writer was very obstinate."

Wooden sat in his living room one summer night, recalling the incident — and all the others that made life in California uncomfortable.

"People drank back in Indiana, of course," he said. "We didn't drink with them, but they didn't make us do it. Back there, we didn't drink — and we were never criticized."

Nell, seated nearby, interjected: "We came out here and we were made to feel unwelcome."

They talked about the "snide remarks," the attacks on his coaching style.

"The writer who forced me to drink with him," he said, "proceeded in his write-ups to say that even when we won we didn't do very well. According to him, we were 'wild' and 'fire-wagon' and 'racehorse,' but later on, this fellow became a pretty good booster of mine. What it all amounted to was that I had to prove myself out here. My style was being criticized. It seemed we did not receive credit for what we were doing."

John Wooden leaned forward in his chair not long ago in his Santa Monica apartment and looked back on the drastic changes of those early years out West — in life-styles, in people, in places:

"It was different for us out here. We'd never been to a city to speak of. Terre Haute wasn't a city like Los Angeles or anything in this area . . ."

His wife nodded knowingly and sighed. "I felt," she said, "like I was coming to the end of the world."

The coach went on. "In many respects, to be quite honest with you," he said, "we were a little frightened out here."

Perhaps that explains the symbolism of a gold charm affixed to a bracelet that Nell Wooden wears today only on "special occasions." That charm — and all the others — were picked out by Nell, while John had them engraved. They signify the eventful moments in their four decades together: nine miniature keys, each sculptured to form block letters that spell "South Bend," hearts engraved with dates of their marriage and their moves to Dayton, Kentucky, Indiana State, and the United States navy, not to mention heart-shaped medallions commemorating their twenty-fifth and fortieth wedding anniversaries, the latter imbedded with a ruby.

But the most telling token of what lay ahead, of the thoughts dancing through John Wooden's head, was the gold charm he gave his wife when they moved west — a four-leaf clover in deference to Nell's Irish ancestry. Engraved on it was the year, 1948, and, intriguingly enough, a question mark.

CHAPTER 5

So Near and Yet...

> Remember this your lifetime through —
> Tomorrow, there will be more to do . . .
> And failure waits for all who stay
> With some success made yesterday . . .
> Tomorrow, you must try once more
> And even harder than before.
>
> — John Robert Wooden

THE FIRST FIFTEEN UCLA BRUIN TEAMS of John Wooden tried, and tried, and tried. Some of them played very well. Eight of them won divisional or conference championships. None of them had a losing season. But none of them achieved the sort of success that has become commonplace for Wooden teams either.

It was a case of almost but not quite over and over again — a missed opportunity here, a key error there. A chain of freak injuries and illness that buried some excellent chances.

But UCLA fans in the early years of John Wooden were pretty much happy with what they had — because they hadn't had much before him. Starting in 1928, and carrying through their first twenty-one seasons in the Pacific Coast Conference under Caddy Works and Wilbur Johns, the Bruins had only *three* winning years. The major "name" players were men who would go on to greater success in other things — Dr. Ralph Bunche and Jackie Robinson.

UCLA went ten years — from 1932 to 1942 — without beating cross-town rival USC. The year before Wooden came to Westwood, John's Bruins had been only 12-13.

Observers predicted UCLA would be a last-place team in 1948-1949 too. Wooden made a promise. "I've never played on or coached a losing team," he said, perpetuating the legend of invincibility, "and I don't intend to start now."

But the brave public words were not what Wooden felt when he took a look at his first "team" at UCLA. Wooden says the turnout was sixty, assistant Eddie Powell remembers it as about half that. But it was a far cry from the 170 prospects that turned out at Indiana State two years before. And both Wooden and Powell were shocked by the caliber — or lack of it — of the players seeking spots on the Bruin squad.

"I took one look at that material and I thought, 'Ohhhh, Lord!'" says Wooden. "The team had not only finished last the year before, it had lost its best ballplayers — Don Barksdale and Dave Minor. I sure didn't see many basketball players among that new bunch. Boy, it looked pitiful, a motley crew like I had in physical education classes back at Indiana State."

"When we saw them," Nell Wooden adds, "we wanted to go back to Indiana."

But Wooden transformed that unlikely mass into a running, hustling squad that rarely seemed to tire. It won twenty-two games and the Southern Division championship of the PCC before losing to Oregon State and Coach Amory T. (Slats) Gill in a three-game play-off at the Beavers' old gym in Corvallis. ("If your first name was Amory and your middle name Tingle, you'd like to be called 'Slats,' too," Gill used to say.)

"That gym was much worse than ours," Wooden recalls. "It's too bad the games weren't down here. I think we'd have won."

Actually, the Bruins were lucky to get as far as they did. Alan Sawyer underwent an emergency appendectomy before a critical two-game series with USC that closed the regular season. Chuck Clustka and Ron Pearson both came down with the flu. So Wooden had to go with three nonstarters. But the Bruins beat the Trojans twice, 51-50 and 63-55.

"That still is my most satisfying year of coaching," says Wooden. "It was not just that we were picked to finish last and won. I was new here, trying to get established and my style hadn't been well accepted."

The player names then are not as memorable as Alcindor, Goodrich, Hazzard, Wicks, and Walton. Clustka, Pearson, Sawyer, Carl Kraushaar, Eddie Sheldrake, and George Stanich would be hard to reel off, even for a basketball trivia expert. But they helped start the Great Turnaround at Westwood. Several stayed to form the nucleus of the next couple of Bruin teams. Stanich became Wooden's first UCLA All-American.

He was not a big man, and — to put it charitably — he was not a good shooter. But he was an excellent athlete, one of the best UCLA ever produced — an Olympic high jumper in 1948 and a standout baseball pitcher who shut out USC's national championship team and star Wally Hood the same year.

"He was extremely competitive," says Sheldrake. "Sometimes he'd participate in all three sports the same day. He was an awfully good rebounder in basketball and you could go around him twice on defense and he'd still be there to bat the ball down your throat."

After seeing George play forty-five minutes of racehorse basketball in a 74-68 UCLA win over USC in overtime, a Trojan player said: "That Stanich looks twelve feet tall out there." (He was 6-3.)

It was obvious that Stanich's skills left an indelible impression on Wooden too.

There was a game one night in 1951 in which UCLA was getting badly whipped on the backboards, whereupon Wooden summoned a key reinforcement from the bench.

"Stanich!" he yelled. "Get in there!"

Ed Powell was startled.

"Coach," he said. "Don't you remember? Stanich graduated last year."

It was a different sort of game in those days. The center jump after every basket and the underhanded set shot were gone but basketball wasn't really intersectional yet. The thinking was decidedly provincial. The Eastern teams employed the "give-and-go" offense and didn't break much. Midwestern teams all ran, as had Purdue in Wooden's playing days. Western teams played rugged defense and controlled the ball. There was no borrowing of concepts; everyone was locked in.

Watching Wooden's teams in those first UCLA seasons was like seeing a rerun of Piggie Lambert's squads.

"John turned 'em loose with the fast break," says Powell. "It wasn't racehorse. It was fast break under control. But nobody had caught up with him yet. I can remember when we'd have not two on one, or three on one, but five-on-zero fast breaks!"

The Bruins under Wooden were uninhibited, blitzing, grind-you-down. They were always in superb condition. They were always aggressive. And they always had the same sort of supreme confidence Wooden had.

"They used to sort of saunter onto the court," says Pete Newell, the ex-University of San Francisco and California coach. "They'd show a disdain for you. This sort of confidence frustrated some opponents and made others play harder. But you always knew when you played the Bruins, they'd be tough."

After turning the UCLA program around in 1949, Wooden was promptly offered the head coaching job at Purdue. He graciously turned it down — just as he was to turn down jobs at Notre Dame, Minnesota, and Purdue (again) in the 1950s.

His second year at UCLA, a team led by Stanich, Sawyer, Sheldrake, Kraushaar, Ralph Joeckel, and a sixth man named Jerry Norman went 24-7 and won the Southern Division and the right to meet Washington State in the PCC play-offs at the Bruin gym.

Washington State had two men — Gene Conley and Ted Tappe — who would play major league baseball, and three other fine players, Ed Gayda, Bob Gambold (who starred in football, too), and Leon Mangis.

But UCLA had "Goggles," otherwise known as Ralph (Bifocal) Joeckel, who turned out to be the most famous astigmatic in school history. The gangling, bespectacled Joeckel was an engineering major who had been beaten out in late season by Norman. But he was in the first of two play-off games against Washington State with the score tied, 58-58, and time running out.

He got the rebound on a missed shot and began dribbling downcourt. He couldn't see the basket but he could see the clock. Or somebody yelled how much time was left. Three seconds. One step behind the center line, Joeckel cast off with a two-handed set shot — a forty-five-footer. It hit the lower part of the backboard, wedged inside the rim, and fell in.

"I knew it was going straight," he said, sounding like the budding engineer he was, "but I didn't know if it was long enough or tall enough."

It was both, and UCLA beat the Cougars the following night, too, in another tense game, 52-49. And the Bruins were suddenly in a most unfamiliar situation — on their way to the national tournament and a meeting with the Bradley Braves, Paul Unruh, and Gene Melchiorre, at Kansas City.

UCLA led, 57-50, with less than six minutes to play. But it lost, 73-59. What happened?

"We were playing tough, really doing a lot better than most people thought we could do," says Sheldrake, "and then some of our guys just tied up — and we fell apart."

There was some small solace. CCNY, a team UCLA had beaten by seven points in the regular season, went on to win both the NCAA and NIT championships.

The Bruins went back to "B.O. Barn," the nickname affixed to UCLA's former home court — the Men's Gymnasium. It was architecturally attractive on the outside, styled after the campus's original Romanesque concrete-and-red-brick buildings, but cramped, stuffy, and noisy inside. It seated a maximum of only 2450 on pull-out bleachers — that is, on nights when the fire marshal wasn't looking. People's knees jutted uncomfortably into other people's backs. And when Wooden's teams ran and ran and ran the enemy into submission and breathlessness, visiting coaches accused him of turning up the gym's heating system to tire out rival teams — a charge Wooden repeatedly denied.

"If somebody did it," he said, "I certainly had nothing to do with it. Which team runs the most? We do, of course. So shouldn't we wear out faster?"

"The place was hotter than hell," says former Los Angeles *Times* writer Jack Geyer, who nicknamed it B.O. Barn. "There was just one little window open in the whole place. But Wooden's teams were always superbly conditioned early in the season. They'd win ten in a row before *you* got in shape. They'd come out roaring in that old gym like it was the one-hundred-meter finals in the Olympics."

"It was nothing but murder in there," says ex-official Al Lightner. "Like walking into an oven. And once the game started, there those fans would go in that little place — booing and hollering and raising the devil. It was something."

"Yes, it was very warm during games," says Don Bragg, a UCLA star of the early 1950s, "but generally, I thought it was a good place to play."

Most Bruin players weren't all that starry-eyed over the bandbox gym, however. Take Johnny Moore, for instance, who joined Bragg as a freshman on the varsity in the 1951-1952 season. Moore was a skillful forward, 6-foot-5 and black, who shot free throws in a flick-of-the-wrists, underhanded fashion and was recruited all the way from basketball territory Wooden knew so well, Gary, Indiana, where he'd worked in a steel mill.

Recruiter Ed Powell said Moore was enticed to Westwood when his wife opened the UCLA yearbook and showed a photo of a black student-body officer to Moore's mother. "She said something like, 'You mean they got a Negro holding office where there are fifteen thousand white folks?' That sewed things up. She looked at Johnny and said, 'That's gonna be your school.' "

On the night of Moore's first varsity game, the Men's Gym was jammed. A reporter approached Moore, who started as a frosh, and asked him, "Are you excited, playing before this full house?"

Moore shook his head. He was asked why.

"Well, sir, the UCLA gym is nothing," he said, "compared to my last high school game in Indiana. They had a crowd of eighteen thousand that night."

Eventually, fire department officials started looking at B.O. Barn.

In 1955, the start of Wooden's eighth season at Westwood, the Bruins had to move elsewhere. Fire officials ruled the building unsafe unless crowds were limited to 1000, thus making UCLA basketball a losing proposition financially.

"Elsewhere" for the Bruins soon became everywhere. That season they played on three "home" courts — the tiny Venice High School gym, Pan-Pacific Auditorium, and Long Beach City College. They spent the next three seasons in the Pan-Pacific and the following six in the new Los Angeles Sports Arena — mostly sharing space in double-headers with USC — with occasional games at Santa Monica City College and the Long Beach Arena.

When Bragg was still in high school, Wooden wrote him, "If you come to UCLA, before your eligibility is finished, you'll be playing in a new pavilion on our campus."

It was twelve years after Bragg graduated when the Bruins' spacious new home, 12,800-seat Pauley Pavilion, opened.

"Wooden says now that when he wrote me he didn't think I'd progress as fast as I did in my classwork," says Bragg, an honor student who had almost straight As in high school.

None of UCLA's earlier gyms was satisfactory. "I think lack of a real home gym and positive thinking were the main reasons we didn't win a championship in those early years," says ex-star center Willie Naulls.

"If we could have played before the home folk in Pauley Pavilion and had that NCAA fever like they do now, I think we could have gone all the way almost any of those seasons. The proper thinking is a big part of achieving any goal, too. It used to be, we only wanted to win the conference. The NCAA, then, was just something we got to if we really did well, sort of a reward. Now, UCLA prepares for the NCAA too."

Much of the preparation in the early years was directed toward survival.

Gary Cunningham, now Wooden's chief assistant, recalls that as late as the first years of the 1960s, when he was a player, the Bruins *still* were practicing in the Men's Gym:

"Dust was always seeping through the roof. And the gymnastics team practiced at one end of the court. There were guy wires on some of their equipment, and we had to drape mats around them to protect ourselves in case we hit them. There was chalk dust the gymnasts used all over the floor. One of my jobs was to spend half an hour before every practice with a pail of water and a push-broom mop, picking up the chalk dust. If I hadn't done that, we wouldn't have been able to stand up."

It wasn't much better when UCLA switched its practices occasionally to the Sports Arena, a modern facility. Logistics was the problem this time. The arena is fifteen miles from the UCLA campus.

"It was such a hassle getting down there," says Wooden, "fighting back and forth through traffic, that often we just didn't do it."

In the doubleheaders, too, a large contingent of fans usually stayed to root *against* the Bruins if USC had played the first game.

"It wasn't really like a home gymnasium," Cunningham says.

"Not having your own facility definitely handicaps you in building the kind of tradition you want," says Wooden, "and in getting the enthusiasm for the team you'd like to have. From the beginning at Pauley, the enthusiasm has helped inspire us, carry us. It builds your confidence, subconsciously. But you must remember, we won two national championships *before* Pauley, and came very close to winning a third."

But all of that still seemed on a distant horizon in the early 1950s, when Wooden battled not only the best of the PCC but an injury-illness jinx.

On the eve of the play-off game against Bradley in 1950, Norman — who underwent an appendectomy earlier in the season — suffered a cut over his eye in practice that required four stitches to close. Stanich played with a bone chip in his ankle.

In 1951, Sheldrake — the team captain — and another starter, Art Alper, missed the first game of the PCC play-offs against Washington and played only sparingly in the second as the Huskies won twice, 70-51 and 71-54.

In 1952, Bragg — the team's leading scorer with a ten-point average — ran into a foot-powder box on his way out of the shower, breaking his toe before UCLA met Washington for the PCC title. Bragg played but was ineffective.

Then there was Dick Ridgway, a brilliant shooter with immense potential, who joined the team in 1950-1951. Complex and talented, Ridgway had set freshman and sophomore scoring records, but he suffered a head injury after his sophomore season.

"Coach Wooden never told us," says Eddie Sheldrake, "but he could play only so many minutes a game. He laid out a year but then he had grade problems and psychological problems because he couldn't play all the time. He was never the same."

With a healthy Ridgway and players such as Ron Livingston, Ron Bane, Norman, Moore, and Bragg, UCLA might have won a national title. As it was, the Bruins won the Southern Division in 1951-1952 and played host to Washington in the best-two-out-of-three PCC championship series.

Bragg, now a savings company executive, was a freshman then, a smooth, smart youngster who had played at the same San Francisco high school as Hank Luisetti and was constantly compared to him.

He had concentration (as a youth, learning the game, he had to shoot through a fire escape ladder near his San Francisco home) and he had cool (he broke up a potential fight between Norman, a senior that season, and a Stanford player).

"Bob Houbregs [Washington's All-American center] took one look at our gym," Bragg recalls, "and said, 'It's not much of a place to play but we won't be here more than two nights anyway.'"

But UCLA won two out of three — despite Bragg's broken toe — and advanced to the regionals at Corvallis, Oregon, where the team was dispatched back to Westwood by Santa Clara and Oklahoma City.

Corvallis was becoming a graveyard. The Bruins lost two straight in a conference play-off to Oregon State and its giant center, Wade (Swede) Halbrook, there in 1955, then bowed to Bill Russell and USF in the first round of the regionals there in 1956.

Russell — a whole new style of basketball. It grew almost automatic. You tried to shoot. Russell's hand was there to swat the ball away. In USF's third game of the 1954-1955 season, the Dons lost to UCLA, 47-40. It was their last loss in the next sixty games over two seasons.

USF, under Coach Phil Woolpert, beat UCLA twice in the 1955-1956 season. The first was a 70-53 win in the Holiday Festival in New York, the second a 72-61 victory in the Western Regionals at Corvallis.

A clue to what was going to happen later came in the first half of the Holiday Festival game. UCLA had a one-point lead, and, according to Wooden, was going to hold the ball if it could get the next basket. The ball went to Naulls, who faked Russell and prepared to slam it through the net. But wait a minute! There was Russell's hand, blocking the ball before Naulls could drive it home.

"Even though it was only the first half," said Wooden, "it stunned us — and it beat us."

UCLA went a perfect 16-0 in conference play, led by Naulls, Morrie Taft, Dick Banton, Connie Burke, and Allen Herring, and Russell's chief aide — guard K. C. Jones — was ineligible for the play-offs. But his replacement, Gene Brown, scored twenty-three points and Russell had twenty-one, to go with twenty-three rebounds. Naulls and Taft: sixteen points each.

The following night, ironically, was historic for the beaten Bruins. They won their first NCAA play-off game ever, 94-70, over Seattle.

But the next two seasons were mediocre and then along came Cal.

Pete Newell and John Wooden didn't share a lot of things. They differed especially on a basic concept of the game. Wooden was dribble, pass, and fast break. Newell was stop the dribble, pass, and fast break.

Newell says he "loved to play" against Wooden's early teams when they used merely the up-tempo style. "But John got tougher offensively," Pete added, "when he went to a spread court offense — a semibreak where his players would come down the court and not take the ball all the way in. Rather, they'd throw in fifteen- to eighteen-footers before you could get set defensively. To me, this was a whole new approach to offense — a good, new avenue. Other fast-breaking teams weren't doing this yet."

But it was Cal that won a national championship in 1959 — and Cal that reached the NCAA final in 1960 before losing to Ohio State.

*

The late 1950s. A time of Elvis and Fats, hula hoops and beatniks, Ike and Khrushchev, crew cuts and trousers with buckles in the back. And years of frustration in Westwood.

Oh, the UCLA Bruins won more games than they lost. Their style was upbeat and entertaining. But the bright lights and headlines fell on Big Brother 400 miles to the north.

Cal was the toast of the Coast. Discipline and defense were strangling UCLA's daring and dazzle. And John Wooden privately cried in his soup at Hollis Johnson's lunch counter over being upstaged again and again by a man he once had conquered seven times in succession, Pete Newell.

"I know Pete really bothered John when Cal controlled the ball against him," said an erstwhile assistant coach. "That really rubbed John the wrong way. I remember when Pete was at Michigan State and he would drive all those other coaches crazy with his slowdown philosophy. I know it bothered John quite a bit. He didn't like it at all."

Compounding Wooden's torment, too, during those years was the absence of any Willie Naullses or Walt Hazzards or Gail Goodriches or Lew Alcindors. Recruiting had been crippled by a chain of events a few years earlier that exploded like a string of firecrackers up and down the Coast. And, to Wooden's chagrin, it was football — not basketball — that ignited the fuse.

It all started in the mid-1950s with the biggest college football scandal in history. Under-the-table payoffs to athletes, beyond the conference's expense limits, were disclosed — first at Washington, then at Cal and UCLA, finally at USC. Charges and countercharges flew like buckshot. The Pacific Coast Conference broke up in 1956.

The result: all four schools were placed on probation and fined. UCLA absorbed the harshest penalty — three years' probation in all sports, not just football. That meant there would be no Rose Bowls or NCAA basketball tournaments for UCLA. So, how does a recruiter convince a blue-chip high school prospect he should enroll at Westwood and play for John Wooden? Answer: he doesn't.

"UCLA was getting decent players and that was about all," recalls a university official. "Certainly we weren't getting any players — especially guards — in Hazzard's and Goodrich's league."

Three times in the 1950s Wooden signed new contracts at UCLA. But the pressures tore at him — no home gym, a cramped office, little recruiting help, the PCC penalties, lack of national success. More than once he thought of accepting one of those tempting Midwest offers. More than once he talked about it with Bill Ackerman, former Bruin tennis coach and university official in charge of student body activities whose voice was nearly as strong as Wilbur Johns's in athletics at Westwood.

"Purdue and Minnesota were offering him the world," says Ackerman. "Any salary he wanted. Big pavilions. Staff. Here he was playing in a crackerbox, and he had an office like a cloakroom. It was hard to compete with those Big Ten schools but we *knew* we had a pretty fine coach. I had to get him in my office and strengthen his backbone to stay at UCLA. How'd I do it? Mostly on the basis that someday he'd have a new pavilion and a six-ten or six-eleven guy and just be patient. Eventually, I told him, he'd be happy."

But as it was, Wooden lost his most distinguished player of 1959 — guard Walt Torrence — by graduation, then suffered through his worst season at UCLA in 1959-1960. The record was only 14-12.

The Bruins clawed back to finish at 18-8 the following year and finished runner-up in the Big Five to John Rudometkin and USC. But there was more trouble on the horizon — from a brash, talented freshman named Ron Lawson.

Lawson, an outstanding prep player and student at Pearl High School in Nashville (which won the national all-Negro tournament four years in a row) was the son of the physics department chairman at Fisk University (where Ron is now head basketball coach). A tremendous outside shooter (he averaged 24.5 points as a frosh, breaking all scoring records), Lawson was criticized for "gunning" too much and his UCLA career never was a happy one.

In December of 1960, Lawson told a reporter that playing basketball at UCLA was "like a job. I once loved to play. I used to sleep with a basketball when I was a kid. I carried it with me wherever I went and I used to dribble it down the street."

But, even in his freshman season at UCLA, he and Wooden clashed. "When I'm criticized, I just react," he said. "I know I shouldn't, but I can't help it. I get mad — at myself. I'm trying to get over it."

He withdrew into himself. A freshman teammate said: "Ron is quiet and sincere but he's a loner — and he's homesick."

Then, in May of 1961, the nineteen-year-old Lawson was called before a New York grand jury, to be questioned about "shaving" points in games. The charge was not that he had accepted a bribe — but that he had failed to inform authorities that he was contacted twice about "shaving," for a sum reportedly as low as fifty dollars.

"The only thing I did wrong," he said when he left school following his sophomore season, "was failing to report the approach. Why I didn't report it, I don't know."

Wooden was quoted after the incident broke:

"In my twenty-six years of coaching," he said, "I've never had a boy who resented instruction and correction as much as Lawson did. He would have preferred to be completely on his own — even practice on his own, and not with the team. He's a boy who was always looking for excuses. And I'm not saying this behind his back or because he's involved in this thing. I've said it to him many times.

"He made tremendous progress as a sophomore but I asked him to quit at one point, over a disciplinary matter. I relented and took him back. I've looked at Ron's record and movies of the games and there isn't a single incident where you would guess he's playing anything but his normal game."

Wooden added he thought the other 1960-1961 Bruins were "clear" too. Then he paused and said, "But you never know for sure, do you?"

Lost in the glaring headlines such as UCLA CAGER LAWSON ADMITS BRIBE OFFER, QUITS SCHOOL was the fact that Lawson had been the team's leading scorer — 356 points for a 13.7 average. And starters John Berberich and Bill Ellis were graduating. It didn't look good.

But out of gloom came the hint of greatness.

Three blonds and two blacks. A poet who was nicknamed "Spider." A midget, overweight center. An extroverted guard dubbed "The Mouth." A frail-as-corn-silk forward. And a showboating guard called "East Coast" because that's where he came from.

Pete Blackman. Fred Slaughter. Johnny Green. Gary Cunningham. Walt Hazzard.

Nobody gave them much chance, not even John Wooden, early in the 1961-1962 season.

"We're a running club," he said. "Of course we don't always bring the ball with us when we run. And I have a guard [Hazzard] who's an excellent passer. He may not throw the ball where someone can catch it but he throws it beautifully."

It was a funny *looking* team too.

Cunningham and Blackman both were rail-thin, Slaughter overly chunky. Cunningham and Green (also known as "The Green Stringbean") both wore their hair in Yul Brynner cuts. "Green doesn't comb his hair," somebody said, "he polishes it."

The Bruins appeared a good bet for something like fourth place in the Big Five that season. By the first of January that prognosis appeared optimistic. Their record was 4-7.

A magazine observed: "The Bruins had no height, no center, no muscle, no poise, no experience, no substitutes and no chance."

Oh, yeah? UCLA won fourteen out of the next sixteen games, the final two victories in the Western Regionals at Provo, Utah, over Utah State and Oregon State.

What happened? Slaughter lost thirty pounds and felt like a gazelle instead of an elephant. Cunningham thus got some help on the boards. Blackman was moved out front on defense, and the rugged, aggressive Green went inside. And all of them started watching Hazzard, catching the machine-gun passes that were bouncing off their heads in early season.

So the Bruins moved into the NCAA semifinals at Louisville against Cincinnati in what was to become one of the most significant games in UCLA history.

"You get to the semifinals on talent," a coach said the night before the game. "But after that you are in the hands of God."

God, perhaps, smiled on UCLA in a strange way.

It had been a season of surprises. Before the Bruins took the floor, another was unveiled on a grateful nation — the UCLA cheerleaders, doing the Charleston, the twist, the prance. Three girls who captured everyone's fancy.

A man noted that two of them were juniors and one a sophomore and said: "Good, the best team in the NCAA may be back next year."

While everyone else was in awe of the UCLA cheerleaders, the UCLA players (who'd seen the girls before) were in awe of the Cincinnati Bearcats.

"We were scared to death," says Gary Cunningham. "Petrified! We'd never seen men as big as Paul Hogue and George Wilson."

Cincinnati burst out to an 18-4 lead, and John Wooden called his Bruins' start "the worst I ever saw." But by half-time, the Bruins had come together on the shooting of Cunningham and the defensive harassment of Hazzard and Green on Tom Thacker and Tony Yates and the score was tied.

It was still tied, 70-70, with ten seconds to play in the game when Hazzard was called for a charging foul.

"Before the foul," says Cunningham, "we were setting up so I'd take the last shot behind a double block. I'd probably have put it right through the backboard if I had got the shot. But Walt was double-teamed and when he reversed his dribble he hit the other defender."

Hazzard was outraged by the call. "I never touched the guy [reserve Tom Sizer]," he said. "He grabbed my arm and pulled me down. It should never have been called on me."

But it was and Bearcat coach Ed Jucker signaled for a time out. He wanted to get the ball in to the bulky Hogue. UCLA thwarted that but the ball went to Thacker, who had missed all of his six previous shots from the floor. He did not miss this one, a twenty-five-footer from the right corner with three seconds left. UCLA was beaten, 72-70.

John Wooden had tears in his eyes as he said: "I've never been more proud of any team that ever won than I am right now of this team."

The basketball fans of the country felt the same way. Letters — many of them from coaches — poured into Wooden's office, protesting the call against Hazzard, saying UCLA had been robbed. The final letter count was more than 300.

"I think this loss may have helped us more than anything over the years," Wooden said. "We got more favorable comment and national publicity than when we won a national championship a couple of years later. It really helped our program."

Wooden lost Cunningham, Green, and Blackman from that team but Hazzard and Slaughter returned and they were joined by three impressive newcomers — Keith Erickson, Gail Goodrich, and Jack Hirsch.

Midway through the next season — 1962-1963 — after two close losses at Washington, Wooden had a premonition. On the plane trip home from Seattle, he wrote a poem to a former player. The last verse read:

> However, there's optimism
> Beneath my valid criticism.
> I want to say — yes, I'll foretell,
> Eventually, this team will jell.
> And when they do they will be great
> A championship will be their fate.
> With every starter coming back,
> Yes, Walt and Gail and Keith and Jack,
> And Fred and Freddie and some more,
> We could be champs in Sixty-Four.

But this was Sixty-Three.

Erickson hobbled most of the season on a sprained ankle he suffered during the Los Angeles Classic. And Wooden was embroiled in a dispute with a disenchanted sophomore, Goodrich, who complained bitterly that he wasn't starting enough and thought seriously of quitting in favor of a baseball career.

But still, the Bruins reached Provo, Utah, and the NCAA Western Regionals. The opponent: Arizona State's run-and-gun Sun Devils, the nation's number-three-ranked team.

It was an intriguing match. The Bruins were only three-point underdogs to a Sun Devil team that had an impressive 25-2 record and two of the nation's finest players. They were Jumpin' Joe Caldwell (6-5), an import from the L.A. playgrounds (he was All-City Player of the Year at Fremont High) who reportedly could leap high enough to place a half dollar atop the backboard, and forward Art Becker (6-8) from Phoenix.

But it wasn't even close. Arizona State blasted away from all over the place. Long jump shots swished through again and again. The Sun Devils raced through UCLA's man-to-man press as if it never existed. Suddenly it was 30-9 and during the second half Arizona State led by thirty-five points! It was over almost before it began. Final score: 93-79, thanks mainly to the Arizonans' sizzling 59 percent shooting from the floor.

"Their shooting in the first half," said Wooden afterward, "was the greatest I've ever seen." The Bruin players stared emptily at the locker room floor. "They were so shell-shocked," said an observer, "that not one of them really knew what happened."

The shock never wore off. In the third-place game the next night, UCLA lost to the University of San Francisco, 76-75.

It was, however, to be UCLA's last defeat in NCAA postseason play. In the ensuing decade, John Wooden's teams have obliterated all records by winning thirty-two NCAA games in a row.

But who would have envisioned such a phenomenal streak back in that winter of sixty-three?

In those days — except for the occasional tournament appearances — Bruin fans got their biggest kicks out of belting that hated rival down at University Park, the USC Trojans.

UCLA versus USC in any athletic endeavor, a wise man once said, is not a life-and-death matter, it's more important than that.

USC still holds the series edge in basketball, 79-74, but when Wooden came to UCLA, the Trojans were ahead, 59-19. He quickly evened things. In his first six years, the Bruins held a 13-12 edge. And then it happened. Over the next seventeen seasons, UCLA won thirty-nine games, USC just eight.

But the Bruin-Trojan basketball rivalry has always been much more than just streaks and numbers. It's been a Hatfield-McCoy feud, a bristling, often bitter sort of thing that consistently has meant supremacy in a conference and a region — as well as a city.

City rule is the big thing. It is impossible to be neutral in Los Angeles. You are a Bruin or you are a Trojan — and that's it.

It's a rivalry that has been marked by streaks and stalls, by fistfights and controversy, and has spanned a lot of locations and a lot of names.

The most dramatic of the pre-Bruin championship years? Well, how about these:

— UCLA riding the play of Don Barksdale to a 42-37 win in 1943, ending a forty-two-game USC streak over the Bruins.

— A twin "main event" in 1951, when UCLA's Bobby Pounds squared off with USC's Bob Kolf in a rouser and then, later in the same game, when Dick Ridgway was knocked to the floor by Bob Boyd, then a USC player. Ridgway threw the ball at Boyd, who caught it and bounced it off Dick's head. The officials made the combatants shake hands but that only started things again. It took sheriff's deputies and the band playing the National Anthem to restore things to normalcy.

— Chet Carr's last-second jumper in 1954 that gave USC a 69-67 win and a sweep of a two-game series (at the Westwood gym, of all places!) for a spot in the regionals.

— A 1958 game at the Pan-Pacific, where players from both teams spilled onto the floor and exchanged punches. Trojan Jim White was reportedly crowned champion but Jim Steffen of the Bruins, who doubled as a football player, comported himself admirably too.

— A basket interference call against UCLA's Ron Lawson in 1961 that helped USC win, 86-85, and perhaps rankled Wooden more than any ruling in the long series.

But the most memorable moment might have come in 1960, in a game at the Sports Arena:

"I blew the whistle for a jump ball with just twenty-three seconds to play," recalls ex-official Al Lightner, who worked the game. "The two players dropped the ball and started swinging and the people poured out of the stands. Somebody from the UCLA band hit John Rudometkin of USC over the head with a trombone.

"I was getting off the floor before somebody got to me when I saw Wooden on his hands and knees, his glasses off and his nose bruised and cut. I said, 'John, what happened to you?' and he said, 'Twogie did it.'"

It turned out that Forrest Twogood, the USC coach, saw somebody aim a punch at Wooden. He tried to get in the road of it and accidentally hit Wooden in the nose with his elbow.

Wooden, perhaps better than any living man, knows what the UCLA-USC series means to the players and coaches involved. "If a player lacks desire for one of these games," he says, "there's got to be something wrong with him."

A bright, fiery assistant coach. His admiration for a famous football coach and a nemesis in the basketball coaching fraternity. The vivid memory of a somewhat puzzling victory and a haunting defeat.

Together they helped turn UCLA from a sputtering bumpkin in NCAA tournament play (the Bruins had won only three of twelve postseason games) to the mightiest dynasty in basketball — or any sport, for that matter.

The assistant coach was Jerry Norman, young, ambitious, personable, fiercely competitive. At six-foot-two, he was a star forward on John Wooden's teams in the early 1950s and once was temporarily kicked off the squad by the Bruin coach because his temper blew up. Later, after a tour of military service, he spent a year coaching the varsity at West Covina High School, about twenty miles east of Los Angeles, where Wooden's brother, Maurice (Cat) Wooden, was principal.

In the fall of 1957, Norman joined the UCLA staff as freshman coach — a position he held six years while also partially assisting Wooden with the varsity. But it was not long until he asserted himself as a skillful, aggressive recruiter, as the man who hand-picked and assembled the championship teams of the Hazzard, Goodrich, and Alcindor years. And it was only a matter of time until Norman's strategic contributions would weigh far heavier than anyone else's in transforming John Robert Wooden into the peerless coach he is today.

Jerry Norman was anything but a yes man. Behind closed doors, he clashed with Wooden over tactics and innovations and changes. Sometimes Wooden agreed; mostly, he did not. But the truth is, Norman became the first assistant coach to whom Wooden listened to enough to change old ways, and he gave Norman vast responsibilities.

It's an open secret that Norman persuaded Wooden to deploy the full-court zone press, the "monster" that revolutionized (and panicked) the college basketball world in 1964. To this day Wooden admits he didn't think the press would work. He had used it successfully but only occasionally as a high school coach, but he was convinced that college guards possessed far more savvy and finesse than their high school counterparts, too much to be harassed or fooled by pressing tactics, man-to-man or zone.

Wooden was partly right. The man-to-man press that UCLA installed late in the 1963 season was only sporadically effective. It created more risks for UCLA than ruination for the enemy. It didn't exert the stranglehold on rival backcourt players the way Norman thought it would. But the zone press — installed the following autumn — did. And UCLA was soon the most discussed (and cussed) four-letter word on the basketball map.

Two games, both within three nights of each other in March 1963, bore a message that most observers — casual and ardent — overlooked. What happened those two nights was enough to convince Jerry Norman that all was not right with the UCLA press. One game was a victory — 51-45 over Stanford in the conference play-off. The other was the shattering defeat, 93-79, to Arizona State in the NCAA regionals three nights later.

Upon returning home from Provo, Norman sat down with Wooden and together they jotted notes about the Stanford and Arizona State games "while they were still fresh in our minds." Mostly, they rehashed what went wrong with the full-court press.

"The Stanford game was something of a mystery," Norman recalls. "Here we created all those turnovers with our press and nothing really happened. Look at the score: only fifty-one-forty-five. That alone was enough to tell us something was wrong. Actually, our man-to-man press had slowed the tempo to a crawl. Why, if we had forced a team to make close to twenty mistakes, we should have been scoring in the eighties or nineties. Against Arizona State, we really didn't have a chance to press 'em. They ran by us so fast we didn't know where they were."

The roots of Norman's reasoning, however, went deeper than the memory of those two games. They touched strongly on the philosophy of Wooden's bitter nemesis, California coach Pete Newell, a man Norman admired more than many UCLA partisans realized.

At just about the time when nearly everybody up and down the West Coast was convinced that "Newell had Wooden's number," Norman began pondering words Newell had spoken at a clinic: "The team that controls the tempo controls the game."

A key figure was the Bruins' playmaker, Walt Hazzard, a smart, slick-passing, clever-dribbling senior who was to assert himself as the nation's superior offensive player.

"We knew Walt was fantastic on the run," said Norman, "especially if we spread the court. But we hadn't been creating that. We weren't scattering the court. The question we asked ourselves was, 'How do we create it?' The answer: by forcing the tempo to our liking. We needed to create more full-court and spread-court situations, to take advantage of all our quickness by using the entire court — from end line to end line."

The solution was the zone press. The man-to-man press had encouraged too much dribbling in the backcourt. A nifty dribbler could elude his man, one on one, and render the press ineffective by slowing the tempo barely enough to beat the ten-second clock and cross midcourt. But the zone press — with each Bruin assigned to a specific area — lent itself to double-teaming and trapping. Suddenly the dribbler was frozen in his tracks. He couldn't dribble past *two* men; therefore he had to pass to a teammate to advance the ball. Passing the ball was faster than dribbling it — but riskier. Thus, UCLA's zone press had created a jitterbug tempo. Rival teams were stricken with haste and panic. UCLA quickly pounced on all those stray cross-court passes — and just as quickly converted them into baskets. UCLA was controlling the tempo, but in a different way than the Cal way.

As Norman says today, "By switching from a man-to-man press to a zone, it meant that fine line between a team using nine seconds to cross midcourt by dribbling and eleven seconds by passing."

Meanwhile, there were other factors that shaped Jerry Norman's thinking and led indirectly to dramatic changes in UCLA's basketball success. One was a football coaching clinic Norman had attended ("I don't remember why I went") at UCLA in the late 1950s. The principal speaker was Bud Wilkinson of Oklahoma, then the most celebrated coach in the land.

"He talked for about a half hour and he was a very, very impressive guy," said Norman. "What he said were things so true, so basic, that most coaches don't even think about them. His main point was that at some time in the game — to be effective as a coach — you've got to have imagination. For instance, the double-reverse play he pulled off against USC a few years ago wasn't so much the play, but the right time, the circumstances.

"In other words, anything you can do that has a surprise factor will give you a better chance of winning. That's what led to the zone press. The idea was to make the other team panic. Then they have to take chances. Our defense eats 'em alive and we get the ball to Walt Hazzard."

Of all the lessons he learned from Wilkinson, Norman said the most profound was: "Always question everything that's done."

The lessons were applied to UCLA in many ways. Norman was able to uproot John Wooden from much of the traditional, conventional thinking that had worked so well for him previously — but had not worked well enough to make him the all-conquering coach he has been for almost the past decade. Another tactical change also involved defense — once the enemy had crossed midcourt. As a kid growing up in Los Angeles, Norman and his high school friends used to chat with the late Scotty McDonald, then the Loyola University coach and a man with whom Wooden did not get along — and vice versa.

"We often talked about defense," Norman remembered. "It was always a big thing at Loyola. Pete Newell had played there. Obviously, the influence had rubbed off in a big way. Anyway, Scotty used to tell us there were only three things your man can do when he has the ball — drive right, drive left, or shoot over your head.

"How many times have you heard coaches say, 'On defense, stay between your man and the basket'? Well, that's only partly true. Scotty's theory was to overplay your man in such a way so that you would challenge his strength and force him into his weakness. For example, if he drives to his right well enough to get past you, then stand a little bit to his right so he *has* to go to his left. And vice versa. What you're doing is making him do what he doesn't want to do. The defensive man is taking the initiative *before* the man with the ball decides what to do with it. It took UCLA exactly ten years to discover and apply this — and make it work."

At UCLA, Norman said Wooden always has tried to balance his practice sessions evenly between offensive and defensive drills, with slightly more emphasis on offense, inasmuch as passing, cutting, and dribbling require more precision and interaction among players.

Nonetheless, two basic assumptions about rival players were incorporated into the Bruins' man-to-man defensive game plan. "The first," said Norman, "was that if your man is right-handed, four out of five times he'll go to his right. The second was, if he doesn't, then we'll call time out and decide whether to play him heads up, meaning straightaway, or 'split' him so we overplay half his body — to his stronger side. Really, you'd be amazed at the number of kids playing college ball who can dribble well only with their right hand!"

The upshot of all these theories is that you hear John Wooden ascribing his success today to defense more than he ever did before.

And the greatest manifestation of that, of course, has been the full-court zone press — the "Glue Factory," the factor that helped make college basketball more a concept than a contest over the last decade.

The 1964 press was about as much a case of exploiting the quickness of five players as it was molding the players to fit the refinement. Artistically, the press performed like a preci-sion-built machine, with all the parts strategically placed in a 2-2-1 alignment.

Much of UCLA's success with the full-court press, says John Wooden, has been based on a simple truism: human nature. "It's often natural," he said, "that when a player makes a mis-take, he'll hurry to correct that mistake. And when he hurries, the more he becomes careless. And the more he becomes care-less, the better we're able to capitalize on his mistakes."

Wooden's application of defensive principles has won the admiration of an erstwhile adversary, Pete Newell: "I always respected Johnny as a coach. But I never felt his defense was up to his offense in earlier years. Defense was just something UCLA kind of tolerated until it got the ball again; it was com-petitive defense but it was predictable. Now, UCLA plays the best defense in the West, certainly, maybe in the country. His teams position well, communicate well, switch well. They're fundamentally very sound."

Newell says of all the Wooden defensive weapons, the most intimidating, the most effective, is the zone press.

"It's like a hammer," he says, "just waiting to fall on your head. They don't give you many easy times. It's a negative pressure. You worry about it all week — and what you're going to go against it. Wooden makes subtle adjustments. He'll go from a three-one-one to a two-two-one. It's like a chess game. Most coaches will prepare for his first move, but not his second."

Actually, the press was nothing new. At Cal, Newell exploited a three-quarter-court press for many years before Wooden installed the full-court zone press. Wooden himself had used other pressure defenses but had never had real confidence in them — or stuck with them a full season.

Wooden's success, says Newell, is attributable mostly to use of what he calls "complementary" presses.

"For instance, Cazzie Russell of Michigan was killing UCLA in their NCAA title game [1965] from shots near the foul line," he said. "UCLA was in a three-one-one. Wooden called time out and went to a two-two-one. The next time the ball went into the key to Russell, it was intercepted. It turned the game around. Wooden does this better than anyone I've ever seen. And it's a change. His philosophy in the early years was that he never initiated a press. If you pressed him, he might press you. But not otherwise."

At the same time the press was changing UCLA's style on the court, telling changes were happening off the court too. The largest came in July 1963, when J. D. Morgan, UCLA's tough-minded associate business manager and tennis coach, was named athletic director to succeed the man who had hired Wooden, Wilbur Johns.

"John Wooden was only a fine line between being a very

good coach and a sensational coach," says Morgan. "The thing we were able to do was take away the concern he previously had to have for the financial aspects of the basketball program — the budget, the equipment, the salaries, the scheduling of games.

"We gave him full-time assistants so he didn't have to recruit and scout a lot on his own, as he had in earlier years. And we gave him a free hand on things like grants-in-aid. We knew he wouldn't abuse them.

"I also felt he was grossly underpaid and I set about a plan to remedy that situation, *before* he won his first national championship. What we wanted to do was remove everything from his way so he could coach to the maximum. We wanted him to do just one thing: Win!"

PART THREE

Glory Road

═══════════════════════════

". . . Caught me a pickup down from Seattle
    through to L.A.
Seems like those folks go chasin'
    a new star every day.
Ain't gonna stay . . . in Nevada. . . .
    through Wyomin' . . . Colorado . . . I'm on my way
Friend, have you seen Glory Road?
Say, friend, I gotta heavy load
And I know Glory Road's waitin' for me . . ."

                — "Glory Road," by Neil Diamond

CHAPTER 6

The Midgets Make It

"The Defenders," Dick Van Dyke, and *Lawrence of Arabia* score on TV and movie screens . . . George Wallace, jaw jutting, blocks a door at the University of Alabama . . . Martin Luther King, Jr., says: "I have a dream that this nation will rise up and live out the true meaning of its creed, 'We hold these truths to be self-evident: that all men are created equal' " . . . "The Singing Nun" parlays a second-hand guitar and happy songs about religion into fame and fortune . . . Women around the world decide that swimsuit tops are passé . . . A couple of call girls, Christine Keeler and Mandy Rice-Davies, put the British government in a stew . . . An old man, Pope John XXIII, and a young man, John F. Kennedy, die in stunningly different ways . . . The day the President is shot down, John Wooden of UCLA, national titles still only a dream, calls off practice as the world mourns.

THEY WORE THEIR HAIR closely cropped at a time when the coach didn't need to tell them to. They willingly wore navy-blue team blazers on road trips because it was fashionable and correct.

They played home games away from home — fifteen miles away at the downtown Sports Arena and twenty-five miles down the freeway in Long Beach. And they looked so hopelessly mismatched physically that rival teams were convinced that UCLA had inadvertently suited up the Glee Club.

But they were quick! Oh, they were quick!

They attacked and pressed and fast-broke like a swarm of

mosquitoes. They scooped up "garbage" and passed everybody dizzy before they shot. They scored baskets like a string of exploding firecrackers. They broke up inbound plays and swiped cross-court passes and turned the enemy's game plan into something that resembled a theater crowd's exodus when somebody yells "Fire!"

Five sawed-off kids from Westwood leaped to the top of the polls and had their fans chanting, "We're Number One!" at just about the time four long-haired kids from Liverpool were climbing to the top of the charts by singing "Yeah! Yeah! Yeah!"

Remember the names: Hazzard, Goodrich, Erickson, Hirsch, Slaughter. And Washington and McIntosh too.

Remember the season: 1964.

Just about everybody knew the 1964 Bruins would be good. The question was: *How* good?

In its annual college basketball preview edition, *Sports Illustrated* did not rank UCLA even among its top twenty teams nationally, although the Bruins were accorded a paragraph under a section entitled "Some Surprise Packages":

"Except for guard Fred Goss, who has quit to concentrate on studies, the whole Bruin team that won the Big Six last year is back. UCLA could repeat, but its lack of height again will make things tough. Flashy Walt Hazzard still leads the Bruins. He is one of the best offensive players in the nation and one of the worst defensive players on the Coast. As he goes, so go the team's chances."

When they opened the season a week or so later, the Bruins looked unbeatable — but were largely unappreciated.

Only 4700 fans watched them smash the school scoring record by blasting Brigham Young University, 113-71, at the Sports Arena, but a fearless forecaster, Frank Finch of the Los Angeles *Times*, was among the appreciative.

"It's going to take quite a quintet to beat the Bruins," he wrote, "off what they showed in their debut. They could go all the way."

They were basketball's Lilliputians. No starter was taller than 6-foot-5, and the average was only 6-3. They were perhaps the most enduring antithesis to the axiom that says you can't win games without a seven-foot center and maybe a Bunyanesque forward or two to control the backboards with headlocks and karate chops.

Most of the firepower came from two backcourt snipers who suffered from nervous stomachs so often they had to eat powdered nutrients in lieu of the pregame meal. The playmaker and premier scorer was Walt Hazzard (6-2), a showboating, sharp-shooting son of an itinerant preacher and a refugee from the playgrounds of Philadelphia, where he grew up trading elbows with such pros as Wilt Chamberlain, Guy Rodgers, and Woody Sauldsberry. His accomplice was baby-faced Gail Goodrich (6-1), son of USC's basketball captain in 1939 and hero of his high school team's victory in the L.A. City championship game despite a chipped bone in his ankle.

The forwards were Jack Hirsch (6-3), a spidery, free-spirited senior from Van Nuys whose father died a month before the season and bequeathed him a chain of bowling alleys, and Keith Erickson (6-5), who slapped away enemy shots like a spiker in volleyball, a sport he played well enough on the beaches near his home in El Segundo to win a place on the United States Olympic team.

At the post was Fred Slaughter (6-5), who came from Topeka as an All-Kansas high school star. With his 230 pounds, he could have set a double screen by himself, yet he was fast enough to have been a decathlon prospect.

They were starters in all thirty games. What they lacked in height they made up in quickness and fanaticism. They had long arms and quick hands and lightning feet — qualities that John Wooden choreographed into the "monster" with which he was to revolutionize college basketball: the full-court zone press.

What also set them apart was extraordinary jumping skill. It was not very often when they were outscrapped on the backboards. In fact, UCLA averaged eight more rebounds than its rivals and was to lead the Big Six in rebounds despite being the shortest team in the conference! Which led one coach to remark, "They sure don't *play* small!"

Why did they jump so well? Well, quickness and timing were significant. But so was an ingredient that hardly anybody knew about: bonus money.

After each game, several Bruins received envelopes from alumni containing monetary rewards for rebounding — an incentive plan similar to one recently installed by coach Bill Sharman of the Los Angeles Lakers. The UCLA scale, says Jack Hirsch, was five dollars per player for each rebound up to ten, and ten dollars for each rebound beyond ten. "It was a helluva great feeling," he said, "to pick up one hundred bucks for a night's work. Believe me, we really went all out for rebounds."

They were a mixture of black, Anglo, and Jew, and they frequently exchanged ethnic barbs — and chortled about it.

Walt Hazzard was the team's self-proclaimed "H.N.I.C." (Head Nigger in Charge). Teammates called Freddie Goss "Blackberry." They called Kenny Washington "N.B." (for Nigger Boy) and Jack Hirsch "J.B." (for Jew Boy).

It all seemed so innocent in those days. Martin Luther King had aroused a nation's conscience, but Watts and Newark and Detroit had yet to go up in flames, civil rights was not yet black power, and nobody was boycotting Olympic teams.

Walter Raphael Hazzard wore his hair so short that his skull appeared Simonized when he went to Tokyo to play for America's victorious Olympic basketball team in 1964.

A minister's son who preached a gentle militancy in the wake of Watts two summers later, Walt Hazzard, as part of a barn-storming program called "Operation Cool Head," appealed for tranquillity among kids in the ghetto when others advocated the brick and the firebomb. At a Los Angeles high school he told students at an outdoor assembly: "You're not really the ones we want to reach. The ones we want to reach aren't in high school. But maybe you will be in contact with them this summer and at least that's a start." He asked them to sign a pledge to: be responsible for their own actions, respect the rights of others, uphold law and order by their own personal actions, stay away from mobs and street gatherings, and engage in "at least one constructive activity during the summer."

Hazzard was a two-year veteran with the Los Angeles Lakers then. He has since dribbled to other teams — to Seattle, Atlanta, Buffalo, Golden State. He also has adopted the Islam faith, has acquired a new name, Mahdi Abdul-Rahman, and would like to coach basketball when he is finished playing it.

But his finest hours were spent at UCLA when he was Walt Hazzard, All-American, the Wizard of "Ahhhs." His magician-ship with a basketball was something to behold, the sleight-of-hand dribbles, the dancing footwork, and, yes, those thread-the-needle passes that whizzed under enemy players' noses and bounced off teammates' ears. It took the UCLA Bruins a while to learn to watch for Hazzard's passes, which seemed to come from out of nowhere. And when they did, UCLA enjoyed three successful seasons and people all but forgot who Bob Cousy was. "Hazzard can make any pro team right now," said Bill Sharman, an ex-teammate of Cousy's, in 1963.

His selflessness — and his showmanship — had roots in the asphalt jungles of Philadelphia, where he had played forward in the shadow of Wally Jones (now of the Milwaukee Bucks) at Overbrook High School, alma mater of Wilt Chamberlain and Wayne Hightower. Hazzard admitted he had been "brain-washed" by the Harlem Globetrotters when he was a small boy. "I saw them play just once in nineteen fifty," he said, "and then I went out and practiced dribbling like Marques Haynes for hours every day."

UCLA did not pick Hazzard. Hazzard picked UCLA, through a couple of ex-pros, Woody Sauldsberry (a distant cousin) and Willie Naulls. He enrolled in the Bruins' so-called "farm school," Santa Monica City College, to elevate his grades, and he threw in thirty-five points almost every night for the Broadway Federal Savings team in an AAU league during his freshman year.

By next season, he was the playmaking sophomore on UCLA's 1962 national semifinalists, although it was not always a happy season for Hazzard. His style didn't mix with John Wooden's (a behind-the-back Hazzard dribble elicited an angry roar from the bench: "Quit trying to show how good you are!"). He thought seriously of quitting early in his sophomore year, but when Hazzard began playing Wooden's way he became, at only 6-foot-2, the nation's very best offensive player. He almost single-handedly carried the Bruins to their first championship when things got sticky in tournament games.

Today, John Wooden remembers Hazzard as "the finest ball-handler I've ever coached." And there never has been a year when Wooden hasn't received a "good luck" telephone call from Hazzard on the eve of the season opener.

Now came the battle of unbeatens that everybody had been waiting for.

It was number-two-ranked Michigan and its front line of heavyweights battling in the L.A. Classic against number-four-rated UCLA and its whiz-bang bantamweights. The brawny versus the scrawny. Height and might versus speed and quickness.

Not many people figured John Wooden's team could withstand all those punishing Michigan elbows and hips. UCLA had the lightning, all right, but did it have the thunder to counteract Michigan's tough guys — notably Cazzie Russell and Bill Buntin — under the backboards? It shaped up as a slugfest between the "Bowery Boys" and the kids from "Our Gang."

But scarcely had the opening whistle blown when UCLA leaped at Michigan with a whiplash fury. In the first nineteen seconds, the Bruins grabbed a 4-0 lead. And it was obvious that December 27, 1963, would be a night to remember in UCLA basketball annals.

With four minutes to play, it was all over. UCLA was leading, 87-70, when the public address announcer told the crowd that defending NCAA champion Loyola of Chicago, ranked number one on both wire-service polls, had been upset by Georgetown.

Suddenly the place was thundering with chants of "We're Number One!" In a few minutes, there was bedlam at the finish. UCLA 98, Michigan 80. An era had dawned.

A man who scouted the game said he had never witnessed any performance as impressive as UCLA's. The man was Coach Harry Combes, whose Illinois team was to meet the Bruins in the finals the next night. "UCLA," he said, "was absolutely the very best basketball team I've ever seen. They were flawless the full forty minutes."

Harmon Gym, where all 7200 seats afford excellent viewing, was packed for the two-game series with UCLA. The Straw Hat Band, which supposedly was "worth an extra fifteen points a game" to California teams during the Pete Newell years, hooted the Bruins as usual with epithets. And the two schools had not been on the friendliest terms since the 1950s, when both were punished in the controversial football "slush fund" scandals and when a star quarterback, Ronnie Knox, quit Berkeley to lead UCLA into the Rose Bowl.

On Friday night, UCLA lost Jack Hirsch — who was sent to the showers for fighting with Cal's Myron Erickson — but won the game easily, 87-67.

"I see now why they're number one," said Cal's 6-11 center, Camden Wall. "But we can beat them tomorrow night."

The Bruins' confidence had been inflated. "We'll run 'em into the ground again," said Hirsch to Assistant Coach Jerry Norman. "Don't be so sure," warned Norman, anticipating a possible Golden Bear slowdown.

Norman was right. Rather than run with the Bruins, the Bears did a soft shoe. They even outplayed them part of the way and had a chance to send the game into overtime. Trailing 56-54, Cal had the ball with forty seconds left, but reserve Chris Carpenter fired a fifteen-footer that missed. Hazzard grabbed the rebound and was fouled. His two free throws in the final twelve seconds sewed up the victory, 58-56.

But emotions remained strong long after the final buzzer.

The next day, Wooden and Norman were severely criticized in San Francisco newspapers. One story said Wooden was "shrieking at officials" and allegedly yelled at Cal players "as they went past the Bruin bench," while Norman was accused of twice grabbing his throat, in the traditional "choke" gesture, when officials came to the scorer's table.

Wooden denied baiting the officials, but confessed he had yelled at California's captain, Dan Lufkin. "He protested every call against Cal whether he was in a position to see it or not. I told him to quit crying and let the officials officiate the game. As to the 'choke' sign gesture made by Jerry, I'll say this: I sat next to him the entire game and I never saw him do it."

He amplified his bench conduct by saying: "Yes, I occasionally yell at other players. But I have never said anything out of line to them. I yell at my own players too. And there's nothing I've said to officials that I'd be ashamed of." He was philosophical about his feud with Bay Area newspapers. "I've won a lot of ball games in the Bay Area," he said, "but I could never tell it by reading their papers the next day. When we've won, you would think we'd lost by the newspaper accounts."

It was victory number twenty-three of a perfect season, and a Yugoslavian coach who saw the game was highly impressed with the Bruins. Aleksandar Nikolic, who coached his country's national team, was touring the United States and observing numerous college teams. His eyes brightened when he said: "Is small team. No big man, no big score like Nash of Coach Roop team in Kentucky. But ziss — pardon, my English very bad — ziss is best I see. Because is *team*. All five."

He held up five fingers.

"*Team!*" he said. "You understand? Is best!"

Tex Winter, the Kansas State coach, knew he was gambling with his luck.

He sent his "lucky" brown suit — the one in which he had watched his Wildcats win thirteen games in succession — to the cleaners on Monday of NCAA finals week, but he would get it back in time for Friday night's semifinal showdown with UCLA.

"If I hadn't had it cleaned," he said, "the suit would have been our biggest offensive threat in Kansas City."

It was now a four-team race to be staged in ancient Municipal Auditorium. And both games would be rematches — a tall Duke team trying to avenge an 83-67 loss to Michigan and Kansas State seeking to atone for its three-point defeat to the Bruins in the Sunflower double-header.

"I was just outcoached," said Winter, recalling his team's troubles with the UCLA press in December. "We just weren't prepared to meet the kind of problems UCLA presented. However, I believe we're as good as any ball club that's going to be there."

The Wildcats, led by Big Eight player of the year Willie Murrell, had asserted themselves most of the game. They led,

75-70, with slightly more than seven minutes left, and it looked gloomy for UCLA. But suddenly the Bruins reeled off five points in a row — free throws by McIntosh and Hazzard and a short jumper by Erickson — to tie it, 75-75, whereupon K-State called a time out.

At that moment, UCLA got some added moral support. The cavalry arrived! Into the auditorium raced four UCLA pompon girls, bedecked in overcoats and costumes, to the muffled cheers of Bruin rooters, who were far outnumbered by the roaring, partisan Kansas State crowd. Two of the coeds were Pat Shepherd (who dated Hazzard and is now his wife) and Sheri McElhany (who dated Erickson), and their arrival had been delayed by a snowstorm.

Did their presence give the Bruins a lift? Certainly the timing was right out of Hollywood.

When play resumed with 6:23 left, UCLA's fireworks kept spewing. Erickson sank two free throws and Goodrich drove past two Wildcats for a fast-break lay-up to make it 79-75. The Bruins had scored nine points in a row — and they went on to a 90-84 victory, their furthest advance ever in NCAA play.

"We haven't been playing well lately," said John Wooden afterward, "but all I ask is one more time."

"If you are silly enough to apply logic to basketball," wrote Dick Wade in the Kansas City *Star*, "there's no way for UCLA to beat Duke. The Blue Devils simply have too much — height, rebounding, shooting ability and defense. But UCLA isn't a logical team. It beats the law of averages with the intangible and the unbelievable."

The stage was set. John Wooden was fifty-three years old and had a history of state titles and national championships eluding him during more than three decades of coaching. Could UCLA do what USF and North Carolina had done in the previous decade — extend its perfect record all the way through the championship game?

Most of the coaches attending the national convention and finals said no. But nobody could convince those Bruin fans wearing "We Try Harder" buttons and chanting "We're number one!" all night along Baltimore Street that their team was overmatched.

In the locker room before the game, John Wooden's message consisted only of one question. "Who can remember," he asked his players, "which team finished second in the NCAA two years ago?"

The answer was Ohio State, but nobody knew it. The Bruins were on the threshold of making history, not taking a quiz in it. "That one question," recalls Gail Goodrich, "was all the coach really had to say — and he knew it."

Convinced that second place in the NCAA is a passkey to eternal obscurity, the Bruins took the floor against a run-and-shoot Duke team led by All-American guard Jeff Mullins and two 6-10 players, Jay Buckley and Hack Tison.

The Blue Devils, who had outlasted Michigan the night before, grabbed a 30-27 lead at the outset, less than eight minutes into the game. But suddenly, spectacularly, UCLA's press turned the Devils into a jittery, frantic team that threw the ball away again and again. Goodrich threw in fifteen-footers, Hirsch stole the ball twice in the backcourt, and Kenny Washington, a bashful black kid from Beaufort, South Carolina — playing for the first time before his father, a career Marine — came off the bench when Erickson got into foul trouble and popped in back-to-back jumpers.

Wham! Zap! And bang again! It was the biggest blitz. Sixteen consecutive points in two and a half minutes. UCLA was on top, 43-30, and it was all over even before half time.

As the finish neared and Washington left the game to a standing ovation, Hazzard rushed to him on the bench and they deliriously slapped hands.

"We couldn't beat 'em! We couldn't beat 'em!" Hazzard shouted. "Man, did you read the paper today? Send Duke back to Dixie!"

Washington, slumping wearily to the bench, wrapped an arm around Hazzard and grinned. "This is sweet, boys. This is sweet!" he said. "We're number one, baby! We're number one!"

A few minutes earlier, Wooden met privately with his players for the last time and told them: "Now you are champions. And you must act like champions. You met some people going up. You will meet the same people going down."

Outside the dressing room, Nell Wooden waited patiently and happily for her husband. Victory number thirty, fittingly enough, had come on the thirtieth birthday of their daughter, Nan.

The first to congratulate Nell as soon as the game had ended was the Reverend Bob Richards, the former Olympic pole-vault champion, who embraced her warmly. Like her husband, Nell is superstitious and she was telling friends of having carried a lucky acorn in her hand through every NCAA game.

Now, at last, she saw John Wooden emerge from the locker room and the mobs of well-wishers and fans and newsmen. When their eyes met, the only words the coach uttered to his wife were, simply, "Isn't that something?"

Their smiles — which seemed to stretch all the way from Martinsville to Westwood — told you it was.

One day's headline screams, "Khrushchev Ousted" and the banner the very next day says, "China Tests Atomic Bomb" . . . A civil rights bill is passed in Washington and three men, two white, one black, are murdered in Mississippi . . . Those mop-haired youngsters from Liverpool wail their way across the United States on two concert tours and take home more than a million dollars . . . James Bond offers escape in *Dr. No* and

From Russia with Love . . . Lyndon Johnson offers a "Great Society" after burying Barry Goldwater . . . Women's skirts go up, up, up, the highest in seventeen years . . . Don Schollander, a boy with an All-American face, wins four gold medals in the Tokyo Olympics . . . Streisand and Channing score on Broadway in *Funny Girl* and *Hello Dolly* . . . "Excellent progress is being made in Vietnam," says Secretary of Defense Robert McNamara, "but it's going to be a long war" . . . "I won't say this year's team is better than last, but we're going to be good," says John Wooden.

He looked so much like a ninety-pound weakling that you expected somebody to kick sand in his choirboy face.

But the face — and the sawed-off, sinewy physique — simply had to be a put-on. Nobody believed Gail Goodrich could find happiness in the rough-and-tumble world of pro basketball, let alone the big-time college game.

"Too small," the recruiters said, shaking their heads, when they saw him outslicker all the big kids when he was a left-handed forward playing for Polytechnic High School in North Hollywood.

Even Gail Goodrich wondered what the future held. As a 5-foot-2 youngster entering high school, he would tell his mother, "I don't understand why God gave me all this ability and not the height to go with it."

Mrs. Jean Goodrich, looking back on those years, remembers telling her son: "Yes, but God gave you much more than he has given others."

And how! Quickness, for instance. That's what John Wooden liked when he saw Goodrich, then only a 5-8 junior, playing in the Los Angeles city high school tournament. Seated behind Wooden — unbeknownst to him — was Gail Goodrich, Sr., former All-Pacific Coast Conference guard and team captain at USC back in the days when UCLA was a basketball nonentity. He and Mrs. Goodrich had eavesdropped on Wooden's conversation with an assistant coach — and that's the first time they had heard that UCLA, or anybody, for that matter, was interested in their son.

Basketball had been spoon-fed to him from infancy. His first lay-up broke a table lamp, and he grew up shooting basketballs incessantly in the backyard court built by his father and reading textbooks by Oscar Robertson and Bill Sharman, now his coach with the Los Angeles Lakers. "My Dad taught me everything I know," he grinned, "except my jump shot."

His Laker teammates call him "Stump," but the nickname is misleading. He has hands that are big enough to make a basketball look like a grapefruit and an arm span that requires a thirty-seven-inch shirt-sleeve length.

Always a fierce competitor, he also has exuded enormous self-determination. "He's not afraid of anything," says a friend. "Gail would drive on King Kong if he had to."

Goodrich entered UCLA as a midwinter freshman — two days after he finished high school — and by then USC had made a belated, unsuccessful recruiting bid for him. As a sophomore, he played in Hazzard's shadow and often clashed with Wooden about not playing enough. He thought seriously of quitting to play baseball or transfer elsewhere. But when Wooden convinced him that he should try to get open so Hazzard could feed him the ball, Goodrich blossomed almost overnight in his junior year.

Now, with Hazzard graduated, he was the take-charge guy, the role he always had savored, and this would be his finest campaign ever — that is, until he and Jerry West and Wilt Chamberlain would propel the Lakers to the NBA championship many years later.

He reminisced over breakfast one morning about the man he played for at Westwood:

"When he made me play forward sometimes during my sophomore year, I couldn't understand it," he said. "But, looking back, it gave me the confidence I have today in shooting closer to the basket against big men. At the time, I didn't know that. And I know he reaches guys in different ways. For instance, I didn't like being yelled at — and he kicked me out of practice sometimes. But he yelled at Keith a lot more. It helped, too, because he realized that it made Keith mad and he knew that Keith played better when he's mad. This is one of the coach's real strengths — knowing how to get each guy to play up to his potential, but reaching each guy in a different way."

It was a new season and there were new faces in the starting line-up to replace Hazzard, Hirsch, and Slaughter.

But they were faces of experience and promise. Kenny Washington and Doug McIntosh stepped into the front line. Freddie Goss, red-shirting year over, moved into the backcourt with Goodrich. And off the bench would come a couple of highly regarded sophomores, 6-6 Edgar Lacey, the former All-City player of the year at Jefferson High School, and 6-7 Mike Lynn, a much-decorated center from suburban Covina.

"I think we'll be an entertaining team," said John Wooden.

He took the Bruins and their thirty-game winning streak to Champaign, Illinois, to open the season, but they ran smack into a fusillade of jump shots that rang out like a scene from *The Longest Day.*

Illinois' Fighting Illini, who had given UCLA a close call the year before in Los Angeles, came out with their guns blazing. Cheered by nearly 12,000 fans who went absolutely daffy, the Illini broke the Bruins' press again and again and threw in shots from all over the place.

It was never close. Illinois, getting twenty points from Skip Thoren, nineteen from guard Bill McKeown, and seventeen apiece from Bogie Redmon and Don Freeman, shot a scorching 60.5 percent — a school record — and ran up the highest score ever on a UCLA team. Final score: 110-83.

Freddie Goss, now head coach at UC Riverside, looked back on the debacle. "I remember I had a fine game [eighteen points], and so did Gail [twenty-five]," he said. "Everybody else was pretty bad. Wooden's reaction? You could probably give me the quote as well as I could give it to you. He just told us, 'The pressure's off now. Just go out and play your game.'"

Anybody looking for Keith Erickson could generally find him in either of two places — under the basket or at the beaches.

"I majored in eligibility at UCLA," said Erickson, now a seven-year pro whose career with San Francisco, Chicago, and Los Angeles has been hampered by injuries. "I was in P.E., and just took enough courses to stay in basketball and volleyball. I made a mistake — I see that now. I was looking through a UCLA catalog not long ago and I was depressed to see what I had missed."

On a basketball court, Erickson seemed to be several places at once — intercepting passes, protecting the goal like hockey's Terry Sawchuk, harassing the first man downcourt in enemy fast breaks and soaring airborne like a trapeze artist to snap up rebounds.

He was a cocky, tenacious senior who played with an indomitable fury during games, but often got into trouble with Wooden for his indifference in practice sessions.

Nonetheless, Erickson had progressed a long way from the days when he was only a second-team all-leaguer at El Segundo High School and came to UCLA on a partial baseball scholarship. Now he had transformed from somebody whom UCLA wasn't really counting on into a fellow who unfailingly rescued the Bruins when their full-court press broke down. Suddenly he had been to Tokyo and back — as a member of the United States Olympic volleyball team — and now his basketball skills had crystallized.

Rival coaches respected Erickson's ability. "I think he's definitely an All-American," said Stanford's Howie Dallmar. "Against most teams, when you get through on a fast break, it's two on one. Against UCLA, with Erickson back there, it's no better than two on one and three-quarters. He has timing, balance, shooting ability, defensive ability — and he's a real team player."

Chicago. Subzero cold. What better place for an ambush?

UCLA's Bruins, returning from a two-week layoff for final exams, battled an Iowa team that matched them fast break for fast break, press for press.

The Hawkeyes (9-5) forged ahead early and UCLA contributed to its own frustration by tipping six shots at the basket in rapid succession — and missing them all! — and by throwing the ball away sixteen times in the first half alone.

Still, the Bruins were very much in the game, slicing Iowa's lead to 79-78 on a jumper by Erickson. But guard Chris Pervall, the game's leading scorer with twenty-eight points, answered with a three-point play, and the Hawkeyes ran out the clock with a stall.

Final score: Iowa 87, UCLA 82. Another win streak broken — and pandemonium on the floor of Chicago Stadium. Coach Ralph Miller, who had beaten Wooden a few years earlier as coach at Wichita State, was jubilantly carried to the dressing room aboard the shoulders of his players.

Iowa's press had forced UCLA into twenty-one turnovers. Goodrich had been held to only two field goals. "We weren't up to snuff," said John Wooden, "and Iowa deserved this one."

Freddie Goss remembers that January night. "There was a lot of pressure again — big Midwestern crowd, defending national champs and all that," he said. "Just going into that area gave you the jitters. But that's also where we threw off the last bits of tension we had from the previous season. It was a loss that brought us together."

The place was the Portland Coliseum, a modern arena nicknamed the "Glass Palace," and now there were four teams left:

Michigan, ranked number one, champion of a Big Ten race that included UCLA's two conquerors — Illinois and Iowa — and a team that Adolph Rupp of Kentucky picked to win the tournament.

Princeton, a Cinderella team in ivy, spearheaded by everybody's All-American, Bill Bradley.

Wichita State, which had lost two big men — All-American Dave Stallworth by graduation at midseason and 6-10 Nate Bowman because of scholastic troubles — but managed to survive the Midwest Regional.

And, of course, John Wooden's defending champions, of whom USF coach Pete Peletta warned, "They are as good as they were last year — and they have better depth."

Everything pointed to a classic showdown between UCLA and Michigan. At least, that was the chatter on street corners, in hotel lobbies, and in taverns, to say nothing of the rumor that circulated among the nation's basketball coaches at their annual convention. The rumor: Lew Alcindor, the 7-foot-1 schoolboy sensation from New York, would choose Boston College out of hundreds of scholarship offers and play for coach Bob Cousy.

Meanwhile, Iowa coach Ralph Miller talked about two teams he knew extremely well — UCLA, which he had beaten in January, and Wichita State, which he had coached the previous season.

"If Wichita can get off to a good start — by that, I mean hit well — they'll be in the game," he said of the Bruin-Shocker semifinal. He also spoke highly of Wichita's remaining star, 6-1 guard Kelly Pete. "Gail Goodrich is very good," he said, "but Pete is one of the best defensive players in the country. He certainly will not be embarrassed in this assignment."

As it was, the game turned into one of the sorriest mismatches in NCAA annals. UCLA raced to a 65-38 lead by half time, then rode Goodrich's twenty-eight points, Lacey's twenty-four (and thirteen rebounds), and Goss's nineteen to a resounding 108-89 victory — mostly without Erickson, who had pulled a leg muscle during the warm-ups and played hardly at all.

It was a dream match. Michigan versus UCLA, Cazzie Russell versus Gail Goodrich, number one versus number two.

Would it be shades of their memorable battle the year before in the Los Angeles Classic?

John Wooden pondered those Michigan heavyweights, who had turned back Princeton and Bill Bradley, 93-76, the night before. "It's hard to imagine a college team that strong," he said. "I really doubt if any team in the pro ranks is bigger or stronger. There certainly are no thin men out there."

Gail Goodrich was wary of the Wolverines' backboard might. "Our problem," he said, "will be to offset them on the boards."

At the outset, Michigan took command by building up a 20-13 lead. Russell, the All-American junior, had scored eight points by repeatedly driving past his man, Erickson, who was limping badly as a result of his muscle pull.

With the game five and a half minutes old, Wooden removed Erickson. In his place went Kenny Washington, a hero in the championship game the year before. At the same time, Wooden made an adjustment in the full-court press, shutting off a vital passing lane to Russell.

Suddenly the ceiling collapsed on the Wolverines.

Washington swished in two jump shots, back to back. Michigan threw away the ball twice against the press, Lacey and Goss quickly converting the mistakes into baskets. Goodrich made a free throw, and Washington stole the ball and sank still another jump shot.

It was a dizzying 11-2 blitz, and when the bewildered Wolverines gazed at the scoreboard, it was 24-22, UCLA's favor. Still, Michigan clawed back on baskets by Russell and Bill Buntin to trail only 32-31, but UCLA went on *another* spree. This time, the Bruins outscored the Big Ten champs, 14-2, with Goodrich doing most of the damage. It was over by half time, 47-34, and Michigan got no closer than twelve points thereafter.

Toward the finish, with his team leading by thirteen, Wooden ordered a stall-tempo game to lure the Wolverines out of their zone defense. And when they came after UCLA, Goodrich made life miserable for them. He sailed past them like a gnat. He sprang toward the basket, hanging, pumping, and twisting his body and befuddling the Wolverines into so many fouls he established a beachhead at the foul line over the last ten minutes.

His last hour was his proudest. Goodrich broke his school record with forty-two points (it was also an NCAA title game record) and UCLA became the fifth team to win back-to-back championships, 91-80.

Again, Washington had played a vital role with seventeen points ("If we get this far every year" — John Wooden grinned — "Kenny will take care of us") and McIntosh and Lynn took turns holding Buntin to fourteen points.

It had been the most spectacular night in NCAA history — and perhaps the most memorable. Bill Bradley had broken the tournament single-game scoring record in the consolation game, hitting fifty-eight points against Wichita State. He was named the tourney's most outstanding player, but many thought Goodrich should have received the honor.

"What's more important?" one fan snapped. "Bradley's fifty-eight points against a team as bad as Wichita State, in a consolation game, or Goodrich's forty-two against a team as good as Michigan, in the championship game?" Gail himself appeared unconcerned — and quite modest.

In the dressing room afterward, he swigged a soft drink and said, "I honestly wasn't sure when we went out there whether we could win. But after three minutes, I knew we were going to take it."

Meanwhile, John Wooden wore a thin smile as he approached Gail Goodrich, wrapping an arm around his shoulder. "You've got a poor record . . ." he quipped. "You should have gone to USC." He shook Goodrich's hand and added, "That was the best move I ever made, getting you from the Trojans."

Weeks later, at the Bruins' awards dinner, Goodrich told hundreds of guests in his farewell speech that perhaps his own best move was choosing to remain at UCLA when his spirit was wounded.

"I admit I even contemplated leaving UCLA and entering that other school [USC]," he said, "but . . . now I'm glad I stayed. I have even found out where the library is. I have found out there is more to life than just shooting a basketball. The Michigan game was my best game. It gave me the satisfaction that a little man can win in a big man's game. And Coach Wooden is remarkable. He was a master controller of five little puppets."

For the moment, the young dynasty at UCLA was a monument to choreography, to two men's skillful moves — John Wooden's and Gail Goodrich's.

The banners reading WOODEN FOR PRESIDENT and BRING ON THE CELTICS had scarcely disappeared in Westwood when all eyes looked eastward.

It was the spring of 1965, and a towering high school player from New York City had narrowed his choice of colleges to five: Michigan, St. John's, Holy Cross, Boston College, and UCLA. John Wooden had made a transcontinental flight to visit the player's parents in late April, but the speculating persisted.

Finally, on May 4, it was official. Ferdinand Lewis Alcindor, Jr., 7-foot-1, the kid every school in the nation wanted, the star of a Power Memorial Academy team that won seventy-

one games in a row, called a press conference in the school's
gymnasium to announce he was going to UCLA.

"I chose UCLA because it has the atmosphere I wanted," he
said, "and because the people out there were very nice to me."

Summer of 1965. While buildings were burned to the ground
in Watts, a $5 million structure rose in Westwood.

Pauley Pavilion, a gleaming facility with blue-padded
bleachers and gold-upholstered, theater-type seats, was ready
by November to open as permanent home for John Wooden's
basketball team.

The inaugural event was the traditional varsity versus freshmen game on a "Salute to John Wooden" night, in which the
coach was honored with speeches and gifts before the tip-off.

But this game held a particular fascination for the 12,051
spectators: Could Lew Alcindor and the rest of a very good
freshman team beat the defending NCAA champions?

You bet! Big Lew was everything he had been advertised
to be — quick, graceful, poised, skillful, intimidating — as the
frosh broke open the game early and cruised to a 75-60 victory.

As a Southern California television audience also watched,
Alcindor held everybody spellbound. He effortlessly scored
thirty-one points (including a whirling stuff shot), hauled
down twenty-one rebounds, blocked several shots, and forced
the varsity into a miserable outside shooting game (35 percent).
The full-court press? Oh, that was no problem. On inbound
plays, the freshmen lofted the ball skyward to Big Lew — far
out of everybody else's reach — and away they ran!

The varsity, which played without ailing Freddie Goss,
looked flat most of the way. "I don't think people really know
how much we lost from last year's team," said John Wooden
afterward. "We'll be all right eventually, but we have a long
way to go."

*

Actually, UCLA's 1965-1966 varsity had not lost all its arsenal. Goodrich and Erickson, of course, had departed, but Kenny Washington, Mike Lynn, and Doug McIntosh were back. Goss was ill with osteomyelitis of the lower back (it was first diagnosed as appendicitis) and lost forty pounds, but up from the freshmen came Mike Warren, a 5-11 playmaking guard from South Bend Central, and Don Saffer, another guard from nearby Westchester. And, yes, the full-court press was back too. *Sports Illustrated* had just published a cover story, quoting numerous coaches, entitled: "The UCLA Press and How To Beat It."

The Bruins won their first two games in the Pavilion, beating Ohio State and Illinois, but they would soon experience tough sledding. The following weekend, they lost two in a row to Duke in North Carolina. They returned to play two games in the Sports Arena as part of a double-header with USC, beating Kansas but losing, 82-76, to Cincinnati. "OK, bring on their freshmen!" chortled a Cincinnati player in the dressing room. John Wooden took the loss hard. "He and Jerry Norman were both so disgusted," said Hollis Johnson. "Coach Wooden felt they didn't put out — rebounding and all [UCLA was outrebounded, 58-39]. He felt they should have won. In fact, that was the worst I've seen him feel after a game. As he walked up the stairs, I remember him saying, 'I just can't imagine the kids not wanting to put out.'"

But there would be more disappointments — and more bad luck.

Goss had returned from his illness, but he was physically below par. And when the Bruins still were very much in the Pacific 8 Conference race, they lost their best rebounder — Edgar Lacey — for the final eight games because of a fractured kneecap. Their chances were alive in February when they journeyed to Oregon, but then McIntosh and Lynn suffered from illnesses and the Bruins lost to Oregon State's slowdown Beavers and to Oregon.

UCLA finished with an 8-4 conference record (and 18-8 overall), while Oregon State won the title with a 10-2 mark and advanced to the NCAA Western Regionals in, of all places, Pauley Pavilion!

To this day, John Wooden believes his team was strong enough at the finish to win a national championship for two reasons: (1) Goss had fully recovered, as had Lynn and McIntosh and (2) he believed the tournament field was "weaker than usual" (Utah advanced from the Western Regionals, and Texas Western beat Kentucky for the NCAA title).

But perhaps the most significant game of the season had been played back in November. John Wooden had sensed it, too, a few nights before Lew Alcindor was to take on the UCLA varsity. The game may have been an epitaph for a season.

"We were uninspired in that game," he said, looking back. "Probably it was my fault. We didn't know what to do about guarding Lew. Do we double-team him and play him aggressively and increase our chances of winning? Or do we make certain we don't get him too aroused — and possibly too upset?"

For reasons of domestic tranquillity, John Wooden chose the latter course, although neither probably would have significantly affected the outcome. As it was, the game was to weigh heavily on three future basketball seasons. Fans everywhere wondered: If Big Lew can almost singlehandedly conquer a good varsity team — the NCAA champs, yet! — then he should be able to conquer *all* varsity teams, right?

CHAPTER 7

The Magnificent Seven-Footer

Ronald Reagan wins the governorship of California, demonstrating he's a more skillful politician than an actor . . . The Watts Festival emerges from the ashes of 103rd Street . . . Holy barracuda! TV's Batman and Robin captivate Mom and Dad too! . . . Stokely Carmichael preaches "black power" in the South, while a "white backlash" erupts in the North . . . For moviegoers, *Dr. Zhivago* warms the heart and *Who's Afraid of Virginia Woolf?* blisters the eardrums . . . American bombs fall on the DMZ, and Communist China explodes a nuclear weapon . . . John Lennon says the Beatles are "more popular than Jesus" . . . It's O.K. for United States Catholics to eat meat on Fridays . . . *Mame* brightens Broadway, and an unmanned Soviet spacecraft hits Venus . . . Meanwhile, everybody in Westwood breathlessly awaits Lew Alcindor's first "dunk" shot, and John Wooden says, "I would be surprised — and always will be — if our team goes all the way without a defeat."

ON A CLEAR DAY, UCLA could see basketball prosperity forever. John Wooden, whose two-year reign in the NCAA's throne room had been overturned by Oregon State, thus clearing Texas Western's path to national preeminence, suddenly found himself sitting atop the wire-service polls by default. The Bruins were accorded the number one ranking even before the first jump shots of 1966-1967 had been fired.

The biggest reason, of course, was Ferdinand Lewis Alcindor, Jr., the sophomore center of such extraordinary skill that just about everybody from Atlantic City to Pacific Palisades was expecting him to spearhead the Bruins to three national titles in succession — and maybe, just maybe, ninety victories in ninety games.

Of course, that was a gargantuan order. John Wooden said so himself. "I don't believe I could even hand-pick a team from the entire nation," he said, "and be assured of doing it."

Nonetheless, you couldn't find many people in Las Vegas or Monte Carlo willing to wager against it. After all, hadn't Big Lew hypnotized a good UCLA varsity into submission a year ago? True, he was now without help from senior forwards Edgar Lacey, who was recuperating from a knee operation, and Mike Lynn, who was charged (and later convicted) with illegally using a stolen credit card a few nights before the season opener. But didn't he have a masterful supporting cast — led by playmaking junior Mike Warren and three sophomores who, like Alcindor, were high school All-Americans, Lucius Allen, Lynn Shackelford, and Kenny Heitz?

Whatever the promise, 1967 shaped up as a good year with Alcindor, a *very* good year with the talented players surrounding him. Warren had averaged sixteen points and played a near flawless floor game the previous season. Allen was a quick, fluid guard of such consummate skills that he already was winning raves as a surefire professional prospect. Shackelford, a superlative shooter whose teammates nicknamed him "The Machine," had shot 62 percent for the unbeaten freshman team, while Heitz was regarded as a fine defensive performer. And coming off the bench were hustling Bill Sweek, a 6-3 sophomore who had red-shirted the previous year, and Jim Nielsen, a 6-7 transfer from Pierce Junior College.

For Wooden, who had abandoned his customary high-post offense for a low-post alignment that exploited Alcindor near the basket, the pressures were obvious. They had cast him in a role unlike any he had experienced in eighteen previous years at Westwood, but it was a role he savored just the same.

"Yes, I realize the position we're in," he said, "but I'd rather be in this position than anywhere else."

At USC, new coach Bob Boyd was plotting for a nonconference season opener against UCLA while Trojan fans nervously wondered if anybody could really stop the Bruins' celebrated center, whom they nicknamed "Godzilla."

On a wall in Boyd's office was a candid photo of the coach with eyes wide and bulging, eyebrows shooting halfway up his forehead and face frozen in open-mouthed astonishment. The picture inspired someone to scrawl beneath it: OH, MY GOD! IS THAT ALCINDOR?

The War on UCLA was imminent. At enemy strongholds such as Duke, Texas Western, and Kentucky, among others, all eyes were gazing at a towering teen-ager who — since his freshman year at New York's Power Memorial Academy — had won 99 of his last 100 games. It was all over but the shooting.

Saturday, December 3, 1966. It was the night the "Magnificent Seven-Footer" rode through Westwood.

His weapons were a spectacular stuff shot and a delicate jumper that banked into the basket again and again. His prey were the USC Trojans, but it probably could have been anybody.

Lew Alcindor, nineteen years old, twisted a good Trojan team around his little finger, but — even with the season only one game old — he seemed to have the whole college basketball world in his hands.

Big Lew poured in fifty-six points, a school record, in an auspicious varsity debut as the Bruins outscored a USC team that played Lew straight up, with a man-to-man defense, 105-90. He not only broke Gail Goodrich's single-game record of forty-two points and the Pauley Pavilion record, but also shattered his previous all-time highs of forty-eight (as a UCLA freshman) and forty-four (as a high school star).

When it was over, Alcindor said he couldn't play his customary game, in which he unselfishly feeds open teammates when he is double or triple-teamed. "There weren't that many opportunities to pass off," he said, "so I shot."

John Wooden was impressed. "He even frightens *me*," the coach said. "If I had to predict before the game how many points he would have gotten, I would have said about thirty or forty." He cautioned, however, that Alcindor was not yet a "complete" player, that his primary weakness was defensive rebounding. "He still doesn't maneuver too well under there," he said. "But that will come in time. People have a tendency to expect too much of this boy — just as people expect a great deal out of the President of the United States."

Meanwhile, Bob Boyd admitted the man-to-man was a mistake. "I knew he was going to be this good," he said of Big Lew, "but next time I'm sure we'll try something else because nobody can handle him one-on-one."

The next day, while the whole town was talking about the "Magnificent Seven-Footer," people wondered whether he might soon make a farce out of college basketball.

But neither Wooden nor Boyd could agree with such a theory. "There's no way he can be as effective as, say, Bill Russell was in college ten years ago," said Wooden, "because the three-second lane was only six feet wide then and the rule on goaltending was not as strictly enforced. Now, Lew has to work with a twelve-foot lane. There's no such thing as any one player wrecking the game. Chamberlain or Russell didn't do it."

Said Boyd: "There's no question that Lew is going to be the greatest college basketball player in history. A guy told me after the game that watching Lew play was like seeing a grown-up play against a three-year-old kid. But I can't go along with that. I respect Lew for his ability, and I realize that people will have to accept him from now on. He won't really disrupt the game that much because it probably will be twenty years from now — or even longer — until another Lew Alcindor comes along."

He jogs lazily toward the basket for his practice lay-ups, usually rolling the ball off his dangling fingers with the nonchalance of somebody dropping a slice of bread into a toaster. He looks oblivious to the electricity he generates around him. His face is expressionless as he vigorously chews a wad of gum, and he will say nothing or betray no emotion until John Wooden has decided the opposition has had enough and mercifully removes him from the game.

This was the Lew Alcindor everybody saw, a young man who called himself "a minority of one." He was black, 7 feet-plus, and Catholic — that is, until he embraced the orthodox Muslim faith during his senior year. His life has been a center stage and he has been stared at, laughed at, and immortalized at age nineteen — which makes it easy to understand why he has found his greatest comfort in solitude.

As a sophomore, he lived alone in a Westwood apartment that had no telephone. He had few friends and no steady girl, and he conveyed his sensitivity about his height by camouflaging it in airport lobbies, slouching uncomfortably as he sat down next to teammates, in a way that his eye level was even with theirs.

"I'm uneasy around people I don't know," he said during one of the few interviews he granted during his rookie year. "I'm learning to live with it, but I'm much better off when I'm with people I know."

The Alcindor personality was sculptured by a boyhood in the Bronx and Manhattan, where people gawked at him and teased him about his height. It was a hard, cruel world compared with the setting he discovered in California, where people were generally amiable — and often overtly friendly — toward him. But the change made him uncomfortable — and painfully uncommunicative.

"There . . . seemed to be a special art form in California: the art of seeming to like people that you really don't like," he wrote two years later in an autobiographical series for *Sports Illustrated*. "It wasn't long before I realized that certain cats who hated my guts were giving me the big Pepsodent beach-boy smile and saying, 'Hello, how are you?' The intensity of the smile and the greeting would never vary, even when I was hearing stories about how much they disliked me. I never could get with this kind of behavior. Back in New York City, you knew who liked you and who didn't. You knew where you were. But in California, I felt like I was in the middle of the ocean on a raft."

Alcindor, who was 6-foot-11 by his freshman year in high school, was the grandson of a 6-foot-8 immigrant from Trinidad, the only child of a 6-foot-3 New York City subway policeman and his wife, a former light-opera singer, who is 5-11.

He admitted to laziness ("I like to goof around a lot"), but he realized his skills were not merely a by-product of his height alone. He skipped rope for long hours to improve coordination. "I realize I have an opportunity to make a lot of money someday," he said, "but I have worked hard for what I have. I could never make it just on my size."

He was an enormously intelligent young man, one who maintained a B-minus average in history and would become an academic rarity in college athletics — a graduate in four years. He was a late sleeper, a jazz enthusiast (among his favorites: Thelonious Monk and Miles Davis), and had taken saxophone and flute lessons. He read almost incessantly, too, searching for answers about the role of his race through classes at UCLA in Islamic and African history and the book *Malcolm X Speaks*. "What I am trying to do," said Lew Alcindor, college sophomore, "is find out all I can about my people."

His story, in ensuing seasons, would weave in and out of controversy and would reach a crossroads in his senior year by his conversion to the Moslem faith and by his signing a $1.4

million contract with the Milwaukee Bucks. Then, later, there would be more plaudits in the pros — NBA Rookie of the Year and Most Valuable Player among them — and then his adoption of a Moslem name, Kareem Abdul-Jabbar.

He returned to Pauley Pavilion for a charity game last summer, his haircut slightly shorter than the Afro he wore as a collegian, and he and his wife of two years, Habiba, formerly Janice Brown of Los Angeles, were the parents of an infant daughter.

Now, as Kareem Abdul-Jabbar, he reflected momentarily on his years at Westwood and on John Wooden, with whom he was never close but had a cordial relationship.

He had, in his *Sports Illustrated* series, for which he was reportedly paid $20,000, been ambivalent toward Wooden, calling him "this fine man, this superb coach, this honest and decent individual [who] had a terrible blind spot. He had this morality thing going; you had to be 'morally' right to play. From that attitude came a serious inability on his part to get along with 'problem' players. If they didn't go to church every Sunday and study for three hours a night and arrive 15 minutes early to practice and nod with every inspiring word the coach said, they were not morally fit to play — and they found themselves on the second team."

Looking back last summer, he said his views in the series were essentially unchanged, but that now he was grateful for having been graduated from UCLA ("I gained knowledge, my game was improved, and I developed and matured as a man") and he respected John Wooden. "He had to change at a time when things were changing very fast," he said. "And he did. He has adjusted with the times and, to me, that's the mark of a real thoroughbred."

The town clings firmly to the side of a snow-covered hill, like the nose of a small boy pressing against an icy window to get a look at Lew Alcindor.

Pullman, Washington, a town of 10,000 college students, 6000 residents, about half-a-dozen traffic signals, and a partridge in a pine tree, couldn't wait for the moment when Big Lew would plant his size-sixteen sneakers on a foreign court for the first time.

It was the Pacific 8 Conference opener for UCLA and a Washington State team led by 6-9 center Jim McKean and capable of pulling off an upset. WSU coach Marv Harshman tried to simulate "Alcindor" conditions in practice on the eve of the game by permitting a defensive player to wield a tennis racket and by stationing a 6-foot-6 offensive center atop a fourteen-inch wooden stool. A marquee at an off-campus motel read, "Go Cougars! Stew Lew!" and kids waited all night in the snow for seats in tiny Bohler Gym despite the fact that the game would be televised in Pullman and five Western states. "They just don't want to see Lew on the tube," said a WSU official. "It means more to them to say they saw him in person."

The game was a tense, ragged affair, and the 5000 Cougar fans hooted and stomped and shrieked at every WSU basket with a roar that split eardrums. And the roar nearly blew off the ceiling when Alcindor, the game's leading scorer with twenty-eight points, was removed midway through the second half after drawing his fourth personal foul. He sat on the bench for nearly five minutes and, for UCLA, they were moments of truth. The Cougars, scratching and snarling, quickly wiped out UCLA's four-point lead and forged ahead, 54-53, on a long jump shot by little Lucius Allen. Bohler Gym was rocking.

But the Bruins promptly stormed back in front on back-to-back baskets by reserve Jim Nielsen and Mike Warren to lead, 57-54. When Alcindor returned, the Cougars continued missing the same easy shots they blew in his absence, and UCLA slowly pulled out of danger and ran out the clock with a stall. Final score: 76-67.

*

For the newspaper reporter who regularly traveled with the UCLA Bruins, it all seemed so perfectly routine.

He would land in Chicago by midafternoon aboard a jet-liner carrying the nation's number one team, which would play weekend games against Illinois and Loyola of Chicago. He would meet his college roommate for dinner at Old Town and then perhaps grab an aisle seat at the latest David Janssen flick.

Well, he had an aisle seat, all right. The only trouble was, it was on car number 3264 of the Norfolk & Western out of St. Louis. The TWA flight had been destined for Pittsburgh because the Chicago airport was snowbound, but J. D. Morgan somehow convinced the pilot he should make an unscheduled landing in St. Louis to expedite train connections for Chicago.

Now, however, the journey began taking crazier twists and turns. Upon landing in St. Louis, the team was met by six taxis ready to whisk everybody to the Chicago-bound train at a small station a few miles away. The timing was perfect — except for one problem. Four players were missing! In their haste to meet the train, Lynn Shackelford, Kenny Heitz, Gene Sutherland, and Neville Saner had told their cabbie, "We gotta get to the train station — *fast!!*" The cabbie drove them there fast, all right, but it was the wrong station.

Meanwhile, back at the right station, as John and Nell Wooden, eight players, Morgan, Ducky Drake, a student manager, and a bewildered reporter boarded the train, an assistant UCLA football coach accompanying the team on a recruiting trip was told to remain in St. Louis to find the players.

Darkness fell as the train crawled slowly across the Illinois countryside, into the teeth of a blizzard. Now the reporter had a problem: there was no way to tell the world that the UCLA Bruins had been stopped, at last — by the weatherman — and that the whereabouts of four players were unknown. There was no telegraph and no available telephone. The train stopped repeatedly so workmen could melt ice on the tracks with blowtorches, and anxious glances out the window revealed nothing but silos and barbed-wire fences and snowdrifts as tall as Lew Alcindor.

Hours passed. The train inched along, stopping again and again in Nowhere, U.S.A., then moving on. The journey seemed endless. John and Nell Wooden had stood in line for ninety minutes at the dining car, only to settle for slices of bread when the train encountered a food shortage. Players chatted with college coeds heading home for the weekend. And J. D. Morgan, furious at the inconvenience, said, "Never again! Never again will we come back here to play in late January!"

Finally, midnight approached. The train had sputtered along for nine hours, and the reporter had missed one edition in which to file his story. Suddenly the train stopped again for the umpteenth time for more repairs, somewhere on the fringes of suburban Chicago. About fifty yards away was a house. Civilization, at last! And maybe a telephone too.

The reporter hastily jumped off the train. "Have them hold the train for me," he said to the UCLA passengers as he plunged into the raging blizzard. He plodded awkwardly through snow that was up to his navel. He rapped on the door of the house. A woman, fiftyish and obese, answered, surrounded by half-a-dozen noisy kids clad in underwear and pajamas. They had been watching the late, late show.

"Quick! I've gotta call the Los Angeles *Times* fast!" he said to the woman. "May I use your phone to make a collect call?"

Her eyes skeptically studied the reporter's face. "Now I've heard everything," she said, slamming the door and almost flattening his nose.

He knocked again. The door opened narrowly. "Lady, please!" he pleaded frantically. "I've got to call my paper before the train leaves!"

She giggled. "Well, O.K.," she said, "but only because I was born in L.A." She pointed to the kitchen. "The phone is out there," she said.

Nervously, he placed his call before an audience of wide-eyed youngsters and began dictating his story. Moments later, a boy darted into the kitchen and yelled, "Hey, mister, your train is leaving!"

The reporter quickly handed the receiver to the boy and said, "Hold this and don't break the connection." He raced out of the house and plodded clumsily back through the snow to fetch his typewriter and suitcase. He climbed aboard the train, whereupon the conductor chewed him out for getting off and then he locked the door.

"I've gotta get off this train," the reporter yelled, with visions of the little boy inside the house, holding the telephone and running up a mammoth phone bill. "You're not going anywhere!" the conductor retorted, stalking into the next car.

With the help of sympathetic passengers, the reporter forced open the door and jumped back into the snow. "Have them hold my things in Chicago," he said, trudging toward the house. "I'll pick 'em up after the spring thaw."

He dashed back into the house, grabbed the telephone, told his angry listener in Los Angeles that he would "explain later," and finished communicating the story about the UCLA team and the missing basketball players. He now envisioned having to spend the night — maybe even the next week — camping out in a snowdrift, whereupon the woman strode into the kitchen and said, "Sir, your train moved only about fifty yards and stopped again."

Relieved, but still trembling, he burst out the door and tried to make like Red Grange dashing through the snow in those ancient football films. He pounded frantically on the train door for several minutes, finally convincing a startled passenger that he really was not a hitchhiker. Then he rejoined the UCLA traveling party for the last leg of the journey — a two-hour, stop-and-go ride through Chicago's railroad yards. "All right, guys, we practice in fifteen minutes!" yelled a voice across the aisle. The voice was Lew Alcindor's.

At 2 A.M., the trip was over. The UCLA Bruins arrived in a metropolis paralyzed by a snowstorm that would last twenty-nine hours, the worst in Chicago history. A hasty telephone call from J. D. Morgan to the hotel where the team had reservations disclosed that Shackelford, Heitz, Sutherland, and Saner had arrived an hour earlier — on *another* train.

The next day, Chicago looked like a frozen ghost town. Industries closed. Cars stalled. Residents snowed in. And there would be no UCLA–Illinois game until Sunday because transportation was at a standstill. On Saturday night, 17,024 dug themselves out of the snow to see Big Lew hit thirty-five points in an 82-67 win over Loyola. On Sunday, he scored forty-five as the Bruins routed Illinois, 120-82.

As if the perils of a snowstorm weren't enough, it was revealed later that Lew Alcindor had been subjected to another kind of danger. He had received threatening letters — two with Chicago postmarks — before the trip, and a secret police bodyguard was assigned to him during his stay in the Windy City. "Lew's bodyguard was a fine fellow, an ex-basketball player," said J. D. Morgan. Then, in a classic understatement, he added, "And Lew wasn't upset in the least by the situation."

Bob Boyd had tried two strategic ploys against Lew Alcindor and Company, both unsuccessful. Now, in a crucial Pacific 8 game, he would try a third — an out-and-out stall.

In a tense, dramatic contest, Boyd's USC team gave the Bruins their scariest fight of the season before a near capacity crowd at the Sports Arena. With seven-foot center Ron Taylor holding the ball under one arm at midcourt and his teammates playing keepaway most of the game, working only for the "sure" shot, the Trojans very nearly pulled off the biggest upset of the season. UCLA partisans hooted and jeered as the Trojans passed and passed and passed, but the crowd soon realized that maybe this was, indeed, the way to conquer the nation's number one team.

It all came down to a stirring overtime period after USC forward Bill Hewitt had cast off a jump shot that would have won the game at the buzzer had the ball not curled quickly around the rim and out. Then sophomore Bill Sweek came off the UCLA bench in overtime to steal a pass from Mike Maggard and make a key lay-up, then intercept another pass from Steve Jennings and feed Mike Warren, who was fouled intentionally and made two free throws to ice the game.

UCLA had won, 40-35, and Bob Boyd was the most disconsolate man in the arena. "We should have won it," he said. "We were very unlucky."

John Wooden, according to one Bruin player, had been nearly outcoached by the man to whom he had yet to lose. "I do think he was baffled," said the player. "I don't think he expected anybody would be able to stall that long or have the courage to stall — and just completely hold the ball. We had practiced against it just a little because of what we'd been reading in the newspapers. But I really think he didn't know what to do. All I can remember him saying during the time outs was, 'Be alert all the time and play hard defense. Stay back.' That's all you could do. I noticed next Monday at practice that he had gone to the rulebooks and had come up with all sorts of defenses about what to do against it. That's why I say he was taken by surprise."

If Wooden was caught with his antistall defenses down, he also voiced mixed feelings about USC's tactics. "It was a good game plan and it was executed well," he said in the locker room afterward, "but something like this is bad for the game. And I'll tell Bob that too. I'm not critical of him for using it from a tactical standpoint — only from the standpoint of how much this can hurt basketball."

He was asked if he expected more of the same from other teams. "Yes, I do. . . ." he said. "But I don't think most coaches will try it. Too many coaches think too much of basketball to do it."

The game, one of the most memorable in the long rivalry

between the two schools, touched off a Great Stall Controversy that reached a stormy crescendo at the weekly basketball writers' luncheon two days later. Wooden was scolded publicly by Jess Hill, USC Athletic Director, for postgame remarks he thought were aimed indirectly at Boyd.

Hill's reprimand came immediately after Wooden had painstakingly explained that he did not "want anyone to draw the inference that I am critical of Bob Boyd personally . . . There might come a time when I might want to do it [stall] myself, although I don't believe it is good for the game."

Wooden appeared on the verge of leaving the luncheon when Hill rose and said to him, "I prefer you stay." Wooden sat down.

Taking the podium, Hill said bitterly: "There is a certain amount of accusation that he [Boyd] doesn't think that much of basketball . . . I have had considerable experience in college athletics throughout the years and I have a philosophy of my own what is good for basketball. I couldn't see anything that wasn't good for basketball [in the game]. Bob had my support in everything he did. Any team that attempts to run against UCLA is doomed to devastation . . . I don't see much difference in stalling in the last four minutes of a game — all coaches do it — or at the beginning."

Wooden sat stone-faced, glaring at Hill throughout his reprimand.

After Hill also deplored the alleged "profane" treatment Boyd received from UCLA fans at half time, then concluded his remarks, Wooden left the room and — on his way out — calmly whispered something in Boyd's ear.

Reached at his home that evening for comment, Wooden preferred to let the matter drop. "I'd be belittling myself," he said, "to comment on his [Hill's] remarks."

It happened during a road game with Stanford.

Lucius Allen and Gary Petersmeyer, the Indians guard, got upset with each other and began exchanging elbows while

both raced downcourt. Suddenly Petersmeyer caught a hard
blow from Allen and tumbled to the floor, so badly shaken up
that he had to be treated momentarily by a trainer.

John Wooden promptly removed Allen from the game as a
disciplinary measure, while a UCLA fan seated behind the
bench yelled, "Atta boy, Lucius! Way to get 'im!"

Moments later, Wooden got up and stalked to the end of
the bench. He angrily yelled at several Bruin players, "Did any
of you encourage Lucius to do that?"

The players sat there, dumfounded, and answered, "No."

"Why would he do that?" said one player, recalling the
incident. "Did he think he heard those words from a
player? Did he think it was a player's friend? Or did the players
really encourage Lucius to do it? Or what? You kinda have to
wonder when you're a second-stringer on the bench. You wonder about double standards. Was he trying to blame Lucius'
conduct on a second-stringer to give him an excuse to play
Lucius? I don't know."

Another player put it more bluntly. "Hell, that was a cop-
out," he said. "The coach knew all the time that the guy yelling
was a fan behind the bench. He didn't want to put himself in
the position of having to tell the fan to shut up. But he wanted
to show everybody that he was concerned. So he took it out
on us."

Were it not for Mike Warren, the UCLA Bruins would not
have been the cohesive team they were all season.

He was the leader, a lightning 5-11 playmaker who, even as
a sophomore, won lavish praise from ex-teammate Freddie
Goss: "Mike was the finest guard I ever played with; he really
understood the game." And Goss had played alongside Walt
Hazzard and Gail Goodrich.

Now Warren was a junior, the guy whose teammates nicknamed him "Flea," a savvy performer with supersonic hands
and feet who scurried around the court like a toy mouse.

He would be team captain next season, and he would date

Mary Wilson, a singer on the Supremes, as well as cultivate a strong interest in theater arts (he has since acted in the film *Drive, He Said* and in a "Marcus Welby, M.D." episode on television).

Warren also brought with him from a black family in South Bend a mature sensitivity to racial concerns that was inspired by a friend he met during his college days, former pro football star Jim Brown.

Black people, he said, "need the extreme elements within the movement today. We need all types of ideas. We need Stokely Carmichael to frighten and make people aware . . . We need Martin Luther King to keep order. What I try to do is listen to everybody. Those ideas I agree with, I accept; those I don't agree with, I discard."

Magazine stories in recent weeks had portrayed Lew Alcindor as being extremely unhappy at UCLA.

When newsmen persisted in asking John Wooden to open locker-room doors so they could discuss the articles with Big Lew, the coach had adamantly refused. "You're just gonna interview him," he said, "and nobody else. How do you think that makes the other players on our team feel?"

Finally, after an NCAA tournament game, Wooden bowed to the pressure. Reluctantly.

Reporters quickly gathered around Alcindor — as Wooden stood by, eavesdropping — and asked him, in essence, if those stories about his discontent were true.

"Right now, I'm as happy at UCLA as I ever could be," he said. "Actually, those are pretty much my quotes, but in many cases I was quoted out of context and they left out a lot of things that I said . . ."

When asked about a *Sport* article that quoted him as saying he would have gone to Stanford, Michigan, or California if he had it to do over again, he said: "That part about those other schools all came up when I said UCLA seemed more

Johnny Wooden, Purdue's three-time All-American guard.

A sign of Johnny Wooden's hustle in Purdue days (he's fifth from left in first row) are bandages on both his knees. (Photo is from the 1930–1931 season.)

Characteristically, John, a rolled-u program in his hand, squats dow to exhort his team during time ol

(2) patting the knee of an assistant coach (in this case, ex-assistant Denny Crum),

The ritual Wooden goes through before every game: (1) turning to wink at wife Nell,

) tugging at his socks,

(4) leaning over to tap the floor.

Wooden with one of his earlier teams, the 1955–1956 squad.
From left are Dick Banton, Ben Rogers, Morris Taft, Wooden,
Willie Naulls (All-America center), and Allen Herring.

John Wooden, seated, with one of his earlier assistants, Jerry Norman. The coach's "Pyramid of Success" and code of loyalty are on wall, background, along with pictures of his two ex-coaches, Piggie Lambert (left) and Glenn Curtis (right).

Tension etched on their faces, Bruins await Western Regionals game against
Seattle University at Corvallis, Oregon, on the way to their first national title
in 1963–1964. From left are Walt Hazzard, Keith Erickson, Wooden,
Fred Slaughter, assistant Jerry Norman, and Doug McIntosh.

pread-eagled as he flips lay-up,
/alt Hazzard scores against Michigan
uring win in 1963–1964 season —
game Wooden thinks is the greatest
ıy of his teams has ever played.
oming up from the back is
eith Erickson.

Demonstrating the nerve-rattling power of UCLA's famed zone press,
Doug McIntosh, left, and Gail Goodrich harass Duke's Steve Vacendak
during Bruins' first championship win, 98-83, at Kansas City.

Wooden with a jubilant 1963–1964 championship team,
after the victory Wooden savored more than any other because
of breakthrough after years of near-misses.

Emerging from the locker room after the 1964 championship game and happily telling his wife, "Isn't that something?" Wooden is greeted by a victory kiss from Nell.

Former star guard Gail Goodrich goes airborne for reverse lay-up
in a game against USC.

Wooden listens intently to the late Dr. Ralph Bunche, former UCLA basketball player in pre-Wooden era and later United Nations undersecretary and Nobel Peace Prize winner.

Jamming in a two-handed, back-handed stuff shot as a UCLA sophomore,
Lew Alcindor unleashes his most spectacular weapon against Stanford.
Largely because of Alcindor, the "stuff" was outlawed in college basketball
after the 1966–1967 season.

Lew Alcindor, right arm high above basket, blocks a shot against Minnesota.

As Wooden looks on benignly, three men instrumental in his success
ponder the game about to be played — UCLA's historic loss to Houston
in the Astrodome. Assistant Coach Jerry Norman, left, chats with
Athletic Director J. D. Morgan, center, while Lew Alcindor gazes warily
at the record crowd of 55,000-plus.

Elvin Hayes of Houston soaring hig
over Lew Alcindor, who was bothere
by an eye injury, to score in Cougar
upset win over the Bruins at th
Astrodome in 196

Sidney Wicks of UCLA grabs rebound away from Artis (Batman) Gilmore of Jacksonville University during Bruins' 80-69 championship win in 1970.

Basket net draped around his neck and finger held aloft to signify "We're number one," Lew Alcindor stands with obviously proud John Wooden after UCLA's third consecutive win of the Alcindor Era, 92–72, over Purdue, at Louisville.

Wooden samples some of his 60th birthday cake in prepractice ceremony
at Pauley Pavilion. Star forwards Curtis Rowe and Sidney Wicks
sample the punch, at right.

In a tense moment, Wooden exhorts his team with a clenched fist.

John Wooden the Competitor explodes in a rage while calling a time out.

Above and right   Bill Walton (1) snares a rebound against Iowa State, (2) turns to look for breaking teammates, and (3) quickly throws "outlet" pass triggering the fast break. Wooden has said Walton is the best player he has ever had in this phase of the game.

The Wooden family group:

Front row, left to right: Caryn Dennis, 13; Cathleen Dennis, 8; Kim Wooden, 6; Coach John Wooden, holding Michael, 3; Johnny Wooden, 8; Gregory Wooden, 9; and Christy Dennis, 15.

Back row, left to right: Stan and Nan Dennis; Nell Wooden; and Jim and Carleen Wooden.

like a commuter school than the others, and I think you'll agree with me, won't you?"

Suddenly John Wooden's words interrupted the interview. "All right," he said. "That's enough."

He ordered the reporters — some of whom were proceeding toward other players for more interviews — out of the locker room. "See? What did I tell you?" he said. "Look who you wanted to talk to. You didn't want to talk to any of the other players."

Before the newsmen could explain they did, indeed, wish to seek out Lew's teammates, the doors were closed. John Wooden had won his argument, but had lost a round in public relations.

It was the week of the NCAA finals in Louisville. Guy Lewis, coach of the very physical Houston team that would meet UCLA in the semifinals, wore his pink sport coat, which he'd worn for good luck in his team's previous fifteen victories. And the Cougars' star player, 6-foot-8 Elvin Hayes, said, "No way Lew's gonna run over me."

John Wooden knew it would be tough. Forward Lynn Shackelford, looking back on 1967, remembers the coach fearing Houston's muscle on the backboards.

"That's all Coach Wooden and Jerry Norman could talk about all week," he said. "They kept saying how Heitz and I were gonna have to rebound and screen off. I was really up for the game. They claimed it was gonna be our toughest game of the year by far and Houston was gonna be the most physical team we played. They were probably right. They were a bunch of monsters!"

The game opened with a flourish. Houston controlled the tip and stormed the basket with Hayes soaring over Alcindor and scoring on a stuff lay-up. "That kinda startled us," recalled Shackelford, "because we had never seen anyone challenge Alcindor that way."

But the Bruins were not startled for long. Even though Houston double-teamed Alcindor with Hayes and 6-7 Melvin Bell, used its height to pass over the UCLA press, and grabbed a 19-18 lead, the game quickly turned the other way.

Shackelford hit an unmolested jump shot against the Houston zone defense, the Bruins stole the ball with their press, and Alcindor scored on a dunk and began blocking shots, including a subsequent Hayes dunk attempt. For the next five minutes, the Cougars went scoreless and came apart against the press. Soon it was 29-19 and UCLA was one step away from another perfect season, 73-58.

Hayes had outscored Alcindor, 25-19, outrebounded him 24-20, and outknocked him too. "I think I really outplayed him," he said afterward. "I can't really say Alcindor should be the number one basketball player in the country . . . he was not too good on the boards. He stood around a lot on defense. I was looking for him to be much tougher . . . I think later on he'll be a real good ballplayer."

Alcindor said he did only what he was supposed to against Hayes. "We thought we'd lose if they got a lot of inside shots," he said. "So my job was to make him go outside. He's a good ballplayer, the best I've faced this year."

The next afternoon, Alcindor and Hayes strolled together among the Easter shoppers. They bought sunglasses and record albums, then returned to Hayes's hotel room, where Big Lew told the Big E he would follow his advice in the off season by building up his upper torso with weights.

But in the meantime, there was one last game to be played — against Dayton — for the national championship.

The Flyers had upset number-three-ranked North Carolina the previous night and had a fine forward in Don May, but were overmatched against UCLA. Their fans knew it, too, by chanting "We're Number Two!"

It was never close. The "Firehouse Four Plus Lew" had too much firepower and sprinted away to a 20-4 lead, then coasted to a somewhat anticlimactic 79-64 victory. It was win number thirty of a perfect season — and with four sophomores and a junior on the starting team, the Bruins became the youngest team to win the NCAA. Moreover, UCLA joined Kentucky as only the second school to win three titles, while Wooden became the first coach with two perfect seasons.

And the dynasty would remain intact. Lew Alcindor, who had seriously weighed leaving UCLA for Michigan, vowed he would be back and was "looking forward to trying to do it again."

"Everywhere you go, you're going to find something you don't like," he said after the Dayton game. "There are things I don't like [at UCLA]. But right now that's where I am, and I'm going to stay."

He would, however, return without his most devastating weapon — the dunk shot. Barely after the UCLA Bruins got their championship wristwatches, basketball's rulesmakers outlawed the dunk shot for college games. Their reasons: the shot was "indefensible" and too many backboards have been damaged and too many players had been hurt.

John Wooden, however, said what he thought was the real reason. "There's no question," he said, "that the rule is designed to curtail the ability of one player."

The "one player," Ferdinand Lewis Alcindor, Jr., poked fun at the rule a few weeks later when he was honored by the Friars Club in Beverly Hills.

"They're trying to protect the little man unreasonably," he said, drily. "I don't see why they don't take action against the little man by letting the air out of the ball."

"Violence is necessary," says Negro militant H. Rap Brown. "It is as American as cherry pie" . . . *Bonnie and Clyde* splatters blood on movie screens, while a photographer wrestles with two seminude nymphets in *Blow-Up* . . . Carl Stokes of Cleveland, great-grandson of a slave, defeats Seth Taft, grandson of a President, to become the first black mayor of a major United States city . . . A fashion model named Twiggy, 31-22-32, admits, in artless Cockney, "It's not really wot you call a figger, is it?" . . . Arguing "I don't have no quarrel with those Viet Congs," Cassius Clay is stripped of his boxing crown for refusing to enter the army . . . United States planes bomb parts of Hanoi, while college kids, their hair longer and patience shorter, chant, "Stop the war!" . . . A girl in Haight-Ashbury says, "Whatever turns me on is a sacrament: LSD, sex, my bells, my colors — That's the holy communion, you dig?" . . . Meanwhile, John Wooden recovers from a siege of exhaustion and says, "We have more depth, more size, more experience. Of course, we'll be a better team."

Gunshots crackled across a South Los Angeles street during bloody fighting between a small pro-Communist group and about fifty young followers of black power advocate Ron Karenga. It was Thanksgiving Day 1967 and the battle erupted outside a small church where the leftist group had been picketing the three-day Black Youth Conference.

Inside the church, in a meeting that was closed to white newsmen and not directly related to the battle outside, a group of black athletes discussed whether they should boycott the 1968 Olympic Games. Tommie Smith and Lee Evans, track stars from San Jose State, were there and refused to comment on the meeting when it adjourned about a half-hour after the gunsmoke cleared outside. Also declining any comment was Lew Alcindor, who hastily departed before the meeting's organizer, Harry Edwards, a black sociology professor from San Jose State, stood at a doorway to the church and announced that the athletes had, indeed, unanimously voted a resolution to boycott the Games because, he said, "the black man has to be given everything that's due him."

Edwards' words — and his feelings — were strong. "This is a significant stand because I know of no other group of people who can make our feelings known," he said. "I hope the country can see what these black athletes have done. This is our last chance to avert a racial catastrophe in this country

. . . If we finish first [in the Olympics], that's beautiful; if we finish fourteenth, that's beautiful too. This country is not for us, so why should we be for the country? . . . This is our way of pointing out that the United States has no right to set itself up as leader of the free world. It's a simple fact that America has to be exposed for what it is. America is just as guilty as South Africa ever was . . . We want to take this question out of the sphere of civil rights and bring it into the sphere of human rights."

At UCLA the next day, telephones rang in the athletic department with calls from newsmen who demanded to know how Lew Alcindor felt about the proposed boycott. At a hastily arranged news conference after basketball practice, Big Lew said the resolution did not bind him personally to play — or not to play — in the forthcoming Games at Mexico City. He seemed rankled by the questioning — and by the forest of microphones poking in his face.

"I haven't made up my mind," he said. "I'll just wait until the time comes. If I competed in the Olympics, I might not be able to attend school — and that would make me ineligible [for college basketball]. Also, I might have to work during the summer to earn money for school and that might affect my decision too."

He said the decision to boycott was reached by acclamation. "I can't comment on what Mr. Edwards said," he explained. "All I can say is that everybody agreed it would be a good idea to boycott. That does not speak for any one person. Everything was done anonymously. Actually, there is no boycott as of now. There can be no boycott until it's time for anybody to boycott."

Alcindor said the resolution was an expression of the Black Youth Conference. "This conference is being held," he said, "because it is looking out for the best interests of black people as a whole. If you live in a racist society, you have to react — and this was my way of reacting. We don't catch hell because we're Christian. We catch hell because we're black."

Meanwhile, John Wooden was asked about Alcindor's involvement in the boycott movement. "How a player of mine feels about society is his own business," he said, "whether he's black, yellow, or white."

And the 1967-1968 basketball campaign was still a week away.

On paper and on the court, the team was much stronger.

Lew Alcindor was back, his dunk shot silenced, but his vast other skills improved. "No other athlete in the history of college athletics," said John Wooden, "had to face the pressure that Lew did last year."

So, too, were the guards, Warren and Allen, improved. And the forwards, Shackelford and Heitz, although they would be pushed hard for starting jobs by a couple of familiar faces, seniors Edgar Lacey and Mike Lynn. Lacey, who had missed the previous campaign to rehabilitate his knee, was saying, "My jump shot is back from the dead," while Lynn had returned from disciplinary exile as a result of his forgery conviction.

Together, they traveled to UCLA's opening game in Lafayette, Indiana, where they would battle John Wooden's alma mater, Purdue University, in the dedication of its new basketball arena. On the bus ride from Indianapolis, they observed a billboard on the outskirts of Lebanon that heralded the debut of a kid everybody from Fort Wayne to Evansville was ecstatic about: "Home of Rick Mount, Indiana's Mr. Basketball." The UCLA Bruins broke into laughter, but Rick Mount, a blond, sharpshooting sophomore, nearly had the last laugh twenty-four hours later.

Opting for experience the next night, Wooden named Lacey and Lynn as his starting forwards. But it was soon obvious they were rusty from a year's layoff. And the Purdue Boilermakers — armed with Mount's fadeaway jumper and a "diamond-and-one" zone defense that collapsed on Alcindor — were on the threshold of pulling off a shocking upset.

It was a thrilling, frantic contest that almost ended with a baseline shot by Mount that would have been heard 'round the basketball world and would have driven 14,200 partisan fans to tear down the new building, brick by brick.

With ten seconds left and the score tied, 71-71, Purdue called time out to talk strategy. Coach George King told his players the ball would go to — who else? — Mount, who was the game's high scorer with twenty-eight points. A few feet away, John Wooden told his troops to anticipate a last-ditch shot from either Mount or forward Herman Gilliam. "We told them," he said later, "to be dadburned sure they didn't foul them, to get a hand in their faces."

When play resumed, Mount dribbled to the right of the basket. He cast off with a fifteen-footer, but the ball thudded in and out. Alcindor nearly leaped through the ceiling to seize the rebound. He alertly threw a long pass to Shackelford at midcourt, whereupon Shackelford fed the ball to Bill Sweek, racing downcourt alone near the top of the circle. In a split second, Sweek cut loose with a last-second jump shot. Swish! The buzzer went off, Purdue fans booed and pelted the floor with debris, and the UCLA Bruins hurriedly exited with a 73-71 victory.

For the nation's number one team, it was the narrowest escape since the USC stall game, which, ironically, ended with Bill Sweek the hero. Alcindor had been held to seventeen points, while Allen and Shackelford threw in eighteen apiece, but now there was hope once again that maybe the Bruins weren't so invincible after all.

"Well," said John Wooden, catching his breath, "I'm glad that's over."

Off-the-court discipline, a trademark of John Wooden teams in other years, was noticeably relaxed during Year Two in the reign of King Lew.

Hair was slightly longer. The dress code no longer demanded coats and ties. And curfew was almost nonexistent.

"It was a much tighter ship the year before," observed a white player, "until the blacks started going out and coming in at all hours. That's when things started changing. The whites were a little backward in that respect. We had been observing the training rules — bed check and everything — but then we got suspect and finally caught on. I guess the coaches didn't care as much as they did before, because they probably realized we could only be hurt as a team from within.

"So, we all started having a good time, especially on road trips. There wasn't much bed check. Oh, there was a curfew, but it wasn't observed consistently. In a way, Ducky was sort of intimidated by what we were doing. The coaches' attitude was different now. About all Wooden cared about was keeping everybody happy. It was like he was saying, 'To hell with the rules. Let's get the season over with and win another national championship.'"

It all seemed so routine, another romp through the Bay Area.

The UCLA Bruins had trampled the California Bears, 94-64, in Berkeley and spent the night across the bay in Palo Alto, where they would face Stanford the next afternoon.

At 3 A.M., Lew Alcindor awakened with a sharp pain in his left eye. It had been inflicted about six hours earlier during the California game when Bear forward Tom Henderson accidentally poked Alcindor's eye when they were battling for a rebound. The game was halted momentarily while Alcindor was treated, but he continued playing.

Now the pain was excruciating and he summoned trainer Ducky Drake. Soon the injury was diagnosed as a scratched eyeball and he was treated at the Stanford University medical center, where doctors applied a thick bandage over the eye and ruled Big Lew out of action indefinitely.

That meant John Wooden had to move Mike Lynn to center and bring the high-post offense out of mothballs for the Stanford game. At breakfast that morning, the players were stunned to learn of Alcindor's injury, but were exhilarated by the new dimensions his absence created for them individually.

"We were kind of excited — not because he was hurt — but because this was a chance for us to go back to the old high-post offense," said one player. "Here was a chance to really prove we were good players even without Alcindor. We felt we were. We felt we had a very good team. We talked about it and said, 'Here's our chance to really have fun and play.' We felt we were somewhat restricted with Alcindor. Wooden wanted us to slow the pace down. Now, we could run a little more and have more individual freedom out there."

As Alcindor watched forlornly through sunglasses from the bench in street clothes, the Bruins sailed past Stanford, 75-63, with Lynn controlling the backboards and Lacey shutting off the Indians' star forward, Arthur Harris.

It was UCLA's forty-sixth victory in a row, but now an intriguing question remained: Would Lew Alcindor be ready for the big game against Elvin Hayes and Company in the Houston Astrodome a week hence?

All week long, John Wooden was confronted by a 7-foot, 1½-inch question mark.

Lew Alcindor had been admitted to the Jules Stein Eye Clinic on the UCLA campus and was confined to a darkened room for treatment. He got a telephone call from the young man who unintentionally struck him, California's Tom Henderson, who wished him a fast recovery.

But the doctors were not yet sure when Big Lew could play basketball again. He remained hospitalized for four days and was allowed to shoot baskets casually in practice on Wednesday — with his eye still bandaged — but he would miss the Portland game the following night. It was won easily (and sloppily) by the Bruins, 93-69, for victory number forty-seven in a row.

The next morning, Alcindor — sans eyepatch — boarded a

jetliner with the UCLA Bruins for Houston, still not at full
strength and complaining of double vision. But now he had the
"green light" to face Elvin Hayes.

The setting was so garishly unreal that probably not even
Warner Brothers or Cecil B. DeMille could have dreamed of it.
From those expensive seats that the management called "sky
boxes" five tiers up, even Lew Alcindor and Elvin Hayes looked
like ants crawling across an eight-cent stamp.

It was the long-awaited shootout at the Houston Astrodome.
Big Lew and those fast-draw artists from UCLA versus Big E
and those Texas-sized big guns from the University of Houston.
A battle of unbeatens between the numbers one- and two-
ranking college teams in the land.

There were dazzling lights and thundering cheers that
swirled inside the cavernous arena and a fireworks-spewing,
cartoon-flashing scoreboard that looked almost as big as the
LBJ Ranch.

John Wooden stood at courtside on the eve of the game and
gazed up into the floodlights that felt as hot on his face as a
sunlamp. "When I was in grade school," he said, "we used to
play in a small place called 'the Barn.' " He shook his head. "It's
hard to imagine," he said, "that a basketball game would ever
be played in surroundings like these."

For more than a year, Texans had been snapping up tickets
faster than free passes to the State Fair, and by the tip-off on
Saturday night, January 20, the Astrodome would be jammed
with 55,000-plus spectators (52,693 paid), by far the largest
crowd ever to watch a basketball game indoors.

Actually, the place was built for football and baseball — not
basketball. The portable wooden floor, which had been trans-
ported in trucks from the Los Angeles Sports Arena, seemed
terribly lonely out there at midfield, at least 100 feet away from
the nearest box seat. As one Houston player said, "We'll be
worn out just running from the dressing rooms to the court!"

What's more, never had so many paid so much for so many poor seats. From the stands, the game looked like a silent movie. The ball was visible, all right, but the patter of feet and the thud of the dribble were almost inaudible. Nonetheless, the game figured to sell out, matching two of college basketball's most celebrated figures with almost as much ballyhoo as a Dempsey-Tunney fight. It would be the most widely seen game of all time (150 television stations carried the contest, even as far away as Fairbanks, Alaska), and certainly the richest, what with the two schools splitting the $200,000 gross receipts, except for a 17 percent cut which went to the sports association that leases the Astrodome.

If there was a favorite, it had to be UCLA, which had not lost since February of 1966 and would be formidable despite Alcindor's eye condition. Houston would be armed with four starters from the team that lost to the Bruins the previous year in the NCAA — 6-9 center Ken Spain; 6-5 Don Chaney, a guard with octupuslike arms; 6-7 forward Theodis Lee; and, of course, Hayes, who grew up in the cotton fields of Rayville, Louisiana, shooting baskets through a bucket that was nailed to a tree. "They won't be able to get away with collapsing on me," he said, with customary self-assurance. "Nobody can. We've got too many other good shooters and, besides, I can always overpower one guy."

He left no doubt that the "one guy" was Ferdinand Lewis Alcindor, Jr., who had practiced briefly with the team the night before the game and still had double vision. John Wooden, however, was minimizing his injury. "I have very few reservations about him now," he said. "In fact, I'm most optimistic." Moreover, Wooden said his team was ready. "Houston is as physical a team as has ever played in college," he said, "but I like to think we will have the edge in quickness and conditioning." Pressure on his team? "Yes," he said, "especially when you figure that there will be less pressure on Houston. We have that long winning streak, you know."

From the beginning, the game clearly was not an artistic success — except for the performance of one man, Elvin Hayes. The players were tense and sloppy, particularly Alcindor, who was sluggish and timid under the basket. But the Big E was throwing in jumpers from all over the place. Edgar Lacey couldn't stop him. Nor could Mike Lynn, who replaced Lacey and got into foul trouble. By half time, Hayes had scored twenty-nine points and the Cougars led, 46-43.

When play resumed, Houston nursed three- and five-point leads, although Hayes was effectively curtailed by the guarding of 6-7 Jim Nielsen. UCLA managed to tie the game, 54-all, midway through the period on a long jump shot by Mike Warren. But the Bruins were playing the game Houston wanted them to play — deliberate and erratic — and Alcindor was hardly a factor defensively.

Nonetheless, UCLA managed to stay in contention, exploiting Lucius Allen's quickness at forward, where he played in high school. He scored on a twisting lay-up to cut Houston's lead to 69-67, then sank two free throws with forty-four seconds left and 50,000 voices cannonading in his ears. Now it was tied, 69-69, and the Cougars looked again to Elvin Hayes. He quickly drove the baseline for a shot from close range, but Nielsen was whistled for a foul by referee Bobby Scott on a play that appeared to be a clean block. Hayes promptly dropped in two free throws — his thirty-eighth and thirty-ninth points of the night — and Houston was on top, 71-69, with less than half a minute remaining.

It remained for Houston to hang onto its lead for keeps when Allen, double-teamed by Chaney and guard George Reynolds near midcourt, hurled a desperation cross-court pass intended for Shackelford, who was in perfect position to hit the possible tying basket. But the ball sailed wildly out of bounds between Shackelford and Warren.

It was over. Pandemonium. It finally happened, just as sure as death and Texas. UCLA, the team that many observers said would not be beaten as long as Lew Alcindor was in uniform, had fallen at last, 71-69. Big Lew, who spent the darkest night of his career (only four of eighteen from the floor, fifteen points and twelve rebounds), was a loser for the first time since 1965. "No, my eyes didn't bother me," he said, "but I didn't feel physically right."

The UCLA winning streak of forty-seven games had ended at thirteen shy of the University of San Francisco's record sixty, and John Wooden stood calmly at courtside and said, "This is a game that will be good for our team. Not only that, but it was a great thing for college basketball."

In two months, Houston and UCLA would be likely combatants in an NCAA semifinal game in Los Angeles — a game that was already the subject of much speculation.

"They call the Houston Astrodome the eighth wonder of the world," wrote Loel Schrader in the Long Beach (California) *Independent-Press Telegram*. "But a victory by Houston over UCLA in Los Angeles would be the ninth."

"Why didn't Coach use Lacey?" yelled Lucius Allen, now a loser for the first time since 1963, his junior year at Kansas City's Wyandotte High School in Kansas. "Why didn't Coach use Lacey?"

His words were directed to no one in particular in the subdued UCLA dressing room. Later, on the bus ride back to the hotel, Allen would ask John Wooden, "Coach, why didn't you put our best forward back into the game?"

Wooden moved to talk privately with Allen, but in another part of the bus, Edgar Lacey was distraught over having been removed from the game midway through the first half and not reinserted. He talked of quitting the team and spent most of the predawn hours talking it over with Mike Warren while teammates sipped wine in their rooms and rehashed the night that was.

While the coach was being second-guessed, he was second-guessing himself the next day. He admitted he "probably erred" by playing Alcindor the full forty minutes. "I think I handled the situation rather poorly," he said. Alcindor thought so, too, and he would say so a year later in his autobiography for *Sports Illustrated*: "And it was the reason we lost! I stank up the joint; I was the worst player on the court, but out of some misguided feeling of loyalty or confidence in me, the coach let me stay in and blow the ball game. I thank him for his confidence, but on that occasion it was misplaced."

But Assistant Coach Jerry Norman disagreed: "Lew played the whole game because his presence would have a psychological effect — and it did. Of course, we wouldn't have played him if he were seriously injured. But without Lew in there, Houston would have stuck a couple of six-nine guys near the basket and it would have been all over in a hurry." A teammate of Alcindor concurred. "Even with one eye and one arm," he said, "Lew should have been playing."

Meanwhile, the following week, John Wooden was featured speaker, as usual, at a meeting of the Bruin Hoopsters, a basketball booster group. A member who attended said Wooden was subjected to pointed questioning by the fans, almost as if he had committed a capital crime, instead of losing his first basketball game in nearly two years.

"You should have seen what they put that poor man through," said a friend of Wooden's, sadly shaking his head. Another loyalist was equally sympathetic. "It was," he said, "almost as if they were asking him, 'Well, Coach, what have you done for me lately?'"

Perhaps the omen was delivered shortly before the tip-off.

The Houston Cougars' student manager, Howie Lorch, reportedly a six-year letterman, was arrested outside the Sports Arena and booked on charges of scalping tickets.

Add to this the unusual behavior of Elvin Hayes on the eve

of the game. He refused to pose for pictures and was reluctant to talk very much about anything — even Lew Alcindor.

As it turned out, it's a good thing Howie Lorch was spared the agony of watching the NCAA semifinal showdown in person.

The Great Rematch became the Great Mismatch. In perhaps the most devastating display of shooting and speed since those blitzes by John Wooden's 1964 team, UCLA demolished Houston, 101-69, with fast breaks galore, a tormenting full-court press, and, yes, a change in strategy that Wooden had insisted would not happen.

It was called a "diamond-and-one" zone defense, which Wooden installed at the suggestion of Jerry Norman, and it turned the Big E to a Little E. Lynn Shackelford shadowed Hayes everywhere but to the men's room and held him to ten points, the lowest total of his career, on a night when just about everything UCLA touched turned to gold.

The game that everybody had been waiting for unfolded before a record Sports Arena crowd of 15,742 and thousands more at six closed-circuit locations. It began with UCLA spurting away to a 12-4 lead, Houston creeping to within 20-19, and then — snap! crackle! and pop! — the Bruins created myriad turnovers with their press and blitzed the Cougars, 17-5, over the next four minutes. And when Lynn Shackelford made a steal and fed Lucius Allen for a lay-up that made it 37-24, Coach Guy Lewis frantically called time out. The heir apparent to UCLA's crown had suddenly been knocked on *its* crown.

It remained for UCLA to pull away to a forty-four-point lead during the second half before Wooden mercifully cleared his bench. The champagne was already on ice, even though UCLA would have to meet North Carolina, a winner over Ohio State, in the finals the following night.

"I feel like a dead man," said Coach Lewis, clutching the polka-dot towel in which he had buried his face during the carnage. "That was the greatest exhibition of basketball I've ever seen."

John Wooden admitted he hadn't expected to win by thirty-two points, but said the margin might have been ascribed to a feeling that "we knew we were better than some of the Houston players thought we were, and not as complacent as some coaching peers of mine thought we were." The latter was an apparent reference to Adolph Rupp, who had called the Bruins "complacent kids."

Certainly there was no complacency in the UCLA camp before the game. "We worked all week on the diamond-and-one," recalls Lynn Shackelford. "This was one time I felt Wooden and Norman were really trying to get me up for the game. Even during the game, they were screaming and yelling at me not to let Hayes get the ball. When he finally did hit a basket — and we were way ahead — I thought Wooden and Norman were gonna just go crazy. I thought they were gonna come out there on the court and kill me for letting him score."

In the finals the following night, the Bruins were not nearly so sharp, although they did not have to be against a North Carolina team that tried to slow the tempo but was clearly outclassed. Alcindor, spearing lob passes from teammates, whirled and scored thirty-four points from close range against 6-10 Rusty Clark to spearhead the 78-55 victory — the widest margin of victory yet in an NCAA title game.

At the finish, there was a standing ovation for little Mike Warren, who played his last college game, and there were chants of "We're Number One!" for a team that finished with a 29-1 record and now made UCLA the only team ever to win back-to-back national titles on two separate occasions.

Lew Alcindor, who emerged from the dressing room afterward, garbed in a colorful African robe, said it best: "This game counted a whole lot, but the win over Houston was our most satisfying victory. They'd had a lot to say about us. I don't think they were correct. We wanted to teach those people some manners."

The Tar Heels coach, Dean Smith, graciously called UCLA "the best college basketball team ever."

Perhaps that was what the tiny gold numeral "1" symbolized on the lapel of John Wooden.

Jackie marries "Ari," and Bob Hope cracks: "Nixon has a Greek running mate and now everybody wants one" . . . The running mate, Spiro T. Agnew, makes a campaign visit to Detroit and says, "You've seen one ghetto area, you've seen them all" . . . President Lyndon Johnson goes on national TV to announce: "I shall not seek and I will not accept the nomination" . . . DeGaulle of France says of LBJ: "He's a cowboy, and that says everything" . . . Tiny Tim rolls his eyes, blows kisses, and sings, sort of: "Tiptoe, through the tulips, with me" . . . Gunfire cracks twice and two men, the Reverend Martin Luther King, Jr., and Robert Kennedy, die, tragically, senselessly . . . Russian tanks rumble into Czechoslovakia amid cries of "Long Live Dubček!" . . . Raising gloved, clenched fists, sprinters Tommie Smith and John Carlos salute black power on the Olympics Games victory pedestal . . . Richard Nixon appears on "Laugh-In," then becomes President . . . UCLA prepares to try for an unprecedented third consecutive NCAA title. Even with the giant, can it win?

Two familiar faces were conspicuously absent as the UCLA Bruins plotted to become the first team ever to win three national championships in a row.

Jerry Norman, who had assembled the championship teams of the Hazzard, Goodrich, and Alcindor years, had resigned shortly after the season to become a stockbroker. He was replaced by Denny Crum, the Pierce Junior College coach who, like Norman, was a spirited, aggressive former pupil of John Wooden's.

Lucius Allen, the lithe, lightning guard who was expected to inherit Mike Warren's playmaking role, was arrested for a second time on marijuana-possession charges during the spring. He dropped out of school because of scholastic difficulties and was later fined and placed on probation.

That left John Wooden in an ambivalent mood about the 1968-1969 campaign. He knew his front line had a lot of exclamation points, one of them 7 feet, 1½ inches tall. But he also was aware that his backcourt, with Mike Warren and Allen gone, would be a question mark.

Wooden immediately moved to shore up the deficiency. He had but one "true guard" in Donnie Saffer, a scurrying 6-1 senior, so he moved forwards Bill Sweek and Kenny Heitz to the backcourt, imported a junior-college transfer named John Vallely from Orange Coast College, and welcomed sophomore Terry Schofield from the red-shirt ranks.

Up front, however, the picture looked rosier. The returnees, of course, were Alcindor, Lynn Shackelford, and Jim Nielsen. And the newcomers were sophomores — and highly regarded: 6-6 Curtis Rowe, up from the frosh; 6-8 Sidney Wicks, the state's fourth-best junior college scorer at nearby Santa Monica City College; and 6-9 Steve Patterson, a red-shirt from Santa Maria who was the heir apparent to Big Lew's job.

"We have the strongest front line in the history of college basketball," said John Wooden. "We have experience, depth, height, and good quickness among them."

But, in almost the same breath, he was apprehensive about the backcourt and his words would be remembered often in the months to come.

"Whoever they are," he said, "they'll be the most inexperienced set of guards I've ever had at UCLA."

The subject was Lew Alcindor's height.

UCLA's press brochure listed him at 7 feet, 1½ inches, but the athletic department had refused to measure him publicly when skeptical reporters swore on a stack of notebooks he was taller, maybe by an inch or two.

Oddly, the subject was raised at a basketball writers' luncheon by, of all people, John Wooden, who had been accused of maintaining a credibility gap about Big Lew's size.

He turned to Lynn Shackelford, whom he had brought to the meeting to answer questions from newsmen, and his words took on the form of Perry Mason interrogating a client.

"Shack," he said, "how tall are you?"

"I'm six-five."

"All right," Wooden replied, "where were you measured?"

"In Pauley Pavilion."

Then came the inevitable. "All right, how tall is Lew?"

Shackelford shrugged. "Seven-one-and-a-half?" he answered, tentatively. ". . . Is that right?"

Laughter rippled across the room.

"And where," asked Wooden, "was Lew measured?"

"In Pauley Pavilion too."

Shackelford explained that his own height was shorter than the one listed in the program. "It listed me one-half inch shorter," he said. "I measured six-four-and-a-quarter, but I'm listed at six-five."

He talked about having been questioned by other players about Alcindor's height. "There have been a lot of games," he said, "when we all line up for a free throw — and a guy on the other team, standing next to me, will say, 'That guy's a lot taller than seven-one.'"

Then, as an afterthought, he added:

"They say he's seven-one-and-a-half . . . but to me, he sure looks taller than that."

No cross-examination, thank you. Case dismissed. Or is it?

The subject was religion.

On a nighttime bus ride from Columbus to South Bend, Lew Alcindor and Steve Patterson were sharing viewpoints.

Patterson: "Listen, Christ died for all men. Christ is the only salvation for men."

Alcindor: "Wait a minute, man, what about all those people around the world that never heard of Christ. Aren't they gonna be saved?"

Soon they were joined by Schofield, a Catholic, and Saffer, a Jew. John Wooden listened, too, offering observations along with those of everyone else. It was then that Alcindor informed everyone he was now an Orthodox Muslim. In his *Sports Illustrated* autobiography, Lew wrote:

". . . nobody seemed to care that I was a Muslim. They accepted it and we talked about it. The world did not come to an end. Coach Wooden did not look at me cross-eyed. He seemed to accept it as well as everybody else. Out of that midnight ride across Ohio and Indiana, we became a different group of men, much more than just a bunch of jocks traveling around the country bouncing basketballs . . ."

The craziest things happen on chartered buses with the UCLA basketball team.

Departing from snow-covered Pullman, Washington, one morning, several Bruins in the back of the bus declared open season on a defenseless reporter in a front seat. They playfully pelted him with snowballs — much to the amusement of everybody, including John Wooden, who knew when to duck.

Then, on another occasion, the team bus was waiting outside Pauley Pavilion to transport the team to its off-campus hotel. Every player was aboard except one — Lee Walczuk, a guard and the team's twelfth man.

One player said the bus driver was ordered to abandon the wait and move on when all of a sudden Walczuk appeared. He raced toward the bus and ran alongside the door, frantically motioning the driver to stop. A witness said Ducky Drake told the driver to keep going, but the UCLA Bruins shouted, "Stop the bus! Stop the bus!" to no avail.

"They could have stopped and let him on," said a player. "I know if Walczuk had been Lew, well, you always wait five minutes. But it was kinda unfair to Walczuk. He was being singled out as an example."

*

Another berth in the NCAA Western Regionals was clinched, but there were two more games against USC's Trojans. And they weren't just games, they were cardiac arrests.

On the first night, at the Sports Arena, the Trojans seemingly had pushed the Bruins over the cliff after successfully executing the same stall-tempo tactics that very nearly beat them two years earlier. In fact, USC rooters nearly tore down the building when guard Steve Jennings' lay-up gave the Trojans a 47-45 lead with only four seconds remaining in the first overtime.

But UCLA alertly called time out, now virtually counted out for the first time in forty-one games. A few feet away, Trojan coach Bob Boyd told his players to play their men closely all over the court. "I thought they'd try to send the ball in to Lew, if anyone," he said later.

As play resumed, the Bruins in-bounded the ball with two crisp passes — not to Lew, but to Shackelford, who had yet to hit a basket all night. He promptly let fly, awkwardly it seemed, with a twenty-five-foot shot that was airborne as the buzzer blasted. It seemed to hang forever up there in the lights before it fell, spiral fashion, into the net. Overtime again! Now UCLA fans were going berserk. The victim had gotten an eleventh-hour reprieve. In the second overtime, Alcindor and Shackelford shot the Bruins into a four-point lead, and they held on to win, 61-55.

"This," said Boyd, who had yet to beat John Wooden, "was the toughest loss I've ever had."

Hardly anybody would have wagered even a nickel that the Trojans could pull off the "impossible" the next night. After all, they were crestfallen and now they would be playing in Pauley Pavilion, where the Bruins *never* lose, right?

But nobody told the Trojans. They used the same delaying tactics. The same drama. The same tension. In a game that seesawed nearly every dribble of the way, Alcindor's free throw tied it at 44-all with slightly more than a minute to play. But it was USC's ball again, as it had been most of the night.

The Trojans passed and waited and wound the clock down to nineteen seconds, then called time.

Bob Boyd told his team to keep the court balanced, set a screen for forward Ernie Powell, let him drive to it and "put the ball in the basket."

As the seconds ticked away, Don Crenshaw quickly set a pick for Powell at the right of the basket, twenty-five feet away. Powell burst for the screen, jumped and let go. The ball sailed perfectly into the net. It was 46-44.

Time remained only for a last-second twenty-footer by Sidney Wicks that fell harmlessly off the rim. Bedlam. Trojan fans were all over the court, crazily jabbing index fingers into the air to signify that — for the moment, at least — *they* were number one.

Records fell. It was UCLA's first defeat ever in Pauley Pavilion, its first loss in forty-one games dating back to the Astrodome game, its first loss to USC in six years, and Boyd's first win over John Wooden.

"I don't feel badly," said Wooden. "The Trojans played their game. They did what they wanted to do, and they did it very well. We just weren't able to do much about it."

The players felt somewhat differently. "It was kind of frustrating to lose that game because we knew we had the better team," said one Bruin, looking back. "It wasn't that important to us — at least to the seniors — because we'd already lost one game. Another one didn't mean that much. I think some of the younger players were more distressed about it than the seniors were because they had never lost."

In the frenzy of the USC locker room, Bob Boyd stood tieless and sweat-soaked in a blue shirt. He smiled and didn't care who heard him.

"They're damned lucky we didn't beat them twice!" he screamed. His USC players, up on chairs, climbing ecstatically on each other's backs and laughing, erupted into a chorus: "Who's Coach of the Year? Who's Coach of the Year?"

A few days later, John Wooden quietly reflected on the hysteria and shook his head. "When winning becomes *that* important," he said, "I'm getting out."

The close calls were not over yet for the UCLA Bruins.

Waiting to ambush them in Louisville's Freedom Hall were the Drake Bulldogs, a team that was more overlooked than overmatched.

They were a quick, scrappy team that pressed and ran and played everybody tenaciously on defense — a "bellybutton" man-to-man, as their coach, Maury John, called it. In other words, the Bulldogs play you bellybutton-to-bellybutton.

Then, too, they resembled John Wooden's 1964 national championship team. The stars were 6-3 guard Willie McCarter and 6-5 forward Willie Wise, but the Bulldogs seemed to send in tidal waves of junior-college transfers (including a refugee from Long Beach, guard Gary Zeller), and they kept the pressure on constantly until rival teams fell apart.

And this was a night when the dynasty tottered.

UCLA was a ploddy heavyweight by comparison — and nowhere did it show more than during its semifinal contest with Drake. Guards John Vallely and Kenny Heitz were harassed frequently into mistakes, but Drake was able to shoot only 38.6 percent and could not convert enough of those errors into baskets.

Still, it was close most of the way — closer than expected. UCLA needed every one of Vallely's twenty-nine points, mostly on baseline drives, and Alcindor's twenty-five to pull it out, 85-82, and advance to the finals against Purdue.

As if the tension of a tight game weren't enough, John Wooden faced still another confrontation during the Drake game — on the bench. It started late in the game when a Bruin guard fouled out. Wooden summoned Bill Sweek as a replacement. Sweek got up slowly, ready to go in, whereupon Wooden suddenly chewed out the 6-3 senior for apparently lacking proper enthusiasm and ordered him to sit down. Sweek yelled back and the two exchanged heated words in the locker room for a long time after the game. Their breach was not mended until the coach called a team meeting before practice the next day.

"He just explained his feelings," said Sweek, looking back not long ago. "That's all that needed to be said. The whole thing was pretty much a misunderstanding. When he called me to go in, I guess he thought I was supposed to leap off the bench and go racing to the scorer's table, like I play in games. What I did was get up slowly so I could gather my thoughts before I went in. I guess the coach misinterpreted my actions as not wanting to go into the game. Really, that was the last thing I wanted to happen. I really *did* want to go in — who wouldn't in an NCAA game?"

Sweek attributed the outburst in part to other off-court tensions confronting John Wooden. "He was really under a lot of pressure that year," he said. "Pressure from alums, I'm sure. Pressure to win three in a row. So he got mad and misinterpreted what I was really doing. Just a misunderstanding, that's all."

It was a rematch of the season opener. The Rocket vs. Big Lew.

Purdue's Boilermakers, who had looked sharp in losing to the Bruins by twelve points in Pauley Pavilion, were ready to challenge a UCLA team that was still trembling from its frightening escape two nights earlier.

They unleashed a full-court press, a blistering fast break led by 5-10 guard Bill Keller, and, of course, all those acrobatic, unerring jump shots from everywhere in the building by The Rocket, Rick Mount. It shaped up as Purdue's outside guns versus UCLA's inside power, speed versus speed, and depth versus depth.

But the Big Ten champs ran smack into one of the finest defensive efforts ever fashioned in a championship game.

His name: Kenny Heitz, a 6-3 guard with eyeglasses and wispy arms and legs, and also the team's intellectual, a senior from Santa Maria who has since been graduated from Harvard Law School and works for a Los Angeles-area law firm. His assignment: stop Rick Mount.

It wasn't easy. Mount, one of the collegiate game's best pure shooters ever, had popped in thirty-six points to cut down North Carolina and now, against UCLA, he suddenly fired in his first two field goals from the corner before the game was minutes old.

"I was scared to death, frankly," said Heitz.

His fright never curtailed him. Perhaps it helped. Whatever, The Rocket suddenly misfired again and again, with Heitz waving arms and hands in his face and getting help from Lew Alcindor when he needed it. Mount finished with twenty-eight points, but he went almost eighteen and a half minutes without a field goal — and missed fourteen shots in a row — during those telltale early stages.

But it was not entirely defense that won for UCLA. Big Lew flexed his muscles at the other end of the court and scored thirty-seven points. He got help from Vallely (fifteen points) and Rowe and Shackelford (twelve and eleven) as the Bruins raced away at half time, 42-31, and piled up a twenty-point lead midway through the second half. Purdue made belated runs at the Bruins, trimming the margin to eleven points twice, but the Boilermakers had to commit fouls in desperation when UCLA delayed the tempo.

It was all over, 92-72. And when it ended, all eyes focused on the towering young man in front of the UCLA bench.

Across his face burst a smile that must have stretched 7 feet 1½ inches wide. Around his neck hung the tangled strings of the basket and he was happily waving his left index finger. And from his right hand sprouted three more long fingers. He waved at the UCLA fans who cheered him from the beginning — and who had waited three years for what seemed like the inevitable.

In a moment, he was arm-in-arm with his father, who had spent the afternoon playing first trombone in the Bruin band, and then he was holding his fingers aloft again. They were the fingers of Ferdinand Lewis Alcindor, Jr., and they had just finished sculpturing the UCLA Bruins into the legend that everybody thought they'd be four winters earlier.

The Lew Alcindor Era, eighty-eight victories in ninety games, was over. A record three NCAA titles in a row — that's what the three fingers symbolized. The number one team in the land — that's what the index finger signified.

"It was a question of attitude," he said of the game he had just played. "We were ready. We were up. I was, and the whole team was. We weren't up for Drake. That was the difference."

In a few weeks, he would sign a $1.4 million contract with the Milwaukee Bucks, then earn his diploma from UCLA and move on.

John Wooden had now won five national titles and was one up on the Kentucky Baron, Adolph Rupp.

One legend was leaving. The other would stay.

CHAPTER 8

Life without Lew

Dwight David Eisenhower, thirty-fourth President of the United States, dies of a heart attack . . . In France, Charles De Gaulle steps down as President . . . A car goes off a bridge at Chappaquiddick Island, Massachusetts, and a twenty-eight-year-old secretary named Mary Jo Kopechne dies in the dark of a tidal pool . . . Neil Armstrong, moonman, takes "one small step for man, one giant leap for mankind" . . . John Wayne swaggers to an Academy Award in *True Grit* . . . President Ho Chi Minh of North Vietnam dies . . . An AWOL Marine sets a distance record for plane hijacking, 6900 miles, San Francisco to Rome . . . A half-million demonstrators gather in Washington, D.C., to denounce the Vietnamese war and President Nixon calls on the "great silent majority" for support . . . Miss Illinois, Judith Anne Ford, 36-24½-36, is named Miss America . . . John Wooden faces a season, the first season in three, without Ferdinand Lewis Alcindor, Jr.

THERE HAD BEEN TRIUMPH for John Wooden in the Alcindor years, but there had been tumult and trying moments too. Most of those happened out of the public glare. Wooden had aged. Some said he had aged a lot.

Wooden usually discounted the pressures of coaching the sometimes sullen giant.

"Problems with Lewis?" he would ask you. "I should say not. He was a very capable player, coachable and very unselfish. The good far outweighed the bad."

But there were other, private moments when Wooden discussed "Lewis" more candidly.

"He told me once that I was understanding toward his feelings but not completely understanding, for one reason — I'm white," said Wooden. "I said to him, 'Well, Lewis, I can at least try to understand, can't I?' He said, 'Yes, Coach, but you can't fully because you're not black.'

"That is something everyone should think about."

Wooden was hurt, however, when he read Alcindor's critical comments about UCLA in the *Sports Illustrated* series.

"I'm very, very sorry to find out that he seemed to be as unhappy as he has indicated," said Wooden. "But I think he would tell you that any player who goes away to any school is unhappy for a while. Generally speaking, that feeling passes. If Lewis felt there were some problems at UCLA, I honestly believe he would have been ten times more miserable at many other places he could have gone."

And still later, Wooden said: "It will be fun coaching to win again, rather than coaching to try to keep from losing."

Without Alcindor, Wooden went back to the high-post, running offense of an earlier day.

"I feel more comfortable with this style," he said. "We used the low-post offense solely because of Alcindor and the personnel we had with him."

His new team was an unusual mixture of personalities and life-styles — Sidney Wicks and Curtis Rowe, the tall, lean aggressive forwards, a pair of immensely talented but volatile young men from a black ghetto of Los Angeles; guards John Vallely, a blond beach boy who grew up in luxury on Balboa Island, and Henry Bibby, a black sophomore, who was reared in near poverty on a North Carolina tobacco farm; center Steve Patterson, an articulate, engaging junior who replaced Alcindor. Or the man who played the same position as Lew.

Patterson had red-shirted one season, playing every day in

practice against Alcindor. Physically, it was helpful. Psychologically, it was damaging.

"Lew really destroyed my confidence," Patterson said. "I began to wonder, 'Am I really that bad, or is he really that good?' I finally realized that he *is* that good."

Patterson thus was realistic. "No one man is going to fill his shoes," said Steve. "It's going to take all of us, working together, to do that."

At the start, that's the way it was. Differences didn't surface right away. A teammate credited Wicks and Rowe — inseparable off the court as well as on — for that.

"They've matured a lot," he said. "Last year, with Lew here, there were cliques and we didn't get along well. It's better, so much better, this season."

Some people had questioned if Henry Bibby were ready for major college basketball. But he was. He had prepared for it a long time.

Preparation began on a tiny tobacco farm in the northeast corner of North Carolina — Franklinton — where the summer sun comes up so early you curse it and goes down late, after the ache of a long day's work has set in.

Henry Bibby worked the dirt with his parents and his brothers, twelve hours a day, scratching out the meager living the earth would yield. And when the 7 A.M. to 7 P.M. shift was over, Henry Bibby would pick up a basketball and cross the dirt yard to the shed and a hand-me-down basketball hoop that older brothers James (now a professional baseball pitcher) and Frederick had used before him.

And for two hours or more, aided by the lone light bulb on the outside of his house, he would dribble and shoot — blotting out the memory of the long day gone and the prospect of the long day to come.

UCLA was a nation away from Franklinton. Henry Bibby was a small-town boy in a big city, groping a little at first to find the truths of a metropolis that sometimes moved too fast for him. But the problems did not include shooting the basketball — long, arching bombs from the stratosphere.

"I don't believe I ever had a player with more range," said Wooden.

"It was my brothers," said Bibby. "They were so big that when I played against them I got nothing on the inside. I had to learn to shoot long. And, you know, it feels good. I have confidence in my ability but sometimes it's instinct. I just *have* to shoot the ball."

The Bruins coughed and sputtered in early season but there was no more serious trouble until a road trip to Washington State. Pullman, the home of the Cougars, is a bucolic town. The pursuits are few. A visit by the UCLA basketball team is not only the major sporting attraction of the winter, it might be the leading social gathering too.

But there are no social niceties inside tiny Bohler Gymnasium. The fans scream from the beginning of the game to the end of the game, regardless of who has the ball. Urged on by the fanatical hollering — "Beat 'em! Kill 'em!" — the Cougars took a thirteen-point lead in the first half. But, at the end, UCLA had another narrow win, 72-70. Again, the Bruin guards — Bibby and Vallely — were the difference. It had been Bibby's first visit to Pullman. He would remember it. "For quite a while," he said, "my ears were ringing so badly I couldn't hear anything. This place is something else."

Wooden was unhappy, shaking his head back and forth and holding a crumpled program in his hands.

"I'm very, very aggravated at my team," he said. "They weren't really ready to play but they had to get a taste of something like this before they would understand."

The winning streak was to last just three more games. Wooden knew the end was coming. Something had happened in that dank dressing room in Bohler Gym.

"What time did you get in last night?" Wooden demanded of Curtis Rowe.

"Why, one forty-five, coach, why?"

"I said one-thirty, didn't I?"

"Yes, coach, but that's only fifteen minutes late."

"Too late is too late."

Wooden walked away and moments later he confided to a reporter: "A loss might help this team more than anything else."

It was Eugene, Oregon, a town not unlike Pullman. A small town, a college town where basketball is usually bigger than antiwar protests and the Rolling Stones. There were two minutes left in the game and Oregon led mighty UCLA, unbeaten UCLA (21-0) by fifteen points.

A time out had been called and John Wooden was striding down the bench to the spot where Steve Belko, the Oregon coach, a man who smoked a pipe and worried a lot, was sitting. Wooden extended his right hand, and said: "It's going to be a little wild at the end, Steve. So I thought I'd say congratulations now. You beat us in every way a team could beat us."

Then, as Wooden had predicted, it was pandemonium, a deluge of well-wishers on the floor, slapping backs, grabbing hands, clutching and pulling at jerseys. Paper and programs were hurled out of the gallery. At each end of the court, guys were hoisted on willing shoulders and cut down the basket nets, to thunderous ovations. "This," said Bruin broadcaster Fred Hessler, "is the kind of student demonstration I like to see."

At Eugene, Oregon, it was New Year's Eve in February.

Belko couldn't seem to believe he'd won. "When John came over to me I was afraid to accept his congratulations," he said, "because even though we had a nine- or ten-point lead with just a minute to go I still respected UCLA's ability to come back."

John Wooden stood nearly alone in the catacombs under the place where the upset had happened and sipped on a cup of Coke. He was calm, gracious.

"Subconsciously," he said, "a team that has won as many games as we have might get a little fatheaded. That's why I consider it almost a relief to lose. When you're number one, there's always the challenge for someone to knock you off. I could see it coming. Really, I expected it before this."

So, apparently, did Nell Wooden. She stood by the door of the bus that would take the players back to their motel after the game and told her husband, "They deserved to lose. They deserved it."

Many of the Bruin players stayed up talking at a Holiday Inn, then went down the road for some food, and finally shared a little wine in their rooms. The conversations continued the next day on the plane trip home and the following Monday at a team meeting. It was frank talk, man-to-man, searching.

It was still a close team. "Together" was the word Sidney Wicks used. But Vallely had his mind on a professional contract. So, even as juniors, did Wicks, Rowe, and Patterson. Starting in midseason, there was a drift away from the unity of December and January. A player would force a shot or not make the pass he should have. Some saw it as a racial problem but it wasn't — except in a minor way. It was more just a team grown selfish, a team that had momentarily lost its maturity. Wooden could do little about it. But a loss — that was different.

"To me," said Patterson, "the loss to Oregon and what came after it was the key to our season. There had been things beneath the surface that no one talked about before — a communications breakdown. After we began winning and winning, it became accepted and we stopped communicating. The defeat at Oregon helped us reestablish our priorities. Everyone had started thinking that if he did his own thing, it would be O.K. We'd win. We were getting an attitude sort of like the professionals have, I think. The situation wasn't good.

"Things were building to a head and Oregon gave us a chance to take care of it. Luckily, we got it out in the open. In the end, all of us agreed that anything was worth sacrificing for a national title."

"We're number one," came the cries cannonading out of the Jacksonville rooting section during UCLA's victory over New Mexico State in the NCAA semifinals. Then the boos erupted from across the floor, where the UCLA fans were sitting. "Just wait until Saturday afternoon," shouted somebody in the Bruin gallery. "Aw, go home, UCLA" was the response. "J.U. can do."

The classic confrontation was shaping up: the discipline of UCLA versus the devil-may-care attitude of Jacksonville, the Establishment versus the Age of Aquarius, Richard Nixon versus Dr. Timothy Leary. UCLA represented everything that was entrenched, solid, ordered, sure. Jacksonville symbolized the new and the now, free flight, the experimental, the who gives a damn?

Wooden took his team on a three-hour bus tour of Washington, D.C., early in the week of the College Park, Maryland, finals. He was asked if he gave his players a choice of whether to go or stay.

"Well, yes," he answered. "They could stay on the bus and sleep if they wanted rather than getting off to tour. But they had to be on the bus."

Jacksonville coach Joe Williams, who wore a white, Good-Humor-Man-style, double-breasted sportcoat, said his players toured the White House but he put no restrictions on them. "They do," he said, "what they want to do."

One of the things they did was put on a Harlem Globetrotters style routine — which they had worked up themselves — during a practice, just before UCLA took the floor. The Bruins sat in the front row, watching with amusement. "Greatest thing I ever saw," said Steve Patterson, smiling broadly.

Jacksonville boasted of having the nation's tallest front line — 7-2 center Artis Gilmore, 7-foot forward Pembrook Burrows III ("That name isn't unusual — my father was named that and so was my grandfather"), and 6-10 forward Rod McIntyre. Gilmore showed that the Dolphins were not exactly wide-eyed about the prospect of facing UCLA. When his teammates were late gathering for a practice, he plopped down into a motel armchair and went to sleep.

Wooden, surprisingly, seemed as unconcerned about Gilmore. The coach had been more comfortable, more candid in postgame interviews throughout the first season without Alcindor. His candor reached a peak after the win over New Mexico State. Dozens of newsmen with pens, tape recorders, and TV lights jammed into an interview room to zero in on him.

"Hey, whattaya think of Gilmore, now that you've seen him?" asked a writer with a thick Bronx accent.

"He's a fine player," said Wooden. "Does a lot of things very well."

"How does he compare with Alcindor?" yelled another writer.

"Alcindor is better," said Wooden, without hesitation.

The writer looked somewhat incredulous. Laughter rippled across the room.

"In what way?" he said, pressing for elaboration.

"In *every* way," said John Wooden.

The Jacksonville publicists had dubbed Gilmore "Batman" and he played opposite a guard with two comic-strip names — 6-5 Rex (Robin) Morgan. Floridians were hoping for a headline that read "Dynamic Duo Destroys Bruins." But the Bruins, instead, deposited "Batman" and "Robin" into the "Bat Car" and sent them on their way back to Florida, 80-69, for a record fourth straight NCAA championship, and sixth in seven seasons.

Wicks slew the giant early in the game and picked up a nickname himself: "Super Sidney." It was hokey but who could argue? Wicks, giving away six inches in height, had blocked *five* of Artis' shots, and thoroughly intimidated him.

It was a team victory and Rowe talked about that. "Everybody was looking forward to playing without Lew," said Rowe in the crowded UCLA locker room. "Right now, if Alcindor was on the team, who would the reporters be talking to? Look around you. The reporters are with five people and that's beautiful. Every time somebody mentions three titles in a row, they say Lew did it. Now we just proved that four other men on the team could play basketball — with the best of them."

Wooden seemed a little smug. Asked if he anticipated a letdown in the coming season, he said, "No. I think we will always have pride in ourselves and when you have that you're going to be all right. Other teams, too, get to thinking the way teams did who played the Yankees or Celtics or faced Sandy Koufax . . . that, 'Oh, oh, those are the *Yankees* out there,' or 'That Koufax! Boy, he looks fast.'"

The coach got two calls soon after the Jacksonville win. One was more or less expected. Every year since he graduated in 1964, Walt Hazzard had called Wooden at the start of each fall practice every season and before every tournament to wish him luck. Now he was calling to say congratulations.

The second call was a surprise. Wooden took it at the home of his daughter and son-in-law, just as he was getting ready to go out for dinner.

"The operator said it was the President calling and that I'd have to hold on for a minute. I choked up a little at that point and replied, 'Oh, in that case, I'll wait.' But I still wasn't sure it wasn't one of my players, calling as a prank."

The doubt remained even when Richard Nixon came on the line because, Wooden said, "We had a faulty connection. I could only ask him, 'Is this *really* the President?'"

It was. Wooden called it a "tremendous thrill — a wonderful gesture on his part."

Stan Dennis, Wooden's son-in-law, brought the coach back to earth. "He wanted to know if the President paid for the call," said Wooden. "Then he said he supposed Mr. Nixon would have written rather than calling, if the Postal Department hadn't been having all those problems."

But it wasn't all presidential praise and family humor for John Wooden after UCLA's sixth national title. A few weeks after the season ended, Bill Seibert, a young man who had been little heard from, on or off the court, got up at the team banquet and rapped Wooden and his program. There had been a "lack of communication" with the coach, he said, and a "double standard" of rules for starters and substitutes. He called his years at UCLA "an unhappy experience." It was a strange postscript to another year of triumph for John Wooden and his Bruins.

Children are starving in Biafra . . . 6000 New York postmen, angry over delays in getting a pay raise, stage the nation's first postal strike in 195 years . . . The movies go "GP," "R," and "X" and parents go crazy trying to figure the ratings out . . . There's a shootout outside a courtroom in San Rafael, California, a judge dies, and Angela Davis, former UCLA instructor, is apprehended for her alleged role in supplying two of the guns . . . Cigarette ads are banned on radio and television and the women of the world are warned of the hazards of "The Pill" . . . *Patton* sweeps the Oscars, even though George C. Scott snubs the Oscar show . . . Everyone takes a walk with Simon and Garfunkel on a "Bridge Over Troubled Water" . . . Nasser of Egypt and De Gaulle of France die and so do four students, in a confrontation with National Guardsmen at Kent State . . . And at UCLA, the national championship basketball team sends a letter to President Nixon, denouncing the Cambodian invasion that triggered the Kent State incident.

It's a different generation of college students — longer hair, shorter tempers, a new morality, and a deeper concern for mankind.

A Bruin player spoke of the letter to the President. "This," he said, "is the most important thing I've done in four years at UCLA."

This is what the letter said:

"We, the undersigned, are 13 UCLA students (12 players and a student manager) who wish to express our grave concern and disapproval over the President's policy of expansion of the immoral, genocidal and imperialistic war the United States is now waging in Southeast Asia. We support the meaningful and peaceful demonstrations held throughout this country. We deplore the tactics of violence of both students and law enforcement agencies that are suppressing the intentions of those who are truly concerned with peace on earth.

"We further wish to clarify that we are not 'bums' as we college students have been so wrongly accused. Rather, we are concerned with the well being of America and its democracy, which should function as a reflection of the will of the American people. But when massive demonstrations concerning the policies of this country are suppressed or dismissed as unwarranted and unlawful dissent, then there is something seriously wrong.

"The President has in the past demonstrated an unwillingness to take into consideration the voice of an ever increasing vocal minority, as exemplified by the statements he made prior to the October 15 Moratorium, in which he stated he would be in no way affected by it. He has once again shown his unwillingness to carry out the will of the people by committing U.S. troops to Cambodia.

"We propose certain measures which we feel are necessary for the alleviation of the social and political pressures that exist today:

"The immediate withdrawal of all the combat troops, advisors and arms from Cambodia. The rapid de-escalation of the war in Vietnam with the goal in mind of removing all personnel from Vietnam by January 1, 1971. The public investigation of the killings at Kent State. The end of harassment of youth by the

Nixon-Agnew Administration, by those in authority at the federal, state or local level."

Rick Betchley	Steve Patterson
Henry Bibby	Curtis Rowe
Ken Booker	Terry Schofield
Jon Chapman	Doug Schwab
Sidney Wicks	Bill Seibert
John Ecker	John Vallely
Andy Hill	

The last two signers of the letter were gone. It was a new season, a season dominated by a man who in his way was as imposing a figure as Lew Alcindor before him and Bill Walton after him.

Sidney Wicks's mother — now Mrs. James Smiley — had three sons, Stanley, Stephen, and Sidney. They were three years apart and, since she was divorced, she reared them alone. Sometimes it was difficult.

"I always tried to teach the boys," she says, "that with humor you can forget everything. When times got rough, we joked with each other. We made each other laugh."

At times, Sidney Wicks retained that humor. The team comedian, he could break you up with an imitation of *Midnight Cowboy's* Ratso Rizzo. He could repeat, word for word with accompanying fast draws and mannerisms, the entire conversation of Butch Cassidy and the Sundance Kid on their flight through South America.

But he was different on the court. When he came to UCLA as a sophomore, just out of junior college, he was about as undisciplined as anyone John Wooden had ever recruited. He grew to the point where Wooden trusted him to run the team, on the court. He was almost an assistant coach — or at least assumed that role.

"I hate Sidney Wicks," said a man traveling with the California Bears.

"Oh, he's not really so bad when you get to know him" was the answer.

"I don't mean it that way. I just hate him because he and UCLA win all the time. I'm afraid if we ever beat the Bruins, I might end up liking him."

Wicks was loathed by some, adored by others. A familiar pattern developed before Bruin home games. Wicks and Rowe would swagger along — usually in flashy new outfits — in front of the Bruin rooting section on the way to the locker room. The crowd would pay tribute to their heroes with horns, shouts, applause. Both had had strong maternal influence in their lives and were outwardly secure and proud, often touching on arrogance their senior seasons.

But Wicks held center stage. He was good and he knew it. He had a glare that could cut diamonds — or turn opponents to stone. Bright (he graduated a quarter ahead of his class) and often engaging, Wicks reveled in being the star attraction. At time outs, he would flex his muscles, clap his hands, exhort his teammates. He knew the game well in a tactical sense and was not afraid to share his knowledge with the coaching staff. Occasionally, his teammates resented his power — but they respected him.

And you couldn't help thinking, when you looked at him take command: "You've come a long way, baby."

In the early years, he was just a skinny kid with pipe-stem legs, competing with older brother Stan — always competing.

"When he was six-foot-one," says Stan, "we started talking about dunking the ball and he told me he couldn't do it. I razzed him pretty bad. He got himself a pair of ankle weights and for a week or so, after school, he practiced and practiced and practiced. Then he bet me he could dunk. We went over to the park on Saturday and the first four times he missed. Then he finally made it and tore his pants, in the back end. You know, he was so happy he didn't care a bit."

*

Vallely was the only starter who left the sixth Bruin championship team. Wooden settled on Kenny Booker, a red-shirt transfer from Long Beach City College and a converted forward, as Vallely's replacement. It would have been no surprise if the introspective Booker were picking a guitar or singing a ballad somewhere, or maybe blowing a sax for a jazz band.

His grandfather, Freeman Davis, a man who entertained as "Brother Bones," did the whistling on the Globetrotters' theme song, "Sweet Georgia Brown." At seventy-eight, Davis got a gold record as the song passed a million sales. Kenny's father, Arnold, was on the record, too, playing saxophone.

"But I can't do anything with music," said Kenny. "I tried to play the trumpet in junior high school, a long time ago, but I was so bad I gave it up."

He was not bad at basketball. Neither did he give UCLA the sort of guard play it had had out of Hazzard and Goodrich and Warren.

Later in the season, Booker was replaced as a starter by Terry Schofield, a bright, sensitive senior whose apartment reflected his artistic temperament. Paintings, including a self-portrait, covered the walls. Collages and sculptures, including one made from a broken-down refrigerator, filled the corners. In a bedroom-office were an electric typewriter and a file of poems. One of them was called, "To Dying Men."

"The newcaster broke in in the middle of a song:
"This is a KHJ news flash — the most celebrated football coach of the decade, Vince Lombardi, has died at the age of 52. Lombardi finally succumbed after a four-month battle with cancer at St. Vincent's Hospital in Washington, D.C.
"The music started again.
"God, Lombardi's dead.
" 'Winning is the only thing,' Lombardi said.
"And so the Packers won.
"But now, after the final gun in the final game
"The winners and losers are all the same.

"And only useless statistics recall it all.
"How winners rise, how losers fall."

The new UCLA machine rumbled over some rocks. Wicks and Rowe sat out the first ten minutes of the second game of the season — a rout over Rice — because of what Wooden called "a minor disciplinary problem." The team captains had been dilatory in getting to the team dinner table, so the coach put them on the bench.

Several players say it was Wooden's way of answering Seibert's "double standards" speech of the preceding spring. See, here he was, benching a couple of his *starters*. Was *that* a double standard? "But you notice," said one player, "he did it against Rice, a team our freshmen probably could have beaten."

Wicks and Rowe apparently didn't mind being benched briefly but Patterson did a few weeks later when he was sat down because Wooden apparently decided Steve's sideburns were too long. Patterson took it personally. Only after several chats with teammates the following week did he decide to stay on the team.

"I've never been a famous entity," he said, "but if I had quit and UCLA lost a championship, I'd have been infamous."

Despite the flare-ups, despite the fact that Booker and Schofield were inconsistent guards and Bibby suffered a long shooting slump, the Bruins won with ease. Again, the team forgot the lessons it had learned the year before at Oregon. It grew blasé. There were close conference wins, against Washington at home and Stanford on the road.

Wooden seemed to sense that another fall was coming, this time on a Midwestern road trip in January. The Bruins won by twenty-five points over Loyola but Wooden said: "We're not sharp. We'd better be tomorrow against Notre Dame, or we're going to lose. I'd say that after this game I've got a great talking point for my team. We're not hungry — not at all."

The Bruins took a bus from Chicago to South Bend. A mid-route stop was scheduled but the driver lost his way and the team wandered, somewhere in Indiana, for an hour. The bus didn't arrive in South Bend until 3 A.M. It was an omen.

John Wooden, favorite son, back home again in Indiana. It's almost a ritual by now. His friends — and those who want to be remembered as his friends — know when he's coming. In restaurants, in hotels, on the streets, they congregate around him. He does his best not to ignore anyone but somebody always feels neglected. It's human nature. At half time of the Notre Dame game, they hand John Wooden a bundle of honors. Smiles, handshakes, backslaps. But meanwhile, the Notre Dame Fighting Irish — who already hold a 43-38 lead — are coming back onto the floor to massacre the Bruins.

Austin Carr, slick and smooth, will do much of it himself. He was strongly recruited by UCLA. "I definitely considered going there," he says, "along with North Carolina and Notre Dame. My parents wanted me to get a good education but they didn't want me to go that far away from home. UCLA is a long way from Washington, D.C., where I grew up."

The previous two seasons, UCLA had beaten Notre Dame and Austin Carr and he said, "Yes, there definitely will be a revenge motive going for us this time."

Notre Dame played the mighty Bruins the way few teams dared to — straight up. Not even a hint at slowing the tempo. No gimmick defenses but rather a very aggressive, exceedingly tough, man-to-man. And Austin Carr.

He had scored more than forty-six points in a game — but never in a game that meant this much. Fifteen of his forty-six points against the Bruins came in the last six and a half minutes. He had all but two of the Irish's last seventeen points in their 89-82 victory. Down the stretch, he toyed with little-used Bruin reserve Larry Hollyfield. Wooden defended his decision to put Hollyfield on Carr.

"He's big and quick and I thought he might give us some spark," said the coach. "He's also left-handed and Carr was doing most of his damage going to his right."

But it looked to many like the master strategist was at work. Wooden has never fretted much about a midseason, nonconference loss here and there. It's the conference race that matters to him and UCLA was getting ready for Pacific 8 play again, this time against a crack USC team.

Notre Dame celebrated its win. "Wooden Barriers," proclaimed one banner, "Can't Stop an Irish Carr." "Even the Pope Wouldn't Pick UCLA No. 1," said another. In the locker room, Austin Carr held the net from one of the baskets and said he was going to hang it up in his room as a souvenir. The Notre Dame game plan was pasted on the wall for all to see: "1. Rebound 2. Position 3. Stop their break 4. Run our offense 5. Break their press."

But as the Bruins got aboard their bus for the return to Chicago and a flight home, there was a more meaningful moment. Johnny Dee, the Notre Dame coach, stepped onto the bus to shake hands with Wooden.

"We'll see you the second game in Houston in the NCAA finals, all right?" asked Dee.

"That sure would be nice," said Wooden, smiling.

The smile seemed to say, "We're gonna get there, Johnny Dee; you're not."

Late Saturday night, the plane bearing the Bruins touched down at Los Angeles International Airport and Curtis Rowe announced: "It's been a good day today." Heads flipped around in the seats near him. Every look was incredulous. But Rowe went on: "Every time I get down safely, it's a good day."

It was a gentle put-on, typical of Curtis Rowe. But that sort of humor always seemed strange, coming from him. Generally, he was quiet and considerate, but he appeared to smolder inside, controlled hostility always just beneath the surface. He was the toughest player — both mentally and physically — of the Wicks-Rowe-Patterson years. If you got in the road of one of his elbows, you got a bloody lip — or worse.

He liked to talk to opponents, trying to "psych" them out. His defense was the pro-style defense — a slap here, a hold there, when the referee wasn't watching. Like Wicks, he was highly competitive, in everything from basketball to poker, clothes to cars. Although he and Wicks were extremely close, Rowe always got second billing. It appeared to bother him at times but he rarely if ever expressed it. He was the hardest of the Bruin starters to know. He revealed little. But over three seasons few players were more important to UCLA than Curtis Rowe. Wooden himself said he might have been the most consistent player he ever coached.

"He's spectacularly unspectacular," Wooden said. "But he's very efficient. He makes a minimum of mistakes, both offensively and defensively. He's a very, very predictable player, in a good sense. He's strong and durable, his shot selection is good, he plays very good position on defense, and he seldom gets into foul trouble."

From the time he would run onto the court with a clenched fist upraised, his moves would be graceful — sometimes almost regal. They were polished on the L.A. playgrounds when he was a kid. He grew up in the ghetto.

"Things were tough at times," he said, enigmatically, "but not that tough. There were no real problems for me; maybe it's that everyone I knew was under the same pressures I was."

The pressure was of a different sort after the trip to South Bend.

There was no crowd in Pauley Pavilion. It was midweek of the first USC game and at the start of a workout a team manager came up to John Wooden and asked him if the practice were really going to be closed, and if he should put up a stack of signs he was carrying and inform the public.

"Put 'em up," barked Wooden. "It's absolutely closed." It wasn't — quite. A reporter or two looked on, and, up in the nearly empty cavern of stands, huddled in a seat, was former star guard Mike Warren.

"The coaches don't really want him here today," a manager said, "but they said not to ask him to leave either."

"Sure wish we had him back on the team right now," somebody else said.

John Robert Wooden, sixty years old, had on a blue UCLA jacket, a whistle at the end of a thick cord around his neck, and shorts — like his players. He looked a little incongruous in shorts — pale legs, knobby knees — until he began blowing the whistle and then he didn't look incongruous at all.

He had conducted perhaps 2500 practices like this one and you'd think he could just close his eyes and tell what was happening by the thud of basketballs. But not today. He got into the action himself, snapping a pass to a cutting guard, demonstrating, teaching, imploring, demanding.

He supervised a one-on-one guard drill. He worked mainly with Booker on how to stop Trojan star Paul Westphal's drives down the middle. But it didn't really matter whether Wooden was talking about Westphal or the other USC guards — Dennis Layton and Dana Pagett. The Bruins got the message.

Later Wooden stood off to one side of the court and watched the action, yelling, "Be alive, be alive!" and occasionally chiding, "Steve, you didn't follow that shot. Do it next time!"

There had been a team meeting on Monday. Wooden doesn't call many — maybe two a season. There had been none this year. No big problems now. Just talk — how to regain the momentum and desire and team play lacking in recent games, how to attack and defend against the top-ranked Trojans.

"I haven't seen the old man coach this much in a long time," said a veteran Bruin observer, "maybe not since the second Houston game three seasons ago."

You looked up on the walls at Pauley Pavilion and saw the six national championship flags. And then you looked down on the court and you saw the gray-haired grandfather and you were caught up in his work.

"If you lose the ball, you give them two points. We can't afford to *do* that . . .

"Help each other. Help each other. Hold it. Run it again . . .

"He'll do that every time if you let him. I'm telling you. Every time . . ."

The city of Los Angeles was up. Hardened, plastic, seen-it-all and done-it-all L.A. Basketball had taken over. USC versus UCLA. The fight for number one.

There was an incredible cacophony of noise in the Sports Arena — USC's home pavilion — on game night. The rooting sections vied with voices and with signs, most of them obscene. Of the printable ones, USC offered: WATCH OUT, UCLA, WE HAVE *TWO* AUSTIN CARRS. UCLA retaliated: SC NO. 1? THEY CAN'T EVEN COUNT THAT HIGH.

Trojan rooters nailed a baby blue Bruin doll to a wooden cross, with the message: THIS IS FOR SAINT JOHN. There were cheerleaders romping around on miniature, mechanized Trojan horses. And there was a real horse — USC's fabled Traveler II — who sauntered up to one end of the court as the Trojan band played "Conquest."

But the Bruin players seemed little daunted by the Trojan pageantry. They had their minds in a slightly different channel.

"Right before the game," said Steve Patterson, "the coach came into our locker room and said that even though he'd been criticizing us all week that we were a good team and he expected us to do a fine job. Just the fact the coach showed that kind of confidence in us meant a lot. When he says you can do it, you think you can do it."

UCLA took a nine-point lead in the first half. But then USC,

a quick, excellent shooting team, burst ahead by nine itself —
59-50, with nine and a half minutes to play. But it got just one
more point the rest of the way as UCLA came back to win, 64-
60, probably its most important win of the season.

"We didn't lose our offense those last nine and a half minutes," said Trojan guard Mo Layton. "We had no offense to
lose. We had no rebounding or spark either. It was a little
like our guys didn't even want the ball. But we should never
have let this game get away."

The guy who hurt USC most unexpectedly was the most ma-
ligned Bruin — Booker — who hit seven of ten field goals and
gave UCLA a lead it never lost after stealing a Westphal pass
and scoring on a lay-in.

Booker's performance was particularly ironic because
Wooden had talked of suiting up red-shirt guard Tommy Curtis and starting him along with Bibby against the Trojans.
But Wooden decided not to at the last minute, "because I
didn't think it would be fair to thrust Tommy into such a high-
pressure game, and I didn't want to waste a whole year of eligibility for him by playing him this late."

Others saw the move as a Wooden ploy to try to get better
play out of Booker and Schofield. Both of them were resentful.
Curtis was chagrined. He had called home, Tallahassee, Florida, to tell "the good news" that he would be playing.

Although some saw Wooden's strategy as callous, it worked.
It was Booker's best game. And Wicks did the expected:
twenty-four points, fourteen rebounds, and the usual defensive intimidation. UCLA was on top again.

When it was over, Bruin fans nearly knocked down the backboards with their cheers and their fingers jabbed the air with
familiar WE'RE NO. 1 signs.

Curtis Rowe, stepping out of the shower, was satisfied with
a lesser position. He said merely: "We're the best team in
town."

*

But this still was to be a tense season, the shakiest of any of the championship years, the one in which many people thought Wooden did his finest coaching job because of the uncertainty at guard and very little bench strength.

Again and again, the Bruins played Houdini, but the team of 1970–1971 did have immense confidence and it was best exemplified by Sidney Wicks in the win at Corvallis over Oregon State.

The score was tied, 65-65, with less than half a minute to play and Oregon State had the ball out of bounds. But guard Freddie Boyd dribbled the ball off his foot and the Bruins got it back, with twenty-six seconds remaining. UCLA went into its control game. Wicks had the ball, directing traffic, dribbling, dribbling. Oregon State's 6-9 sophomore center Neal Jurgenson moved in to challenge him. It was the matador versus the bull. Wicks fixed Jurgenson with that well-known "glare," daring him to come closer. Jurgenson made little thrusts but never got too close. Then it was time to move. Sidney sprang left toward the key, stopped, and soared high with the shot. It dropped through the net perfectly.

"Just a plain old jump shot." Super Sidney grinned. "I knew it was going to go in."

The confidence of Wicks and his teammates was so large that they tested Wooden in subtle ways. He sometimes held his ground but he also would concede points, without really wanting to, in areas such as dress. The Bruins wore pretty much what they wanted.

On a flight back from a Northwest road trip, Wicks was dressed in Levis and white T-shirt. He was leaning over in the aisle, talking to Rowe, and the elastic band on his shorts was showing over the top of his Levis. Wooden looked up, shook his head, and said quietly, out of Wicks's hearing range: "Isn't that disgraceful?"

The Great Rematch with USC was a Giant Bust. The Bruins'

margin was 73-62, but they led by twenty-four points before the reserves came in.

"The one thing I feared would happen did happen," said Bob Boyd. "We got behind early in the game. When we did, we had to abandon any game plan we might have had."

USC, 24-2 and with perhaps the finest team in its history, was going nowhere. UCLA, 25-1, was on its way again to the Western Regionals and another meeting with Cal State Long Beach.

Brigham Young University and Kresimir (The Wild Giraffe) Cosic, the Yugoslavian center, stood in the way of that confrontation, but only briefly. UCLA breezed past the Cougars, 91-73, while Long Beach was sluggish in a 78-65 win over Pacific.

Coach Jerry Tarkanian, preparing to meet the Bruins again, seemed as nervous as he had been the previous season. "You know," he said, "beating Brigham Young or Kansas would be beautiful, but beating UCLA would be history."

His 49ers almost made it. They had stage fright in 1970 at Seattle. They did not have it in 1971 at Salt Lake City. With fourteen minutes to play, Long Beach was ahead by eleven points, 44-33, and Sidney Wicks was on the bench with four fouls.

"At that moment," said John Wooden, "I thought Mrs. Wooden and I could leave for Houston a day early next week and just have a good time at the nationals as spectators."

The 2-3 zone — rather than Long Beach's normal 1-2-2 — was what hurt UCLA most, forcing outside shots from too great a range and taking away the Bruins' vaunted inside game. UCLA had had those specific strengths and weaknesses all season long. The guard play was erratic, the outside shooting inconsistent. But if a shot hit the rim and bounced away, Wicks, Rowe, or Patterson would usually have a hand there to swat it into the basket. Other teams had some success shutting off the inside trio — a group California coach Jim Padgett nicknamed "The Rejectors" — but none did it as well as Long Beach. The eleven points looked insurmountable the way the 49ers and Bruins were playing.

Then Wooden made the move of the game, inserting the little-used, 6-6½ Ecker into the game. That left Bibby as the only Bruin guard, but as Wooden said, "The type of defense they were using, we really could employ only one guard anyway." Ecker didn't score a point. But he made a difference. When he came into the game, the Bruins began to come together; the 49ers began to come apart.

With six minutes to play, UCLA pulled into a 50-50 tie — and, soon after, Ed Ratleff, the 49ers' sophomore star, fouled out. It was a critical loss.

With 3:07 to play and the score tied, 53-53, Tarkanian ordered Long Beach into a delay game, to seek only the good shot. But Dwight Taylor, who had replaced Ratleff, cast off from the corner and missed.

It gave UCLA the advantage — and an eventual 57-55 win that probably was the most amazing of a cardiac-stopping two seasons. Wooden was asked how UCLA was able to escape, again and again and again.

"Defense, more than anything else," he said. "This isn't as fine a defensive team as the ones with Alcindor but it's a good one. We haven't had many games in hand but we haven't been out of range in many either. And we're a veteran team. I sometimes feel the players are more confident than the coach."

The Bruins were to meet Kansas in the NCAA semifinals at Houston. As they debarked from their plane, Wicks and Rowe wore huge, wide-brimmed hats. Wicks also wore a stubble of beard.

"You're wearing that in the game?" a reporter asked Super Sidney.

"Yep," he answered.

By tip-off, Wicks was clean-shaven. Coach's orders.

*

Rough, bullish Kansas was 27-1, the same record as UCLA, but it wasn't a comparable team. UCLA's first five bolted into a 68-53 lead before Wooden put in his reserves and the Jayhawks made the final score respectable, 68-60. The Bruins, who hadn't shot well against zone defenses, destroyed a Kansas zone in the first half — and took command. Wicks, as usual, was the commander.

At one point, he hollered at Kansas star Dave Robisch, "Look out, here I come!" At another, he screamed, "Halt!" Robisch did. Bibby — an outstanding tournament player throughout his UCLA career — helped out with eighteen points and the Bruin defense again was outstanding, "taking Kansas out of the things it wanted to do," according to Wooden.

The night before UCLA met Villanova in the final, Steve Patterson dined with relatives at a seafood restaurant. As a reporter walked by, they were sharing a bottle of vin rosé wine. Steve looked a little sheepish, then took a sip.

He was never a smooth ballplayer. "He looks like a robot," a fan once said. "A smirking robot. Isn't it disgusting?" But he may have been the most complex member of the Wicks-Rowe teams, part free thinker–free spirit, part searching young man who didn't want to be deified — or defiled — just because he was an athlete. He was grateful to the world of sports but not bound nor particularly beholden to it or anything else — such as classwork. Often, he stood apart from hooplah of every sort.

"I've seen students who have long hair, smoke dope, dig rock music, and flash the peace sign who are still from the success mold," he said. "But I believe there is a percentage of people who are getting away from the idea that the performance and success ethic is the most important thing — who cringe at the thought of living in middle-class suburbia. I'm one of those."

He was sometimes frustrated by it but he knew his role on

the Bruin teams. "I can't make the spectacular block like Sidney or the smooth tip-in like Curtis but I can do other things," he said.

Against Villanova, he showed the other things. For several games, he had been shooting poorly. In the first half of the title game, he shocked the Wildcats with twenty points as UCLA took a 47-35 lead.

It was a much tougher second half, when UCLA went into a stall-tempo offense in an attempt to bring Villanova out of its zone. The fans didn't like it. The Wildcat players yelled, "You're the national champions! Play ball!" Wooden's strategy very nearly backfired. Stalling, the Bruins lost their momentum. They had to hold on for a 68-62 win, their closest championship win up to that time, over lithe Howard Porter and the Wildcats. But Wooden said he hadn't been concerned.

"I didn't feel, in any way, that we would lose it," he said. He admitted that the slowdown was at least partially motivated by one of his pet peeves — the lack of a time clock to prevent stalling in college games. "Maybe now," he said, "the Rules Committee will think a little more about putting in a thirty-second clock."

Standing in an unusual spotlight was Patterson — twenty-nine points, thirteen of eighteen shots from the field, and three of five free throws. The reason? He said it could have been the trout he had eaten the night before. Then he looked over at Wooden, the teetotaler, and winked. "Or maybe," he said, "the vin rosé did it."

As Steve's parents — the Bob Pattersons of Santa Maria, California — rushed onto the Astrodome floor to embrace him and whirl in a mad dance, one of those minor moments that perhaps make the major challenges of coaching worthwhile was happening at courtside. Sidney Wicks, who had confronted and questioned John Wooden — not always subtly — over three seasons, walked to where Wooden was sitting, leaned over, and said: "It's been a nice three years." He turned, then came back and added: "You're really something."

Minutes later, a reporter who had not been with the Bruins during the regular season approached the other half of the Wicks-Rowe tandem, Curtis Rowe.

"Was there any racial trouble on this team?" he asked Curtis.

The answer was instantaneous.

"Coach Wooden sees basketball players," said Rowe. "He doesn't see color."

But Wooden had seen one color during the game. Red. He and assistant Denny Crum had argued over strategy and substitutions. Crum told Schofield to go into the line-up for Booker. Wooden told Schofield to remain seated. Eventually, Schofield replaced Booker but not until Wooden had raged at Crum: "I'm the coach of this team and don't you tell me how to coach my team!"

Wooden threatened to exile Crum to the end of the bench. It took a peacemaker named Henry Bibby to cool them off.

Crum would be the head coach at Louisville University the following season. And Wooden was already thinking ahead to the new year and the latest challenge too. "Well," he said, "all I can say is that there certainly shouldn't be any pressure on us to win it all next season. But you writers will put pressure on us. You'll pick us to win everything again.

"I really can't understand it. Everybody knows USC will have better material than we will. They had better material than we did this year too. Only a lamebrain would pick us for national honors, with a completely new team."

CHAPTER 9

The Ride of the Walton Gang

Mainland China is embraced by the United Nations, Taiwan booted out . . . Everyone is puzzling over what the lyrics to "American Pie" *really* mean . . . TV brings you "The Selling of the Pentagon" and Daniel Ellsberg brings the *New York Times* the Pentagon papers . . . Broadcast journalism's credibility is questioned, while Archie Bunker thumbs his nose at the world . . . Death mutes Louis Armstrong's trumpet and stops Igor Stravinsky's baton . . . Nixon devalues the dollar and imposes wage-price controls . . . Americans continue to die in Asia, and a nation turns to three different tales of love, *Summer of '42*, *Carnal Knowledge,* and *Love Story* . . . A crowd of 200,000 marches on Washington, bearing signs, END THE DRAFT — END THE WAR! . . . And in Westwood, the question is: Can four new UCLA starters, including three sophomores, beat those veteran USC Trojans across town?

A KNOCK on John Wooden's office door.

"Come in," he said.

Into the room strode a wide-smiling, 6-foot-11 sophomore named Bill Walton, his thick, curly, red hair draped around his shoulders like Tiny Tim's.

Three days later, when the Bruins posed for pictures on the eve of preseason practice, the locks were clipped. The off-court problems with the latest Bruin giant were far in the future.

It was an almost entirely new UCLA team, and coaching was fun again for John Robert Wooden. They were a bright, closely knit team that frequently elicited smiles from Wooden and even the admission: "This may be my greatest team."

The school's sports publicists weren't sure whether to call them "The Bibby Bunch," in deference to the senior leader, Henry Bibby, a hustling, tenacious player with a middle guard's physique and an artist's shooting touch, or "The Walton Gang," in honor of the precocious center from suburban San Diego.

Despite Bibby's talents, the press and the public quickly adopted the latter nickname. Obviously, the man riding shotgun was Walton, a gangly kid with bony shoulders, sharp elbows (and opinions), and tender knees that had to be treated with heat and ice before and after each game, and for which Wooden gave him Mondays off to convalesce. As a freshman, Walton led his teammates to a perfect season, although he often complained about his mistakes (and those of officials) and showed only glimpses of the greatness that would come in 1971-1972. But Walton, the sophomore, had improved markedly and he displayed all sorts of quick, acrobatic moves that prompted many observers to say, "He's the best Caucasian center ever to play this game."

There was also Keith (Smooth as Silk) Wilkes, a shy, frail sophomore forward who excelled at scooping up "garbage" rebounds and hitting medium-range jumpers — even though he was only eighteen years old.

The point man in a revamped offense was Greg Lee, an honor student in high school at Reseda and a slick, deceptive passer — and, like Walton and Wilkes, only a sophomore. And the other forward was a junior, Larry (Moose) Farmer, a quick jumper and rebounder from Denver.

And off the bench came at least three players who could have been starters most anywhere else — Larry Hollyfield, Tommy Curtis, and Swen Nater.

The 6-11 Nater made the United States Olympic team and, before abruptly leaving camp, he impressed some foreign coaches so much they asked USC's Bob Boyd, a visitor to the camp: "How do we stop him?" Boyd's answer: "I can't tell you. We only see the *other* guy [Walton, the All-American center]."

Together, the 1971-1972 Bruins were a team that wreaked devastation among foes, winning all thirty games, *and* by an average of thirty-three points, obliterating the major-college record of 27.2 by Kentucky's 1953-1954 team featuring Cliff Hagan, Frank Ramsey, and Lou Tsiropoulos, not to mention the 26.2 spread by Alcindor's junior-year (1967-1968) team.

The Bruins also outrebounded their opponents by 18.6 a game — far superior to the edge compiled by any of Wooden's previous teams.

Over and over you heard the name . . . Walton . . . Walton . . . Walton.

"If you're picking any all-star team, you'd *have* to start with him," said Oregon's Dick Harter.

"The guys on our team kept telling me how tough and strong he was," added Ducks' center Al Carlson, "but he's so quick too. It's hard to believe because guys that big aren't supposed to be that quick."

"That kid," said Howie Dallmar of Stanford, "destroys you. He's better than Bill Russell at their comparative age and development. My center, Mike Mann, is six-nine and Walton appears to be seven-one next to him. But to me he looks like he's seven-eight. Against Washington we had six turnovers. Against UCLA we had twenty-five and most of them were caused by the big man. All I saw was Walton. Not degrading any of their players, it all goes down to Walton."

"He's the best college basketball player I've ever seen," said Carroll Williams of Santa Clara. "He's better at both ends of the court than Lew Alcindor was — he dominates like no college player in the history of the game. And that includes Bill Russell, whom I played against."

Walton outclassed the Pacific 8's second-best center — Steve Hawes of Washington — so badly in a Los Angeles meeting (holding him to one basket and volleyball spiking his first three shot attempts into the French-horn section) that Husky coach Marv Harshman grinned when he heard newsmen comparing Walton with Lew Alcindor and said: "Alcindor? You know, I kinda wish he was back."

Wooden himself was completely unsparing in praise of Walton, the player. "I've never seen a shot blocker the equal of Bill Russell," he said. "But imagine what Walton would do if he were playing under the same rules Russell did — with the narrower lane and the absence of basket interference rules."

Wooden wasn't even bothered when Denver University tossed up a 1-3-1 zone that collapsed around Walton and held him to eight points. UCLA won, 108-61, as Bibby and Farmer scored nineteen points apiece.

"As I've said before" — Wooden smiled — "Walton is the type of player who wouldn't have to score at all — yet he'll dominate the game. And the pleasant thing is, he enjoys not scoring."

The kids' first road trip. Oregon State and Oregon.

They are a loose, free-wheeling, good-humored group, more tight-knit than teams of the Alcindor years. And they love nicknames. There's "Nate the Great," Swen Nater, the resident punster. There's "Moose," the tag given Larry Farmer because one player said he bore a vivid facial resemblance to "Bullwinkle" of comic-strip fame. There's "Charlie," Henry Bibby's first name. And there's "T.C." — reserve guard Tommy Curtis, the gaudiest dresser and most animated spirit. He fends off those who tease him by saying, "Thanks, I needed that."

The bus ride from the Portland airport south through the Willamette Valley to Corvallis is customarily tiring. Two hours of farms and paper mills and tedium on a chill, overcast afternoon.

It is a quiet journey, except for amiable chatter and "acid rock" music shrieking from reserve forward Jon Chapman's tape player. But most everybody drifts asleep.

When the bus rumbles into Corvallis, the coach — seated

near the front alongside Nell Wooden — rises and addresses his players: "We didn't have a meeting about this before we left, but because this is our first road trip, I hope you will act as gentlemanly as you do in your homes. You're always to be on your special best behavior with those you come in contact. And I want to impress upon you to keep your rooms neat — even after you check out. This is directed at two of you — and you know who you are — who had to be called back to your rooms about this last year."

There is brief laughter as the bus arrives at the motel. Corvallis again. For John Wooden, it remains the way he left it last year — and the year before that, and the year before that. For most of the UCLA Bruins, it is a new adventure.

The Bruins lost their poise. They lost their footing. They lost the basketball — on turnovers — thirty times! But they didn't lose the game.

"Well, we played like sophomores," said Wooden, after a 68-62 win. "That's by far the most turnovers we've had in a long, long time."

Later in the year, however, UCLA was to beat Oregon State at Pauley, 91-72. And *nobody* in the remaining seventeen games of the regular season would come closer than thirteen points to the Bruins.

For first-year starters, they showed unusual poise and polish.

Keith Wilkes, Larry Farmer, and Greg Lee hardly ever stole the headlines from Walton and Bibby. But each contributed mightily to John Wooden's eighth national championship, as did Larry Hollyfield, Tommy Curtis, and Swen Nater.

Wilkes, a minister's son, and Lee, whose father was his high school coach and used to usher at Bruin home games, were exceptional scholars before arriving at UCLA with "A-minus" and "straight-A" records respectively.

Their intelligence helped acclimate them to varsity competition so quickly they could have passed for embattled seniors. "So many people were pessimistic about us," said Wilkes, quiet-spoken and boyish looking. "But . . . we have an awful lot of pride. We all believed we were better than people thought." Said Lee of the team: "We get along together and we're intelligent. We might commit a lot of turnovers sometimes, but at least they're not the stupid kind."

Farmer, a superb leaper who had played well coming off the bench during the NCAA games the previous year, is an affable fellow and a stylish dresser who brought enormous self-confidence to the line-up. As a Denver schoolboy, he solicited UCLA's attention by sending a newspaper clipping about himself. "I guess it was sort of an ego thing," he said. "UCLA is the best and every guy wants to prove he is the best of the best."

Hollyfield, an eccentric personality who performs with lots of flash and dash, starred on unbeaten teams at Compton High School and Compton College and is a strong bet to be chosen early in the pro draft. He has been called a "great talent" ("Why, he could play for any team in the NBA right now!" say his staunchest admirers), but also "spoiled" and "selfish." Says a source close to the team, "Even when he plays a lot, he bitches about being taken out."

Like Bibby, Wilkes, Farmer, and Hollyfield, Tommy Curtis is black, but not "too black," in the opinion of one insider. Outgoing and friendly, Curtis has been described as an "All-American boy, just what Wooden desires in his players." He grew up in Tallahassee, Florida, in a broken home, which, he said, was "deprived socially but not financially . . . my grandfather, so I'm told, was the South's first black millionaire."

Curtis also is active in the Fellowship of Christian Athletes and was his high school's first black player. When those facts were reported in a local newspaper, Curtis' life was threatened one night before a game. "My buddy and I were at the concession stand," he wrote in an FCA magazine, "when this white guy walked up and growled, 'Hey, nigger, you sanctified basketball player. If you score thirty points or more tonight, I'll kill you after the game.' He reached into his pocket and I could see the bulge of a pistol. My teammate wanted to run, but I said, 'No, man, let's get our drink.' I still get teased about how brave I really was that night — I scored twenty-eight points! I wasn't afraid, however, because I had something special working for me . . . this man Jesus Christ."

It was a portent of things to come in the Regionals and the Nationals.

"That was the cheapest shot I've ever seen," stormed Bill Walton, complaining that USC's Ron Riley had intentionally struck him in the mouth while attempting a hook shot during the Bruins' 79-66 win over the Trojans in the season's final regular-season game.

The blow, Walton said, jarred a tooth loose, and he added he had been "elbowed five or six other times" during the emotion-charged game. "It's supposed to be a basketball game," he said, "not a boxing or wrestling match."

Next door, Riley was insisting the blow was accidental. "I wasn't trying to hit him. If he feels that's what I did, that's just his tough luck."

John Wooden was furious. "I suppose that was a 'phantom punch' that caught Walton," he said with bitter sarcasm. "He [Riley] should have been kicked out of the place." (No foul was called.)

And somebody in the Trojan locker room muttered a word that was to be heard a lot in the next couple of weeks concerning Walton: "Crybaby."

There was no repetition of the hostility when UCLA beat Weber State in the regional semifinals at Provo, Utah, 90-58. Walton spent half the game on the bench, in foul trouble, but even without him, UCLA hardly took a deep breath.

Then came what was getting to be a habit — a UCLA–Cal State Long Beach tournament confrontation.

Typically, emotions ran high between UCLA and Long Beach moments before their third postseason showdown in as many years — the Western Regional finals.

From the Bruin rooting section came a handmade banner that infuriated the 49er coach: READ "THE BEST COACH — JERRY TARKANIAN" BY CLIFFORD IRVING. And when the UCLA team made its customary getaway prior to the National Anthem, Long Beach fans yelled, "Where ya going, Bruins?"

Then came the war of insults and elbows.

When it was over, Ed Ratleff, the Long Beach star, quietly and wearily cut the tape off his ankles just after UCLA had cut the heart out of the 49ers, 73-57. His words were soft-spoken but came through clearly.

"The officials protect UCLA," he said. "They were fouling us a lot and we didn't get the calls. They get away with so much on defense but every time you touch them, it's a foul."

Later, Long Beach coach Jerry Tarkanian was to say: "Ratleff is black and blue. His arms are sore — he's sorer than he has ever been after a game. And he says he's never been knocked down so many times."

Both Ratleff and UCLA's Henry Bibby spent considerable time on the deck and it was rarely their own momentum that put them there. And at one point, Bruin center Bill Walton left the game briefly, holding his ribs, after an alleged blow by Long Beach center Nate Stephens.

At that point, Wooden met with Dwight Jones, the 49er assistant, in front of the scorer's bench. Jones remembers the dialogue this way:

"Wooden told me it was 'disgraceful and unethical' the way our kids were playing. He then went to one of the officials and told him that we were elbowing Walton and that it was an 'intentional, flagrant foul.' The referee came over and said, 'Coach, sit down,' to me. Then he turned to Wooden and said, 'John, don't go down there to the other official. I'll watch for it.'"

Asked to comment about the incident, Wooden said, "I'll pass on that."

Bibby appeared with Wooden in the interview room after the game, briefly, but the rest of the Bruin players were spirited out a back exit. The 49ers talked long, loud, and freely.

The most vocal was burly forward-center Leonard Gray, transfer from Kansas. He was asked about Bibby.

"That little squirt was mouthing off all day," he said. "But I couldn't do anything because he's small and I'm supposed to be a bad guy. If I'd done anything, I'd have gotten sent right out of the country to Cuba."

And Gray then had a curt remark for Walton too: "A crybaby," he said.

But the words, while strong, were hollow in the end. It was an emotional, bitterly fought game that drove a wedge for a while between two friendly coaches and two basically friendly schools. UCLA, with Bibby shooting up the Marriott Activities Center gym like Butch Cassidy, advanced surely if not easily to yet another NCAA final round of four.

Bibby blasted at the 49ers' 2-3 zone for twenty-three points, mostly from the corners, Walton got nineteen from the interior, Keith Wilkes fourteen from what was left.

Wooden's strategy on the 6-6 guard, Ratleff, was perfect. Afraid Ratleff would tire out and then overpower the Bruins' smaller guards, Wooden assigned 6-5 forward Larry Farmer to him and had Walton quickly cover him if Ed tried to maneuver from the low post. The result: Ratleff hit only one of eight shots in the first half — and finished with just seventeen points, the only Long Beach player in double figures.

Tarkanian, who had been awakened at 9 A.M. on game day by the UCLA band, which was staying — and playing — in the same motel as the 49ers, conceded that the Bruins were "a very, very difficult team to play. For us to win we had to have a great shooting game [they hit only 42 percent] and hope that Bibby wouldn't have one [he was ten for seventeen]. They got a few passes in to Walton that we almost intercepted. But we knew if Bibby was hitting we'd be in trouble."

It was obvious Bibby, the senior, the leader, reflected a sort of confidence that has become commonplace along with all the championships.

"He's so cocky," said 49er Eric McWilliams, "he just fires from wherever he happens to be on the court and it goes in. He seems to just *know* he's going to make it. The same is true of Wilkes and Farmer. They're not really that good as shooters, but they have confidence they're going to make the shots."

For most of the Bruins, however, this was their first taste of tournament glory and they showed it — even though they played for a man who insisted, repeatedly, that "I never want my players to display excessive jubilation when they win or excessive sorrow when they lose."

At courtside, while awaiting the trophy presentations, they giggled and embraced and gleefully exchanged hand slaps, while Wooden smiled broadly and unreproachfully, shook a few players' hands, and whispered in Henry Bibby's ear. The players tossed cups of water at each other and when some of it splashed on trainer Ducky Drake, he yelled, "Hey, knock it off!" And reserve guard Tommy Curtis grinned and sighed, "We're goin' home . . . Oooohhhhhh! It's good."

Never had a UCLA team displayed so much frivolity after a play-off game — not even after any national championships. This was more than just the usual cutting-down-the-nets-to-signify-victory routine. This was genuine emotion. It was obvious how badly the Bruins wanted to win this one — a game many of them considered would be their toughest hurdle on the road to title number eight.

*

Teacher versus pupil. John Wooden of UCLA versus Denny Crum of Louisville. The man who had exploded the season before, "I'm the coach of this team and don't you tell me how to coach my team!" against a man who now had his own team to coach. A veteran Louisville team against a young UCLA team — but young only in years — in the NCAA semifinals.

Both Wooden and Crum play a mean game of pool. Both favor running, shooting, pressing basketball. Both are intensely competitive. But the resemblance ends there. They are of different generations and life-styles and personalities.

Wooden once told Crum: "Denny, you're the greatest card player in the world — from nose to chin."

Like Jerry Norman before him, Crum was anything but a yes man assistant to Wooden, however. Their disagreements came mostly on strategical grounds. (Crum, for instance, favored using a zone defense against certain teams; Wooden did not because "a man-to-man has always worked well for us.")

Crum inherited excellent material in his first year at Louisville (including All-American guard Jim Price) but of the twenty-one rookie head coaches of the class of 1971-1972 he had the best record (24-3) and it was an open secret he got his job because of his years at UCLA.

"Here in Kentucky," said Peck Hickman, the Louisville Athletic Director, "we like to judge by bloodlines. With Denny's background, you've got to say he has a good one."

The UCLA-Louisville game — thanks largely to a man Crum had recruited for the Bruins, Bill Walton — wasn't close. It was 96-77 and it was easy.

UCLA committed twenty-one turnovers and had trouble shaking the stubborn Cardinals for a while because of their scrappy, man-to-man defense. But Louisville simply had no one who could contain Walton near the basket. He scored thirty-three points against 6-9 center Al Vilcheck, who fouled out with twelve and a half minutes left, and assorted other challengers. Walton missed only two of thirteen shots — and swept off twenty-one rebounds as well.

In style, it was a repetition of the Long Beach game the week before — fists up, no holds barred — more like the NBA or boxing at the Olympic Auditorium than college basketball. There were swings and elbows swapped and the Louisville players yelled "Foul" when it was over — just as the Long Beach players had.

"Walton is strong," said Vilcheck, "but you can't touch him. The officials put him in a cage. He cries a lot. I just don't think a man of his ability should cry so much. He wasn't hurt when he went to the floor in the second half. He was just resting."

Florida State, UCLA's opponent in the finals after a surprise 79-75 win over North Carolina, had been as good as dead for three years — barred from tournament play because of NCAA probation for recruiting violations.

The shadow still hung over the Seminoles during tournament week in Los Angeles.

A strong blast was fired by Bill Wall of MacMurray (Illinois) College, President of the National Association of Basketball Coaches.

"I resent the fact that they're here, and a lot of other coaches do too," said Wall. "Our coaches are amazed, disgusted, and disillusioned at this. Their coach was caught with his fingers in the till, not once but twice."

Coach Hugh Durham, who had heard a lot of criticism since he began recruiting mostly black players at a mostly white school, responded mildly. "He doesn't know what he's talking about. If he infers our players have been bought, well, this is a time when anybody is saying that a good player at a big-time school has been bought.

"It was speculated that Lew Alcindor got more than he was supposed to receive [Durham referred to an NCAA investigation of UCLA that proved no impropriety]. It's all right with schools like UCLA, North Carolina, or South Carolina. But if it's Long Beach State or Florida State, somebody's eye gets cocked and he says, 'Why did he *really* go to Florida State?'

"We've got ten guys but only two of 'em have cars. And one of those is a DeSoto! I'll match that with any team in the country."

Then Durham added, "We've paid the price. We accepted it. We didn't debate it in the press or in public."

An NCAA spokesman concurred, saying as far as that group was concerned, Florida State once again "enjoys full rights and privileges."

Actually, it was UCLA that was on probation, *not* Florida State. The Bruins were serving a one-year sentence over a recruiting incident involving football-track star James Mc-Alister. But the penalty did not carry restrictions, as Florida State's had, so the Bruins were eligible for tournament play.

At a Friday afternoon practice, Wooden consoled Durham. "I'm sorry about all this," he said. "I want you to know we don't feel the same way [as Wall]."

But it didn't end there.

Dr. Stanley Marshall, the Florida State President, called a press conference directly before the UCLA-FSU game to say that Wall's remarks were "very damaging" and that he and Durham were considering legal action. Wall's statement, Dr. Marshall said, "was inaccurate and totally untrue. I asked Mr. Wall this morning if he had proof Florida State was guilty of any infractions. He denied he had such knowledge. I felt it was incumbent upon him to apologize to Coach Durham and the university, and I felt it was incumbent upon the NABC to apologize and censure Mr. Wall."

It was against that backdrop — and under that large cloud — that Florida State, whom many thought was still just a run-and-gun, "renegade" team, took the floor against UCLA.

Few would have suspected that this would be the closest final in Bruin championship history, 81-76 (UCLA's forty-fifth straight win, the third longest streak in major-college annals). The Seminoles were tall, they were quick, and — most surprising to those who hadn't seen them before — they were disciplined. At one point they held a 21-14 lead — the largest anyone had over UCLA all season. And they rode the brilliant outside shooting of Ron King and the inside scoring of 6-11 Lawrence McCray (when Walton got into foul trouble) to make it close until the end.

Wooden had to summon guard Greg Lee off the bench to run a keep-away tempo game the last five minutes and protect a 79-72 lead. But the Seminoles blew several chances to make it closer — or even end the dynasty — by committing costly turnovers. And while they were losing the ball, UCLA was not losing its poise.

"The most pleasing thing to me," said Wooden, "was that when we got behind early, we showed patience."

But the wine was not nearly as sweet for UCLA — it seemed — as it had been after the Regional win over Long Beach State. There were pouting faces over the closeness of the score — and Lee and Larry Hollyfield sat disconsolately on the bench during the trophy presentation.

"There are some things in this world," a bystander said, "that never change. And UCLA winning national championships has to be one of them."

A reporter approached Walton and asked him, "What is the ingredient that makes this team so invincible?"

The redhead turned to Lee, who was seated alongside him, and said: "You're the word man, Greg. You tell them."

"We're integrated," Lee said drily.

But there still was another surprising note to come in this most bizarre of UCLA championship weeks.

It should have been a happy scene — Bill Walton, the giant redhead, meeting reporters after UCLA's title win over Florida State. But Walton, named the tournament's most valuable player, arrived in the Sports Arena interview room not joyous but testy.

Asked by writers in the back to raise the microphone and

speak louder, he snapped: "I can hear myself. My voice is bouncing off the back wall." Asked again to talk louder, he said, "There are a lot of empty seats up front."

When he finally talked about the game, he said, "I'm not that elated because we didn't play that well. Florida State is an excellent team but we didn't dominate the game like we know we can. If we had played our game the way we can, it would have been different. No excuses but I don't like to back into things. I like to win convincingly."

Then he added: "I felt like we lost it."

Wooden wisely intervened at this point, moving captain Henry Bibby to the microphone. Henry coolly handled predictable questions in predictable fashion: "We made mistakes we shouldn't have made but any team would like to be in our position right now."

Meanwhile, Walton had crossed the Sports Arena to the UCLA dressing quarters and pushed through autograph seekers at the door, snubbing them. He was heard to say: "Whose locker room is this anyway?"

But Walton's outbursts were only minor explosions compared to what happened a few weeks later to college basketball's Player of the Year — his arrest for participation in antiwar demonstrations on the UCLA campus.

At the weekly Los Angeles basketball writers luncheon the Monday after UCLA won championship number eight, Coach Gary Colson of Pepperdine asked a question: "They didn't mean it personally," he said, looking at Wooden, "but a lot of coaches here for the NCAA tournament said they thought the fact UCLA keeps on winning is hurting college basketball. What do you think about that?"

Wooden was composed, articulate. "The same thing was said about the Yankees in baseball," he said. "Whether it's an individual or a team, whenever you reach a plateau of excellence there are always a lot of people who want to see you knocked down. Then, when it happens, they don't know what they were complaining about.

"There were those who wanted to see Joe Louis get whipped when he was heavyweight champion all those years. Then, when he did, many of those same people were sorry.

"How many people are mourning for Arnold Palmer right now because he's in a slump? A tremendous number."

The Yankees. Joe Louis. Arnold Palmer. John Wooden was in good company and *he* was still on top. And one of the first people to recognize it — again — was that guy who always seemed to have one eye on the nation's playing fields and courts. His latest letter hangs on the wall in the Wooden apartment:

DEAR JOHN:
What a season and what a tournament! Basketball fans across the country are running out of superlatives to describe your accomplishments at UCLA and the championship game, last Saturday, seemed only to emphasize how firm your hold is on being No. 1.

It goes without saying, of course, that heartiest congratulations are in order — not only to the Bruins for their unprecedented victory — but also to you for the esteem that players, coaches and spectators alike have for you. And you may be certain I am counted among those who think John Wooden is just about the finest coach in the long, exciting history of the game.

WITH WARM GOOD WISHES,
RICHARD NIXON

The "just about" appeared a strange choice of words. You wonder if the President was being pragmatic, or if Adolph Rupp has a letter hanging in *his* den too.

CHAPTER 10

"Be Quick! Don't Hurry!"

"The team that makes the most mistakes probably will win."

— Ward (Piggie) Lambert, former Purdue coach

FOR SOMEBODY who wins and wins and wins as much as John Wooden has over the past decade, it is a news event of considerable proportion whenever he loses a basketball game.

A UCLA defeat almost defies the laws of nature. It seems to happen about as often as a solar eclipse, a massive earthquake, or, well, maybe about as often as California slides into the Pacific Ocean.

Not once in the last six years going into the 1972-1973 season had Wooden lost a game he *needed* to win, the losses occurring in meaningless nonconference games or when UCLA already had clinched — or all but clinched — a postseason tournament berth. And if you throw out 1966, a year when Wooden was on the outside looking in, you have to go all the way back to March of 1963 — the thrashing by Arizona State in the NCAA regionals — to find him losing on a night when it really mattered, when a chance for national preeminence truly hinged on the outcome.

Now, before anyone assumes that John Wooden is one of those "winning-every-game-is-the-only-thing" tacticians, consider the following: John Wooden discreetly plots — or secretly wishes — for some of those defeats.

it is very true that there have been occasions I haven't done
everything that I thought was in our best interest to outscore
the opponent, in that particular game. It doesn't mean I
didn't want us to win. But sometimes I think we needed to be
knocked down to win later on."

This, then, is a measure of John Wooden, coach and master
psychologist. Translated, he does not try to "throw" a game;
rather, he simply does not pull off every magic trick or strategic
maneuver or psychological ploy possible in order to win.
Maybe, he believes, a defeat every now and then will help
more than harm.

At least three games come to mind: the resounding setback
from Oregon at Eugene in 1970, the slowdown 46-44 loss to
USC at Pauley Pavilion in 1969, the nationally televised defeat
at Notre Dame in 1971.

Tactically, there was probably nothing Wooden could do to
avert the defeat at Oregon. UCLA was simply outshot and
outplayed by a superior team that night. Psychologically?
Perhaps Wooden could have done something to arouse his
players, but he didn't. He truly believed — and said so be-
forehand — that a defeat would be good for his team. As it
turned out, he was proved right in the weeks that followed.

The USC loss? Rival coaches have said Wooden could have
won that one, too, had he wanted to break up the Trojans' high-
post delay game with a trapping zone or a harassing, nose-to-
nose defense. "All he had to do," said one, "was tell Alcindor,
'Lew! Get out there and shut off those passes to [Ron] Taylor
on the high post!' That was what USC's game depended on —
the passes to Taylor, the other guys cutting past him."

Looking back, Wooden accepts the blame. "It wasn't my
team's fault, it was my fault," he said, "and I wasn't upset about
it. I felt it would be good for us. If we had the conference title
riding on it, I would have handled it quite differently. I'm not
saying we would have beaten them, but I would go about play-

226 THE WIZARD OF WESTWOOD

ing the game entirely different. We still might have lost; how can you say that we might have won? But, under the circumstances, things worked out for us eventually . . ."

The journey to Notre Dame also found a UCLA team that was ripe for defeat. Austin Carr wheeled past the bewildered Bruins to the basket again and again as if they were nailed to the floor. Could he have been stopped cold by a zone defense, rather than a man-to-man that, late in the game, assigned an inexperienced swingman, Larry Hollyfield, to guard Carr? Perhaps. At least, it might have been worth trying. Carr already had made a shambles of UCLA's man-to-man. But Wooden has scarcely ever deployed a zone defense in all his years of coaching. His team hadn't practiced it. He wasn't about to call for one now, certainly not in a game that meant nothing as far as keeping alive the UCLA dynasty was concerned.

There was, however, a footnote to Austin Carr's finest hour. The very next weekend in Chicago Stadium, an uncelebrated Illinois team threw up a zone defense that drove Carr into the corners and far beyond this shooting range. He shot miserably that night. And Notre Dame lost.

Meanwhile, back in Westwood, the beat goes on and on and on. UCLA, going into the 1972-1973 season, had not lost a game since that day John Wooden returned to South Bend.

The scene: Pauley Pavilion, any midweek afternoon, any winter.

The bespectacled little man in warmup jacket, white trunks, and sneakers stands there at midcourt. His voice transcends the thud of bouncing basketballs and thundering feet with a roar that is right out of Rockne or Lombardi, without the profanity.

"The worst thing you can do is hurry!" John Wooden yells to his UCLA Bruins. "Be quick! But, for gracious sakes, don't hurry!"

For everybody who plays for college basketball's mightiest dynasty, those are words to live by — and to full-court-press and rebound and hit the open man by.

They are the hallmarks of the Wooden Way, the rigorous one and a half hour practice sessions that help sculpture a dynasty and keep those championship flags and cards and fan letters coming.

He stands there, eyes riveted on rangy young men in T-shirts and trunks as they fire jump shots at glass backboards in a shooting drill. They retrieve their own shots and quickly pass to a teammate. Shoot . . . rebound . . . pass. Over and over. They are in groups of six at each basket, playing one of Wooden's favorite games. The first group to make twenty baskets wins.

The whistle blows. Everything stops. "I want all of you to be in balance when you shoot!" yells the coach. "If you are not in balance, for gracious sakes, don't shoot! . . . And make that head follow through — toward the basket — when you shoot!"

Moments later, in a brief scrimmage, he is imparting the Wooden Law for rebounders: "If a shot's taken, always, always assume it's gonna be missed! We don't want spectators out there!"

He prides himself on being what he calls "a good preparation coach." His practice sessions are meticulously organized and fast-paced, with no more than five or ten minutes devoted to any single drill because, as he points out, "If you make them too long, they'll lose interest."

The painstaking preparation by a Wooden team, he says, does not take as much time as that of other teams, although Wooden drilled his teams much longer during the Indiana State years.

"We do, however, get a great deal accomplished," he says. "It's like the saying that goes: 'Don't mistake activity for achievement.' In my opinion — and I have no real proof of this — there's far more overcoaching in basketball than under-coaching."

Basically, Wooden prepares his teams by following three tenets: conditioning, fundamentals, and teamwork:

1. "Get 'em into condition — and make our players believe they're in better condition than our opponents."

2. "Teach them to execute fundamentals properly and quickly. In other words, in our shooting drills, we do *every-thing* quickly — shooting, passing, and rebounding."

3. "We play as a unit. We always try to think of passing the ball before shooting it."

Fundamentals, too, are synonymous with the Wooden Way. Rather than rely heavily on simulated, game-type conditions, he estimates he spends 65 to 75 percent of practice time on fundamentals — shooting, passing, cutting, dribbling — mostly in three-on-three or two-on-two drills. They are drills his players will be executing in March, just as they did back in October.

Why so much emphasis on fundamentals? Wooden's answer seemingly could apply to the way he tackles life off the court, as well as the way he wants his players to respond on it. It re-quires a reflexive, right way or wrong way, black or white sort of snap judgment because basketball doesn't give you time to weigh decisions and fill in the "grays." Says Wooden: "A thorough proficiency in the fundamentals enables each player to adjust quickly and counteract whatever the opposing player might throw at him. That way, we can execute something without thinking too long about how we're going to do it."

Wooden's defense — apart from the zone press — has not been much discussed. But it has been a stronger factor in recent championships than the more-publicized press. It stresses basics and discipline and discourages "reaching," which, in turn, makes UCLA a team that commits relatively few fouls — another important Bruin edge.

Wooden's offense, in effect, breaks the game down into two-on-twos and three-on-threes — mostly off high-post plays, or

high-low post patterns. It isolates two or three players on
one side of the court, there to exploit scoring chances. "That's
essentially all he's doing," says a former player. "He believes
if you can get two players, three players in good position on
one side of the court, they should be able to get into good position to score . . . If you can get enough continuity in the
offense where everybody knows where he's going and what
he's supposed to do, it's two-on-two or three-on-three. That's
when he wants the player to have some freedom and initiate
something on his own. So you *are* restricted — but you are *not*
restricted too. It's a pretty nice feeling. You know what your
teammate is supposed to do, but you feel you're on your own
to do something too."

It all appears very simple in reality as in theory. Wooden
says he tries to keep it that way, a throwback to the Green Bay
Packers' "we're-coming-right-at-you–you've-got-to-stop-us" approach. "My feeling," says Wooden, "is that if we execute
soundly — exactly the way we're supposed to — they'll have a
rough time stopping us. We're an easy team to scout, but
we're not easy to stop."

That is the opinion, too, of a scout, Bill Bertka, a former Kent
State coach who operates the nation's biggest college scouting service (Bertka Views — "We Scout 'Em, You Play
'Em"). "This may surprise a lot of people," said Bertka, "but
UCLA is one of the teams for which we get the fewest scouting
requests. One reason is that everything they do is so predictable."

To encourage teamwork, Wooden says he doesn't want his
players to criticize each other. And he insists that the player
who scores acknowledge the man who set him up with a perfect pass — by nodding, waving, or saying "good pass" to him.

Wooden subscribes strongly to the teachings of his college
coach, Piggie Lambert, who taught his players the "Lambert
Theory": "The team that makes the most mistakes will probably win."

Most mistakes? That's right, says Wooden. "If you're not

making mistakes, then you're not doing anything," he says. "I might not go as far as Lambert, but I'm positive that a doer makes mistakes . . . I'd rather have a fifty percent shooting average with one hundred shots than eight percent of sixty shots."

Additionally, the Lambert style — attack, gamble, fast break, and run, run, run — enables Wooden to see himself as a salesman, a purveyor of an entertainment form in Southern California, where the amusement dollar can stretch only so far.

"Our style is entertaining," he said. "We have an obligation not only to try to win, but to entertain the customers, especially here in Los Angeles, where there are so many other attractions. When people cease to be entertained, they'll go elsewhere."

His theories, he believes, also have much to do with vocational longevity. "A coach who plays an up-tempo style, as opposed to ball control," he said, "is less likely to be fired."

He calls them his "list of normal expectations." Specifically, they are the off-court rules, the do's and don't's imposed on players by John Wooden, and they forbid drinking and smoking.

"I tell our players, 'What you do between practices will tell how you'll play,' " he said. "I put the onus on each individual. My telling him not to carouse, for example, is only the guideline. The rest is up to him. I won't say I'll kick a player off the team for smoking — although that was my policy years ago — but I hope I don't find out about it . . ."

Another rule on road trips: players, if they go shopping or strolling, must go in pairs, particularly in large cities. "We believe in the buddy system for personal safety," says Wooden. "I want to know all I can about them, but I don't want to invade their privacy either . . . I make no threats. All I have is a list of expectations which I feel are fair. Also, I tell our players, 'When you come to practice, you cease to exist as an individual. You're part of a team.' "

The players, for the most part, seem to tolerate Wooden's rules, although they have ignored some and clashed with the coach too. Says one player: "I got kidded at a New Year's Eve party when they started serving champagne. They'd smile and say, 'Hey, what's Wooden gonna say if he finds out?' Well, that's something that hasn't really been spelled out. Does 'no drinking' mean you can't take a once-in-a-while social drink too? But I've found that his rules are tolerable. The coach isn't checking on us all the time. If a player wants to deliberately break a rule, he'll do it. If I break a rule, then I have to expect some kind of reprimand. You've gotta know you're hurting yourself. Personally, I think it's up to the individual."

Wooden argues that his rules are not unreasonable. "Whether our players like it or not," he says, "they're representing other people — people who reflect a university. There's no way to get around that. Sure, some players might say I'm harsh. But look at it another way. They're looked up to by others and receive a great deal of adulation. Is that a hardship? They're getting a grant-in-aid for their college education. Is that really a hardship?"

John Wooden's willingness to share his coaching secrets has made him money, has endeared him to young coaches, and has moved others to call him "terribly naïve."

He is a speaker very much in demand on the coaching clinic circuit, an exhausting schedule that keeps him airport-hopping with almost as much intensity, if not more than, his in-season travels. Moreover, his book, *Practical Modern Basketball*, has sold extremely well — even without much promotional assistance.

He appeals to many young coaches despite some differences

in life-style and philosophy. Example: Furman's Joe Williams, who was beaten by him in the 1970 NCAA finals when he was coaching at Jacksonville, was radically dissimilar to Wooden in areas of team discipline and personal dress. Now, he has sort of attached himself to Wooden, staying in the same hotel with him and observing him during the 1972 NCAA finals in Los Angeles and once driving 100 miles to meet him at an airport and take him to a coaching clinic where he was speaking.

The naïveté? A friend of Wooden's says: "At clinics, he tells them everything he knows. He's willing to share his knowledge. I remember him saying after one game that John Vallely could be stopped by playing him a certain way. Well, for the next few games, Vallely was in a slump because they defensed him the way John had said. It's the same at clinics. When he's finished lecturing, I know a lot of people who are shocked by what he's told all these other coaches and they'll say to him, 'Why on earth did you tell them *that?*' John's response is something like, 'Oh, they know that already. Everybody knows that.' But they really don't. John doesn't give himself credit for how much he really knows. This is why I say John is terribly naïve in this respect."

And how do his peers judge him?

"He may be sixty-two years old," says Joe Williams of Furman, "but he's the most modern coach in collegiate basketball. He stays ahead of the trends. He adjusts to the changes.

"Some people talk about a UCLA mystique. I don't think there is a UCLA mystique as much as there is a John Wooden mystique. He's taught us all about quickness in basketball — from big men to guards, from offense to defense, where his teams trap, overplay, and cut off the passing lanes while still keeping the basket covered.

"But the real key to Wooden's success has been more than coaching techniques; it has been his ability to get each player to play toward his maximum potential. It is John Wooden the

man I feel most people are interested in now. It is to see how
he is able to handle the problems in coaching, how he is able to
deal effectively with the players."

No man has been a closer witness to this effectiveness than
USC's Bob Boyd. Boyd has coached the Trojans six years.
Each year, UCLA has won Pacific 8 and national champion-
ships.

Boyd has turned down several other coaching offers —
some say because of his gnawing desire, bordering on obsession, to topple Wooden and the Bruins. He says no: "We're
involved in a very tough market in Los Angeles with the Lakers
and the Bruins, but I like it and that's why I've stayed at USC
— it's not because I'm hung up on beating the Bruins."

But he recognizes UCLA's achievement: "I'm convinced the
streak is so phenomenal it will never be duplicated. We've
done as well as anyone else in the league the last six years. Our
program was way down and now it's up. But we've gone almost unnoticed because UCLA has been so overwhelming.

"Sure, they've had the players. But coaches often cite players as a crutch for something they haven't done themselves.
The significant thing with Wooden is that he has done what
has been expected. It's a helluva lot easier sometimes to surprise and do what is *not* expected. Even with the players
UCLA has had, a lesser coach could have screwed it up. He
hasn't overreacted to changing attitudes, life-styles, and
times."

Boyd is the only coach ever to have beaten UCLA at Pauley
Pavilion. He's done it . . . twice and it doesn't bother him
that both wins came after UCLA had clinched the league title.

"In spite of what's been said," he says, "I take great pride
in what we've done at Pauley. I've heard it said the wins
weren't meaningful or pertinent. I don't care. You have to
identify with something successful."

Wooden has had differences with coaching rivals — Pete
Newell, for a time, Scotty McDonald, Adolph Rupp, and Tex

Winter, notably. But most coaches speak of him almost in reverence. Some examples:

Phil Woolpert, who guided USF to NCAA championships in 1955 and 1956: "I think that only the purists fully appreciate what a great coach Wooden has become. It's easy to say that he had Alcindor and now he has Walton. But he won titles with centers of ordinary height, like Fred Slaughter.

"Wooden always did some things exceptionally well — conditioning, offense — but now he does *everything* exceptionally well. Like great defense and the ability to instill an amazing degree of efficiency of execution into his players. Their performance on the court is as beautiful and hard to achieve as the finest ballet."

Marv Harshman, Washington coach: "My most sincere tribute to Wooden's greatness as a coach would be not just the winning of so many national championships but his unique ability to mold a collection of blue-chip players into a blue-chip team. I highly admire and greatly respect John as a man, a friend, and the one *great* coach I have met in my twenty-seven years in the profession."

Jerry Tarkanian, Cal State Long Beach coach: "He's unique. His theories wouldn't work for everyone but he does a tremendous job of organizing and getting teams ready to play. He makes very few adjustments during games but maybe the major part of his success is that he's very, very basic.

"Before we were going to play Southwestern Louisiana last year, I was a nervous wreck worrying about their one-three-one extended zone. On the way down to the game, we were going to practice against it and I thought to myself, 'Wooden wouldn't be worrying. Other teams worry about what *he's* going to do — his press, his fast break.' You're extremely conscious of them. They're hardly conscious of you at all.

"Sure, he's had great players but I don't believe if you gave most any coach his choice of the five best high school seniors in the country one year that he could take them and win three straight championships.

"There's a lot more good than bad in Wooden. If anything does disturb me it's that he has the image he never does anything bad. He does but so does everybody else. So it bothers me to have coaches knock him because his faults are so small. What coach isn't hypocritical? What coach doesn't yell at officials? But losers are always going to knock winners, I guess."

Abe Lemons, Oklahoma City coach: "I think he knows talent better than any coach that ever lived . . . he also handles this talent better than any coach in the history of the game, both on and off the court. The pressure on him and his team has to be the greatest ever . . . I think his secret is not to overcoach; he seems to give them just what they will need. No one is perfect but John comes close to it in his profession.

"We all miss John around the coaches' convention floor. His teams have been in the finals so often no one has had a real chance to visit and find out what the real John Wooden is like. We refer to the finals as the UCLA Invitational now.

"I think people try and read something complicated into John Wooden's life, but I think it's so simple that people can't believe it. He has a personal character like so many other great men in history. I think he would have been a success in anything, a general in the army or the head of a great business empire. We're lucky he chose the coaching profession. He has made money for a whole lot of people — full gyms, money in the till for everyone.

"I have seen him get emotional, tough, and demanding with his team. I have seen him fight for his club when he thinks an injustice has been done. But this is not a fault. He is a rare man. It will be difficult to imagine the day when John Wooden is not coaching and sitting on the bench at a UCLA basketball game."

Judgment Day

"Holy rolling down that holy road
Singin' songs of glory
To ease the heavy load
And they all kept on livin'
Livin' in the same old way
Holy rolling straight to Judgment Day."

— "Holy Rolling," by Cynthia Weil and
Barry Mann

Judgment Day

CHAPTER 11

A Quartet:
Harmony and Disharmony

FOUR MEN — four strong men who have affected John
Robert Wooden's life in a manner like the four of a much earlier day: Joshua Hugh Wooden, Earl Warriner, Glenn Curtis,
and Piggie Lambert.

They are of a faster moving, more complicated generation,
four visible — and not so visible — forces and counterforces
that have done much to shape the Wooden story just before
and during the championship years.

His bitterest nemesis, a top lieutenant who got out, the boss,
and the man in the shadows.

Each is much different from Wooden in personality. None
has been the molder of character and life-style the earlier four
(whom Wooden describes as "the four most important men in
my life") were. Each has exerted pressure, but he has learned
from each, lessons that transcend the simple values of Midwest
America half a century ago.

The man is silver-haired now — handsome, well-dressed,
smooth. Pete Newell's game has changed from college basketball to professional basketball, from coach of the California
Golden Bears to general manager of the Los Angeles Lakers.
But he remembers the duels of a different day, between two
bitter nemeses.

"My concepts and Johnny Wooden's have always been close
in a lot of areas," he says, stirring cream into his coffee in an

airport motel restaurant, "even though people used to regard him as an offensive coach and me as a defensive coach.

"I always thought I had the better conditioned team, for one thing. So did he. I always thought you won on 'do's' rather than 'don't's.' So did he."

It is 1957, at the University of California's bandbox — Harmon Gymnasium. Wooden has beaten Newell's Cal teams seven straight times. Newell is to best Wooden's Bruin teams eight times in a row but no one is looking that far ahead when the game begins. As usual, it is just about like two generals preparing for a world war.

"I remember telling my team going into the game that we weren't going to call the first time out," said Newell. "I told them I didn't care if they were running on their knees. No time outs. That would be putting up the white flag.

"I know Wooden gave his team the same instructions. We were both absolutely confident. There were no time outs in the first half. In the second half, we'd played sixteen minutes, the score was tied, and there still hadn't been one. Then we got a quick eight points — pressing baseline to baseline — and Wooden finally called time out."

The Bears eventually won, 73-68, to start the long Cal streak, but Newell felt satisfied only until he got to his office the following Monday morning.

"My athletic director called me in and told me he'd just been given hell," Newell said. "I asked why and he said one of our radio sponsors was hot because he couldn't get in the allotted number of commercials. I do know one thing. It was the quickest game in the history of basketball. But, you see, what Wooden and I were both trying to do was communicate to our players what we believed ourselves."

Newell was one of the most nervous coaches in his sport. He gnawed a wet towel throughout every game. He lived off coffee and cigarettes. While leading USF to the NIT championship in 1949 he lost fourteen pounds.

Most people think of Wooden as very composed, in comparison. Newell says he wasn't, for a long time: "He is much more restrained now but he used to be given to emotional outbursts on the bench, and his teams used to question officials and rag them too. Funny . . . the last half dozen years his teams have comported themselves better than any teams. I think it was UCLA's lack of success in NCAA competition in the early years. When he finally won, Wooden relaxed a little. The Bruins had always been able to reach one step but not go beyond it. Winning that first one, the tension was taken away. Wooden was more confident."

For several years, Wooden didn't seem to fit the style of West Coast basketball either, Newell intimates. "When he first came west," says Pete, "he was provincial, a little aloof, probably not comfortable in a strange area. The coaches he was closest to were Midwesterners, the Branch McCrackens, the Tony Hinkles. He may have considered himself an outsider and some Western coaches did too. He's never involved himself much in national or international basketball matters. And I wouldn't call him a prude but he never spent much time with the boys at NCAA conventions and places like that. At national meetings, his wife was almost always there with him. ("He's the sort of guy," another rival coach once said, "who goes to the convention with his wife and they sit in the lobby and watch *you* come in drunk.")

"What Wooden felt was important," Newell said, "he did; what he felt wasn't important to him, he stayed away from."

Newell has formed a deep respect for Wooden's coaching ability in recent years: "He's operated with different types of teams under different conditions in different times and he's maintained the same winning feeling. He uses his strengths exceptionally well, and he camouflages or minimizes his weaknesses.

"A lot of teams get to the point where they accept winning — because they're *supposed* to win. Wooden has been able to adjust so his players haven't done that. And that's the sign of a great coach. The hardest thing is to give each team a new objective, to keep it going, especially when you win that much.

"You have to have concern for your players as people, rather than just as guys who can win for you. But you can't win consistently unless you have their respect. If you get too close to your players you can lose their respect. Wooden has adjusted to styles and modes of life but he hasn't capitulated."

Newell sees Wooden's accomplishments as a victory for maturity. "I'm very glad to see his success come in the later years of his life. If you're a doctor or a lawyer you're supposed to get better as you get older. The old theory was if you were a fifty-year-old basketball coach you were ready for the graveyard. Wooden has defeated that kind of thinking."

It is perhaps ironic that Wooden, an intense rival of Newell's for so long, now expresses for Newell the admiration his nemesis expresses for him. Aside from Marv Harshman of Washington, who Wooden believes gets more out of his material than anyone he's coached against, the man Wooden most often expresses regard for is Pete Newell.

When he talks about the long winning streaks he and Newell had against each other, he is guarded, competitive: "The results are valid, correct, but not really indicative. There were games in our streak that we shouldn't have won, games in their streak we shouldn't have lost. Probably the ratio should be more balanced. An awful lot of those games were toss-ups."

But then he adds, sincerely, it seems: "I have a lot of respect for Pete. I liked his style, his discipline. And I felt that I learned from him, too. While my teams didn't play like his, I believe he helped me become a better coach."

The news arched a lot of eyebrows outside the UCLA family: Jerry Norman was resigning as John Wooden's top lieutenant shortly after the 1968 season, Lew Alcindor's junior year, to become a stockbroker. To insiders, the move was inevitable. During his final campaign, Norman was spending less time on the recruiting trail than he was at the Beverly Hills brokerage firm where he worked part-time.

Inevitably, too, rumors quickly circulated as to why a bright, energetic, thirty-eight-year-old coach who had been offered several head coaching jobs at other major universities would leave the profession altogether. One theory was that Norman had tired of waiting for that faraway "someday" when John Wooden would hang up his coaching whistle. Another was that he was making far more money selling stocks than selling UCLA to 6-foot-8 All-Universe forwards from Anywhere, U.S.A. Others had to do with family reasons and another, unfounded, surfaced across town at USC that Norman had been quietly asked to resign in exchange for leniency from the NCAA toward UCLA in the wake of a recruiting investigation.

But Norman said, in effect, that the thrill was gone. "We had won four national championships in five years," he recalled, "and when you're on top that much in sports, there's not much else left. There's not the same challenge anymore; I needed a challenge."

And a change. Norman said he wished to remain home more often with his wife, June, and children.

He sipped a beer over lunch one day in a hotel restaurant not far from his seventeenth-floor office in a plush suite leased by the brokerage firm for which he now works in Century City, just a few miles away from Westwood.

It was worlds apart from the front-row bench at Pauley Pavilion, where he sat alongside John Wooden and helped engineer a dynasty, fanatically exhorting players, haranguing officials, and leading the planet in technical fouls.

Even as a star forward for UCLA in the early 1950s, Norman elicited such adjectives as "hothead" and "spirited" and "fireball." He was remembered as one of the few players just over six feet who could stuff the ball in pregame warm-ups and, by Wooden, as a "profane youngster" who in later years as an assistant coach "never used one word of profanity."

But the Norman temper exploded often in his playing days

and it incurred the wrath of Wooden, who briefly suspended him and would sometimes sit him on the bench. An early UCLA watcher remembers an incident in which Norman protested an official's call by angrily slamming the ball to the floor so hard it nearly vanished into the ceiling. "Wooden jerked him out of there in a hurry," he said, "so fast, in fact, that Norman was practically on the bench before the ball came down."

The officials will never forget Jerry Norman, the assistant coach, either. "Some of those assistants were really terrible — especially that Jerry Norman," said Al Lightner, a long-time Pacific Coast official. "He was something else. Used to really raise hell." And a UCLA fan remembers, "Where could you find a more honest, nice-looking guy than Jerry Norman? But, gosh, he'd kill you when he got upset, eat you alive!"

A teammate, Eddie Sheldrake, says Norman — with whom he used to publish game programs in the early years — was "such a great factor" in UCLA's success. "He and I sold tickets for the first varsity-freshman game and the profits went to send Jerry out recruiting during Easter vacation," he said. "Few know how he helped get all those players. When Jerry started recruiting that way, things became organized. I grew up with Jerry and, to tell the truth, I was dumfounded with his ability to follow things through the way he did. Coach Wooden didn't always agree with him, but he was able to listen, to give him the rein he needed."

The players who were recruited and tutored by Norman listened to him too. To a man, they hold him in high esteem even to this day, an approachable, likable man who heard their problems and commanded by suggestion.

Jerry Norman appears almost as youthful today as he did then, save a crop of hair that is slightly grayer and thinner. The easy grin remains. So does his conservative, narrow-lapeled clothing.

He reminisced about the man he played and worked for,

the man he convinced to deploy a gimmick defense — a box-and-one — that shut off Elvin Hayes in the Great Rematch with Houston, the man he called then, and does today, "the coach."

"He hasn't changed much from a coaching standpoint," Norman said. "The coach always felt you had to be sound fundamentally. And we were. He also was very good at handling players, giving them the opportunity to show what they can do. Also, he exercised good judgment on who can play certain positions and who can't. But it's hard to term him an imaginative coach."

He talked about John Wooden's receptiveness — or lack of it — to change: "We had differences of opinion, yes, but they were mostly on minor points, such as changing a player to a new position. The coach will listen. He's definitely that type of person. And two things will usually happen: You might convince him. Or he thinks you're right, but he won't change, anyway."

Off the court, Norman says Wooden has changed just enough to accommodate new ideas, new mores, new thinking of players more inclined to challenge authority than they were in the 1950s and early 1960s.

"He's particularly changed in the last five or six years," he said. "Really, you couldn't survive in coaching today if you didn't change some. It's getting so that the athlete doesn't need the coach as much as we need him. Also, as you get older, you think differently — and that's another way the coach has changed."

As for the observation that Wooden is a far superior "practice coach" than a "game coach," Norman is ambivalent. "He does a good job of substituting," he said, "but he tends to believe that you play as you practice. That's why he emphasized practice so much — and that's where we differed somewhat. Of course, you play as you practice, but if you're down by fifteen or twenty points, that's when you may have to adjust and use some strategy."

John Wooden has, of course, adjusted through the years. He bought many of Norman's theories and will be the first to tell anyone that one of his strengths has been that he's surrounded himself with good assistants, coaches who are not yes men.

Still another ingredient has been recruiting, which Norman today calls "ludicrous" but also a major reason why UCLA wins championships year after year.

When Norman joined the staff at UCLA, he was shocked to learn the recruiting budget was "only $150." He convinced Wooden and other Bruin officials that more money and man-hours needed to be expended in romancing top high school prospects.

"You'll note," he said, "that there were an awful lot of years when UCLA didn't win in the NCAA and got knocked out in the first round. When we finally won, the big reason was: Players. I don't care who's coaching, you've got to have the right players. Oh, you might upset somebody every now and then with ordinary players. But you can't win consistently without good players."

Sheer numbers corroborate Norman's theory. Before UCLA ever won a national title, the only Bruin player to succeed professionally was Willie Naulls. At the moment, no fewer than nine Wooden pupils — all from NCAA championship teams — are on pro rosters: Lew Alcindor, Lucius Allen, Sidney Wicks, Curtis Rowe, Steve Patterson, Gail Goodrich, Walt Hazzard, Keith Erickson, and Henry Bibby.

UCLA, says Norman, has emphasized *selective* recruiting — for needs rather than availability. "We made an effort to determine who was *really* interested in playing for us," he said. "If he was a kid who just wanted a free ride to the West Coast, or to enjoy the weather in L.A., we didn't go for him. You end up making a lot of mistakes that way."

Another factor, he said, was telling recruits they would not necessarily be starters at UCLA, but would be given the chance to become one. "That's one of the coach's strengths, I feel," said Norman. "He has, for the most part, been able to get the player to feel he's had the opportunity to do what he'd wanted to do — be a starter. I feel most of our players have thought they had a fair chance. Naturally, there are a few exceptions where guys complain they didn't get a chance.

"They might say something like, 'One reason I never made it at UCLA was because I didn't get to play with the better guys. Anybody who plays with Alcindor is going to look better out there.' But most of them have been given a fair opportunity — maybe not in games, but certainly in practice."

The chief criterion in UCLA's recruiting, Norman said, has been a long-time Wooden staple: quickness. "He's got to be a highly skilled athlete, of course, but he also has to have quick hands and feet. He has to have these things in high school. A college coach can't really teach him these things. He might be able to make a few refinements along the way. We'd rather have him quick to start with — and then let him develop into a good shooter later."

At times, when he talks about UCLA, Jerry Norman still uses the word "we." But an era is gone with his boyishness.

It is no surprise that UCLA has had the nation's most successful collegiate athletic program over the last decade (nineteen NCAA titles). J. D. Morgan, at fifty-four the prototype of the modern, major college athletic director — a man who knows business at least as well as he knows sports — has willed it, *commanded* it, that way.

He has engineered a rise in the UCLA athletic budget from $1.3 million to $3 million, one of the half-dozen largest budgets in collegiate sports. His motives and some of his methods have been questioned. His competence has not.

Morgan speaks in sonorous, pontifical tones, even when he whispers in your ear. And he speaks a lot, on almost any subject, sometimes using a bear hug to emphasize his points.

"I have the feeling every time he talks to me," says a UCLA alumnus, "that he's about to break into a speech."

He has been called pompous and egotistical. "I don't want to appear that," he says. "But I *do* have confidence in my own ability."

"A forceful, high-voltage type," tennis star Arthur Ashe says of Morgan in his autobiography, *Advantage Ashe*: "J.D.'s will to win was contagious. He kept reminding me that I had to sacrifice to be a champ and I knew he was right. So we got along O.K. even though he had warned me in advance, 'I'm not the easiest guy in the world to get along with.' He was that way with all his players. They all felt his wrath. I didn't mind but some couldn't stand it.

"He sat down with me one day and we had a heart-to-heart talk, with his heart doing most of the talking. We talked about goals — not just in tennis, but in life. 'Self-discipline is the key to success in any line,' he told me. 'Why not start organizing your time, making it count?' I think part of his personality comes from having had a hard climb himself. He found out that the best way to be sure of getting anywhere is to work and sacrifice."

He also prefers to win arguments. Ashe again: "One time a group of us were discussing snakes when somebody asked what the fastest snake was. Allen Fox, who'd studied snakes, said it had to be the sidewinder, which travels five or six miles an hour, faster than a man can walk. J.D. snapped, 'You're wrong, Fox! The fastest snake is the Australian hoop snake that bites itself by the tail and rolls downhill at forty miles an hour.' Was he kidding? You look it up."

Oklahoma born and reared (he played football, basketball, baseball, and tennis at Cordell [Oklahoma] High School), Morgan is a stout man with a large nose and short, graying brown hair combed up in front. He was a four-year tennis letterman at UCLA and later coached the team to seven national titles.

Not only did he free Wooden from many administrative duties when he took over in 1963, he has continued to take far more than an ordinary athletic director's part in the basketball program. Wooden wins the championships, Morgan runs the show. The Boss — without question.

He knows that basketball is the cornerstone of his eighteensport empire. It grosses more than half a million dollars annually — more than football at many major colleges. When he became athletic director, the ratio of dollars spent on football at UCLA to other sports was seven to one. Now it's three to one. Football is budgeted at about a million dollars a year, basketball at $350,000.

Morgan is one of a handful of the most powerful men in college sports. He's a member of the prestigious NCAA basketball tournament committee. He helped get the NCAA tournament a lucrative, lasting commitment from NBC. He helped get Television Sports network (TVS) off the ground. UCLA made three appearances on national TV in the 1971-1972 season and its game against USC drew the highest sum ever paid for a regular-season game.

Morgan makes almost every road trip with the basketball Bruins, and, until the league's coaches balked, he sat on the bench next to Wooden for several seasons and was characteristically unhesitant to express his opinions from that vantage point.

A few months ago, long after most employees had gone home, a UCLA basketball assistant coach walked into Morgan's office to talk about recruiting a prospect in Texas. Wooden and his staff had found the youngster, but the decision on whether to offer him a scholarship obviously would rest with Morgan. And the decision probably would be based on the premise stated by a sign on J.D.'s desk: WINNING SOLVES ALL PROBLEMS.

Publicly, Wooden and Morgan praise each other. Says Wooden: "J.D.'s taking away the other responsibilities I had in nineteen sixty-three probably helped, but his presence — just showing his interest and talking with the players in the dressing rooms and so on — that helped too. Also, he is more of a fighter than Wilbur Johns was. For instance, we fly first-class on long road trips. That helps our program. The word gets out. Other players find out.

"We have had no clashes. Never! J. D. Morgan is a tremendous director of athletics. I can't feature a better athletic director. He knows the players on our team and on all the other teams at UCLA too. How many athletic directors can you say that about? I'll bet he knows more first and last names of athletes at our school than any athletic director in the country. He runs the department for a lot of people — the way it should be run. I wouldn't hesitate to go to him if I thought we needed anything."

Says Morgan: "I'm very close to John. He's the greatest fundamental basketball coach ever in the game. He stresses fundamentals over and over and over . . . just about as strongly with his seniors as he does with his sophomores. Couple that with his ability to evaluate the strengths and weaknesses of his players — to exploit the strengths and defend the weaknesses — to teach his players where they should be under all conditions at all times on the court.

"He molded Lew Alcindor, for example, exploited his personality and his ability as a team player. And he took advantage of the situation Lew created on the court — while still letting the other players get their fair share of points and attention. His balance of offense and defense is superior to anything I've ever seen.

"Through all of this, he develops the ultimate of confidence in his players. They think he's the greatest, so, consequently, they should be the best too."

He is asked whether Wooden relates well to his players — something many recent Bruins question.

"I don't know if he relates to his players as well as some other coaches," says Morgan, "but his teams have performed magnificently for him over the years. And the older they get, the more appreciative they are and the more they praise him. The days of iron-handed discipline are gone. If you still tried to operate like that, there is no way you could have success in college athletics.

"Wooden has exerted a great balance of hard discipline — on and off the court. He has always been careful his players get the proper rest, diet, and such. But he's adjusted to the modern athlete too. He doesn't make them run one hundred laps after a mistake. He takes time to explain why they should do certain things — to grow, expand, and continue to produce great teams, great results, and great people.

"Maybe some younger coaches are more the buddy type. If that's relating, then John doesn't relate. He's not that type — never has been. I've heard the talk about double standards on his teams, for star players and reserves. There are always going to be double standards in athletics. It can't be helped. When I coached the tennis team, there were triple and quadruple standards."

The words of mutual admiration notwithstanding, there are those who say that Morgan and Wooden are not strong fans of each other — that Morgan got along better with ex-UCLA football coach Tommy Prothro, that Wooden has not been happy with the pressures put on him by Morgan, despite the unparalleled success of the program.

"In effect, the coach has been working for a tyrant," said one former assistant. "Winning has just become too important."

When the Pacific 8 coaches asked that Morgan be banished from the bench, he reportedly was far more upset about it than Wooden. And when UCLA was trailing Cal State Long Beach in the 1970-1971 play-off game it very nearly lost, observers said Morgan was yelling at Assistant Coach Denny Crum — not Wooden — from the stands a short distance away, exhorting Crum to make the substitutions.

Then, too, there was a shocking emotional outburst by

Wooden at a luncheon of the Southern California basketball writers early in the 1971-1972 season.

Ostensibly, it was an attack against a Los Angeles *Herald-Examiner* writer who had poked fun at UCLA in print for scheduling cream-puff nonconference opponents. The writer, Doug Krikorian, had said that The Citadel, which the Bruins had thrashed by fifty-six points in the season opener, would have been "short-enders" against a local high school team.

After praising the late Grantland Rice as a sportswriter he always admired as "a positive influence on athletics," Wooden eyed Krikorian and angrily accused him of asking "belittling and demeaning" questions of UCLA players about the caliber of The Citadel team. The coach was upset by quotes attributed to guard Greg Lee, who described The Citadel as "like a real good junior college team."

"It's belittling and demeaning," he snapped at Krikorian, "the way you try to pull things out of our players, things they don't mean to say. I've never done this before, but I had to say these things now. I've only got a few more years left, and I won't always be around."

The truth was that Lee, a bright, scholarly sophomore, was *not* coerced by any writer. He merely gave a candid answer to the question: "What did you think of The Citadel?"

Some observers — reading between the lines of Wooden's tirade — interpreted it as a subtle slap at the Boss, who usually accompanies Wooden to the weekly luncheons but was out of town.

"I suppose," said Wooden, "I should apologize for J. D. Morgan, who is not here, for okaying our schedules."

Later, his voice dripping bitter sarcasm, the coach added, "I guess I should apologize for our record over the past eight years. Nothing seems to please people anymore." When the meeting had adjourned, Wooden elaborated: "Yes, I was upset. There are a lot of fellows around who are about to die because we've been doing so well. I think we have a tremendously entertaining product, but they've been demeaning and belittling us. I don't like it at all. I don't have any respect for it."

Morgan's name surfaced again when Wooden was discussing UCLA's next opponent, saying Iowa State would "be ideal for us to play at this time." He paused and deadpanned: "You might not believe that . . . but you can ask Mr. Morgan why they're on our schedule."

Actually, UCLA had not always ducked formidable opposition before the Pacific 8 season. The Bruins played nationally ranked Purdue, Notre Dame, and Ohio State on the road during the Lew Alcindor years. But economics dictates playing as many games in Pauley Pavilion as possible — a full house is virtually automatic, no matter who the opponent — and J. D. Morgan deals in dollars and sense. Thus, it's no secret that Wooden had felt uncomfortable alibiing for UCLA's preconference schedule and not being able to blame Morgan openly.

In fact, one insider said Wooden carefully plotted his remarks before lashing out at the writers' luncheon.

And there is a footnote to the Wooden outburst. Upon returning to UCLA later that afternoon, he called his players together and told them: "You're going to read a story in the paper tomorrow that I'm very sorry for." A week later, he apologized to the writers, saying: "My emotions transcended reason, and I'm sorry."

Asked some time later about scheduling differences with Morgan, Wooden said: "I like to play one tough road game before the conference season. I prefer to play as tough a competition as we can get. I see J.D.'s right — he's got a budget to meet. If I ever put my foot down, I'm sure he'd say O.K., but I don't think it's right for me to do that."

Wooden said Morgan came to him before the historic UCLA-Houston game at the Astrodome in 1968 "and asked if I'd be interested in playing there. I said no because I thought it would be nothing but a spectacle. But J.D. pointed out to me what a great thing it would be for intercollegiate basketball, that we could possibly have the largest indoor crowd ever to see a game, and that there might be more people watching on TV than for any other sport. He also explained how the revenue would help finance our other sports and make more money for athletic scholarships. That convinced me that it would be all right. But I'm sure that if I had still said no to the game that it would have been all right with J.D.

"A year or so later, when he asked me if I were interested in playing Houston again in the Dome — since we owed them a return game — I said yes. I knew it might mean another hundred thousand dollars. But he said no, that we could be accused of exploitation this time. That shows money doesn't rule. And that surprises many people, I know."

But what of the open trouble spots, the incidents and the critics that have begun to surface publicly only in the last few seasons? What of the remark that "In the last five or six years, John Wooden looks as if he has aged twenty"?

It all started one November evening in 1966 — a few nights before the opening tip-off of the Lew Alcindor era. The news broke while members of the press and their wives and dates were guests of UCLA coaches and officials at a dinner in the Cave des Roys, a swank private club on Restaurant Row.

J. D. Morgan introduced his coaches and their wives, then sadly announced the news that had been telephoned to him during the cocktail hour. A UCLA player had been arrested at a Sears Roebuck and Company store in the late afternoon. His name: Mike Lynn, a 6-foot-7 forward, a standout on the Bruins' previous two teams and now the only senior starter inasmuch as Edgar Lacey was sitting out the season to recover from knee surgery.

A stunned silence swept the room. "None of you will need to telephone your offices," Morgan told the guests. "We've already notified the wire services. Your papers already have the story."

The charges: Lynn and his roommate, Larry McCollister, a former UCLA freshman teammate, had been arrested on suspicion of forging a credit card that had been reported lost the previous month. They were taken into custody by a store detective when they tried to purchase phonograph records at the West Los Angeles store. Lynn told authorities he had found the card — which belonged to a West Covina woman — in a purse near an off ramp of the San Bernardino Freeway.

Lynn and McCollister were placed on probation for two years and fined $300 by Judge Vernon P. Spencer. And J. D. Morgan announced that Lynn would not be reinstated as a player for the 1966-1967 season.

Beneath the public pronouncements the Mike Lynn case created internal combustion at UCLA. In a sense, it represented a crucial turning point for the image-conscious athletic department — described, ironically enough, by J. D. Morgan a few months before as "the last bastion of student discipline on this campus."

Until Lynn, the only major disciplinary problem involving a Bruin basketball player had occurred in the spring of 1961, when star sophomore Ron Lawson was dismissed for not having reported a bribe offer to fix a game. But now, the punishment in the Mike Lynn caper would be a sort of precedent, a yardstick against which any similar incident in the future would be measured.

Lynn rejoined the varsity the following season — after diligently practicing with the Bruins during his exile in 1966-1967 to get them ready for the NCAA play-offs. At the same time, Lynn was often a source of anguish for Wooden on and off the court. The coach frequently chewed him out for loafing. And Lynn's free-spirited life-style — the beach apartment, the long hair, the moccasins he wore "just to be different" — did not endear itself to Wooden either.

If the Lynn experience had stirred uneasiness within the UCLA family, it also gnawed at the disciplinarian, John Wooden. While many partisans were delighted that Lynn's skills would strengthen an already strong varsity, the coach had to answer critics who accused him of sacrificing his principles for allowing Lynn to return. Wooden's response: "I'm doing what I believe is right for the boy."

At the 1968 basketball awards dinner, where seniors traditionally give farewell speeches, Mike Lynn shamelessly talked about still having to visit his probation officer and how the discipline had made Mike Lynn a better person. As Lynn sat down, Wooden stepped to the microphone and told the 800-odd guests in the Student Union Grand Ballroom: "Mike, there's not a person in this room who hasn't made a mistake at one time or another. At least, you have admitted yours — and have done something about it."

Tuesday morning, May 23, 1967: The day dawned no differently from any other for sophomore Lucius Allen, the superlative guard on UCLA's newly crowned national championship team.

Except for one thing: Allen walked out the door of his off-campus bungalow — where he lived with a family in Los Angeles' black neighborhood near Western Avenue — to leave for school, only to discover his car missing.

He promptly called police to report a theft.

"What was that address?" asked an officer on the telephone.

"Two-six-two-seven South Hobart Boulevard," Allen answered.

"Hold on," said the officer. A long pause. And then: "Wait right there, Mr. Allen. We'll send somebody over right away."

Within an hour, there was a knock on the door. Los Angeles Police Department officers had arrived to inform Allen that his car had been impounded overnight — and that he was not going to school, but to jail!

Lucius Allen was under arrest. The charge: suspicion of possession of marijuana. More anxious moments — and an intriguing dilemma — for John Wooden and UCLA.

Officers said they noticed the car, registered to Allen, parked on the street in front of the house and said it bore no license plates. Upon making a routine investigation, they reported finding three marijuana cigarettes in a plastic bag, plus a substance that appeared to be marijuana in the pocket of a coat draped on the rear seat.

Allen spent the day in Central Jail. When he was released in the late afternoon on $1000 bail — and ordered to appear in two days for arraignment — he emerged from his cell, unshaven, puffy-eyed, and hair crazily festooned with tufts of white wool from having slept on a blanket.

Meanwhile, Wooden's phone was ringing. He told reporters that Allen's arrest in no way affects his status on the team "until we find out what the whole story is. If this happened during the season, then I'd take immediate action. But because we're in the off season, we'll have to wait."

On June 23, the charges were dropped because of insufficient evidence. A black woman judge, Vaino Spencer, ruled that Allen was improperly advised of his constitutional rights regarding his access to an attorney. The arresting officer, the judge said, had told Allen that he could request an attorney, when, in reality, he should have said, "You have the right to request an attorney."

At UCLA, however, Allen's case wasn't closed. Officials were still grappling over whether to let Allen play basketball next season. Allen was granted permission to play in 1967-1968 — but only after considerable debate.

Again, UCLA was confronted with a turning point, a crucial decision. Marijuana was a reality of the Now Generation. Campuses were inundated with it. Allen's arrest, inevitably, triggered rumors about teammates "blowing pot" at parties. Demands to legalize marijuana already had surfaced throughout California. And John Wooden said he had "done a lot of reading about its pros and cons" and admitted privately he questioned how harmful it really was.

Still, the major question in Westwood was whether Lucius Allen should — or should not — play for UCLA. A source close to the team said the decision was weighed against the backdrop of the Mike Lynn case only six months earlier — and against racial overtones.

"The difference," he said, "was that Lynn was *convicted*. Lucius was not. I'll tell you this: if Lucius had been told he couldn't play, UCLA would have had an all-white team. And maybe some or all of the whites would have quit in sympathy too."

For UCLA, however, an image was besmudged. Two star basketball players — one white, one black — had appeared on police blotters within six months of each other. People wondered if the moralist, John Wooden, had lost control. J. D. Morgan insisted that his athletic department was blameless and unfairly criticized for the two incidents. "The one thing you can't judge about a prospective athlete," he said, "is his character."

Lew Alcindor's picture never appeared in post offices. He never needed bail money. He was never subpoenaed by the student conduct committee. In truth, his endeavors at mischief were pretty much confined to his elbowing of reserve Bill Seibert in the teeth at practice, or to the time (a few weeks after his final season) when he smashed the jaw of Dennis Grey, a reserve center for the old Los Angeles Stars, with a well-directed fist during a pick-up game, or to tales of his harmless harassment of waitresses at an off-campus coffee shop.

Indeed, the Alcindor magic produced far more assets than liabilities for UCLA. Eighty-eight wins, two losses, three NCAA titles. And millions of spectators nationwide. But for all the artistic and financial windfall, Big Lew's very presence also created a nagging sore spot beneath the surface — sort of a "four-year itch" that cropped up in so many places you didn't always know where to scratch.

It formed during Lew's freshman year with the no-interview policy, which caused an inflammation among the Los Angeles press corps. It festered when rival schools cried "Foul!" by complaining that his living quarters, his 1958 Mercedes Benz, and his summer job at playground clinics simply *had* to be illegal recruiting enticements (a top-secret NCAA investigation proved nothing improper). It quickly spread to the headlines with his pronouncements on behalf of black power, his allegations of racism at UCLA, his tacit approval of the Olympic boycott, his discontent with life in California, and rumors that he might transfer elsewhere.

Add to these the Alcindor personality, which was as mysterious as it was complex, his occasional refusal to face the flag during the playing of the National Anthem, the accompanying relaxation of Wooden's rules on such items as curfew and dress, and what the coach ruefully described as pressure "to keep from losing, instead of trying to win."

It was a high irony of the Alcindor chapter that most problems arose off — not on — the court. Nobody exhibited more unselfishness than Big Lew as a "team" player, especially considering that he had the size and skills to score fifty points a game. And for someone who was elbowed, jostled, and pummeled by rival centers, he generally comported himself admirably and uncomplainingly.

But the torment lingered just the same. While rival coaches privately chortled and snickered — perhaps to salve their wounds from all those Alcindor hooks and dunks and thirty-five-point losses — UCLA nervously held its breath. "The athletic department," said one observer, "treated him as if he were ticking."

And he was. Team disciplinary rules, for instance, were drastically relaxed, and Alcindor was accommodated more favorably than any Bruin athlete before him. All of which was not necessarily in accord with Wooden's wishes. "I really don't think Wooden would have compromised quite so much," said a source close to the school, "if it hadn't been for J. D. Morgan and Bob Fischer [assistant athletic director] telling him he had to. They realized Lew was no ordinary athlete and that they were dealing with someone who was highly intelligent. So it became very convenient for Wooden to go along with them. The problem was removed from his hands. It makes things a lot easier if you can say your boss told you to do it, rather than say it was your idea."

Barely after Alcindor arrived from New York City, UCLA officials imposed a no-interview ban on the press, curiously adding that the restriction always had been policy with regard to *all* freshman athletes. To this day, there are conflicting versions of whose idea it was. UCLA, assuming correctly that Big Lew would be inundated with requests for interviews, says it left the matter squarely up to him and that Lew said no. Not so, says Alcindor. In his autobiographical series in *Sports Illustrated*, he said: "The press interpreted this as my idea — it wasn't — and after a while they tried to make a career out of sticking it to me." In ensuing years, the restriction was tempered. Requests for interviews went to the UCLA Athletic News Bureau, which relayed them to Alcindor. He granted them selectively, although turning down most because of demands on his time.

There were anxious moments in Westwood, too, when Lew and Lucius Allen were rumored to be considering transfers to Michigan and Kansas respectively. They were disenchanted with life at UCLA and, as Lew called them, "all those cracker kids." Again, in his autobiography, he wrote, "I remembered how nice it [Michigan] had looked when I'd visited there in my senior year of prep school, with all those trees at Ann Arbor and a representative enrollment of black and white kids. I figured I would be able to relax and enjoy myself socially for the first time in my college career. So it was decided. Lucius and I would spend our junior years elsewhere."

Still another reason for their unhappiness — not publicized — was possible broken recruiting promises. Lew and Lucius went to a friend, ex-Bruin and pro star Willie Naulls, who had briefly assisted the basketball coaching staff and had spent long evenings with the two sophomores, discussing life and race and society. Naulls in turn introduced them to a wealthy UCLA alumnus who had helped him get started in business.

Enter the "man in the shadows," Sam Gilbert. After talking with Gilbert, Alcindor and Allen decided to stay. Exactly what was said, or whether Gilbert actually talked them into remaining, isn't known. But among the reasons they didn't leave was the inconvenience of the one-year "sit-out" rule for transfers and the very real convenience of a UCLA basketball education when it came to negotiating for professional dollars. The result: UCLA's basketball empire was rescued, thanks partly to Gilbert. And John Wooden's championship team returned intact for the 1967-1968 campaign.

He is the invisible yet visible man, although he was mostly invisible in John Wooden's first two decades at UCLA.

Sam Gilbert's involvement with Bruin athletes was only casual then compared with what it would be later. Who is Sam Gilbert? Well, he's a baldish sixty-year-old father of three, a UCLA alumnus who sits near the basketball team's bench every home game (and sometimes on the road), wearing his "rooter's cap" — a Bavarian fedora with a pheasant-feather band. He also is an avowed atheist and a millionaire Jewish contractor who calls himself a "fat little matzo ball."

It wasn't until NCAA trophies and Lew Alcindor when Gilbert became more than peripherally involved. His contacts then, however, were pretty much confined to Alcindor, for whom he became sort of a paterfamilias and confidant away from home, and partly to Allen. When both players agreed to remain at UCLA, Gilbert gladdened more than a few hearts in the school's athletic hierarchy. His entrée into the basketball program was assured. The question was: to what extent? The answer would come later.

Remember the name, Sam Gilbert, the "man in the shadows." He is the last — and most oblique — of the four strong forces and counterforces in the John Wooden dynasty.

The telephone rang early one January evening in 1968 at the Los Angeles *Times*. Someone called to report a missing person at UCLA's basketball workout. His name: Edgar Lacey. "He hasn't been to practice for two days," the caller said. "Nobody knows where he is or how to get in touch with him."

Of course, that wasn't really so unusual with Lacey. True, he practiced regularly, dependably, diligently. On game days, he arose before wake-up calls at the hotel and engaged in pre-breakfast jogging to increase his stamina. But when the Bruins were neither playing nor practicing, Lacey often abandoned his teammates and coaches — and disappeared. Which is why they nicknamed him "The Phantom."

On this Wednesday night, however, Lacey's disappearance seemed to be less than a mystery. Edgar Lacey, a placid, slender young man with a soulful face and chocolate skin, a star 6-foot-6 senior forward who had turned down a contract offer by the Boston Celtics to stay at UCLA, was obviously perturbed. Only the weekend before, he had played with little distinction — and spent the whole second half on the bench — in the historic loss to Houston in the Astrodome. And only the day before, he had read remarks in the paper by John Wooden, who had been asked at a writers' luncheon why Lacey never went back into the game: "Edgar got his feelings hurt early. He wasn't effective in our high post and he wasn't effective guarding his man [Elvin Hayes]. He didn't especially feel like coming back in anyway, so I didn't feel it was right to use him."

Meanwhile, a reporter went to Lacey's parents' home that evening in South Central Los Angeles. The only occupant was his father, a small man wearing coveralls, his uniform at a construction job. He not only confirmed that Edgar was upset, but that he also was thinking of quitting the team.

"I told him I didn't think that would be a good idea," he said, "but he's really warm about this whole thing." He also told of Edgar's having read Wooden's quotes about him in the *Times* and disgustedly flinging the newspaper to the floor. "He told me," said the elder Lacey, "that he was bouncing up and down on the bench and he told the coach he wanted to play."

A half-hour later, a VW with two young men in the front seat stopped in front of the small house. Edgar Lacey emerged from the passenger's side. He was asked about his feelings. "I'm not talking — I have no statements," he said, refusing to confirm or deny that he was quitting. Then, he said softly: "It's his move."

A wedge obviously had been driven between Wooden and Lacey. Reached later that evening at his home, the coach said Lacey would not accompany the Bruins on their New York trip the next morning for games with Holy Cross and Boston College, but that he had not been dismissed from the squad. "Had he joined us today, he would have made the trip," said Wooden, "but he cannot go with us now. I think it would be ill advised to dismiss him now because he is hurt enough already. He has to sit down and think it all over. I can understand how he feels. I hope he can think it over and come back." Asked whether he had discussed the matter with Lacey, the coach said, "No, I haven't."

At a news conference in New York the next day, John Wooden said he would not "chase" Lacey down and described him as a "fine boy who is also very quiet and sensitive. I would like to talk to him, but only after he thinks it all over ... He's been hurt and from what I've heard, he was kidded by a few people about his performance against Houston. I think he would be making a mistake to close out his college career this way. I don't think it will help him any."

Meanwhile, 3000 miles away, UCLA's second-best re-bounder and third leading scorer was smoldering. Edgar Lacey, a refugee from the playgrounds of Watts, wondered what he should do. Quit? Come back? Make peace? Or war? He sought advice from friends. A strong UCLA booster pleaded with him to stay.

By Sunday afternoon, two Bruin victories later, Lacey's mind was made up. He telephoned the reporter who had visited him four nights before. In embittered tones, and with words he spoke deliberately, Lacey leveled a scathing attack on John Wooden and announced he had quit the team.

He said he had, indeed, talked it over with the coach the previous week — which conflicted with what Wooden had said on the eve of the New York trip. What's more, Lacey said the roots of his discontent grew deeper than the loss to Houston, that they stretched all the way back to his rookie season in 1965. "I've never enjoyed playing for that man," he said coldly.

The Houston game, he said, was only the "last straw" in a string of grievances. "It all started in my sophomore year," he explained, "when he tried to change the mechanics of my shooting . . . And now, I have no one to blame but myself for staying this long. He has sent people by to persuade me to reconsider, but I have nothing to reconsider. I'm glad I'm get-ting out now while I still have some of my pride, my sanity, and my self-esteem left."

He upbraided Wooden for his remark that he did not "feel like coming back in . . . That statement is too foul for words," said Lacey. "With about eight minutes to go in the game, I asked Coach Norman, 'Am I going to go back in the game?' The answer was negative."

He also complained about strategy against Houston. "The real UCLA coaches stood up that night," he said. "Even a numbskull who knows anything about basketball knows that you don't play a high-post offense against the kind of zone that Houston was using. I think a lot of it is because he wanted to play 'Shack' [forward Lynn Shackelford]. He is sacrificing my ability and Mike's [forward Mike Lynn] ability to promote Shack."

He talked about being "misused" in the UCLA offense. "The coach makes me play the high post because I'm a good passer and can get the ball to the big guy [Alcindor]," he said. "I think I'm a better player from the corner, where I can drive and shoot. But ever since I've played for him, he's always discouraged me on my shooting."

The words had an icy, disdainful ring to them now. "I'm sick and tired of being appeased by the coach," he said. "He's on the brink of ruining my confidence, and I think I'm better off getting out now."

John Wooden had to be informed of the news, the first — and most damning — public attack on him by one of his players. He was at home that Sunday afternoon, relaxing and unpacking from the team's transcontinental flight. When asked about his reaction to Lacey's remarks, he said only that his feelings were unchanged. "I'm never going to run a boy down," he said. "He should come back because I think he's making a mistake. I have never said anything but that he's the best forward we have. I wish he'd think it over. Regardless of how he feels about me, I do care about him."

The coach emphasized, too, that he did not want to answer Lacey's specific complaints publicly. Then, he paused and asked his interrogator: "You aren't going to print any of this in the paper, are you?"

"Why, of course," came the reply.

It was explained to the coach that the thrust of Lacey's outburst — coupled with the enormous public interest in him as a sports figure — demanded an airing that readers had a right to know about, just as everyone had a right to know what John Wooden's sentiments were too.

But the coach said he couldn't buy that. He likened what

was, in reality, a reportorial responsibility to the kind of sensationalism that exists among disreputable journalists.

The next day, the wounds were deep and excruciating. They showed on the face of John Wooden when he made his customary remarks before the weekly luncheon of the Southern California basketball writers. He appeared neither resentful nor grief-torn — if anything, baffled and perhaps remorseful.

"I can't help but believe somebody might be putting words into his mouth," Wooden told the writers. "I can't feel that, so suddenly, he would take this point of view."

He disclosed that he had received a letter from "an ex-basketball coach in Ohio" a short while earlier. "He indicated that a copy of the letter had been sent to Edgar too," he added, "and he wrote that I had badly misused Edgar by playing him on the high post . . . He said that any coach should know better than that. Perhaps that's what started Edgar thinking about it, I don't know. I'm not upset over receiving advice. At least, it shows people are interested."

The coach admitted that he may have erred in the manner in which he had commented on Lacey's performance — comments that were untypical of Wooden, who praises players publicly far more than he criticizes them, and that caused much commotion in the UCLA athletic department.

"My remark was correct and I stand behind what I said," he explained, "but oftentimes, you can be correct, but be better off not having said it." He confirmed that Lacey had, indeed, visited him the day the remark was published. "He asked me if what I had said was true," he said, "and I said that essentially it was. So he said, 'Well, I think I'll drop off the team.' And I told him to think it over first before he decided what to do. Apparently he wasn't upset the previous day because he came to practice and we had a fine practice."

Wooden added that he asked guard Mike Warren to talk with Lacey. "Mike is a steadying influence," he said. "He's also a senior and he's been around. But Mike was not able to get in touch with Edgar . . ." He paused a moment, then added: "Maybe I handled it wrongly . . . because he's not with us."

A writer asked whether the Lacey incident bore racial overtones, inasmuch as the University of California team was having black-white problems. "I have no knowledge of it," said Wooden. "I have no indication of a choosing-up of sides."

The room was even quieter when Wooden spoke philosophically. "Last year was difficult — my most trying year in coaching," he said, "and there have been a couple of things happen that I didn't anticipate this year. But everybody has problems. I know that a lot of coaches will say they would like to have the problems I have, but it's not all gravy with this kind of record . . . The only worse thing is when you are losing all the time."

Lacey was not a proficient outside shooter — even though he had said, before the season, "My jump shot is back from the dead." Wooden preferred Shackelford, less agile and mobile, but a deadly shooter, certainly far deadlier than Lacey, for the corner. With rival teams trying to double- and triple-team Big Lew near the basket, Shackelford was devastating from long range. Therefore, Wooden found another place for Lacey, a place where he could shoot from medium range and feed Alcindor.

But Wooden's tactical judgment caused no end of anxiety for Lacey, and it gathered inside him for months until he unleashed the pent-up fury into the headlines. "The guys on the team could sense it," said one player. "Edgar was pressing. That's one reason why he was fouling so much."

But the damage had been done. Feelings were hurt. A coach had been blistered, but his dynasty lived on. And Edgar Lacey drifted into obscurity — to an AAU team called the "Kitchen Fresh Chippers" a month or so later, to the Olympic trials, and to an uneventful year on the bench of the old Los Angeles Stars before quitting to return to school. It was a sorrowful contrast to the promise of earlier winters, to the hopes held for him by his ex-teammate, Lew Alcindor, who had written in his autobiographical series, "I wouldn't be surprised if Edgar Lacey turned out to be *the* Los Angeles Star."

Today, Lacey is reportedly employed by a Los Angeles–area insurance firm after having worked as a teller and in the loan department of a savings-and-loan association. When asked about his feelings on the events of five years ago, he declined to comment. "As far as I'm concerned," he said, "the Edgar Lacey case is closed."

The kid who came from Kansas City, Kansas, to become the best three-cushion billiards player on his block in Westwood fidgeted somewhat as he engaged in self-analysis.

Lucius Allen said he had changed. He said he was not the same Lucius Allen who had spent three days in a courtroom the previous summer, successfully clearing his name from a narcotics division blotter. It was the winter of 1968.

"I think I've matured and settled down a lot more this year," he said. "I used to go out to a lot of the clubs last year because it was all a new experience for me. Now, it's not new anymore and I don't go out as often. Perhaps that incident last summer also has helped me to mature."

Another NCAA championship and three months later, however, Allen's name flashed across the headlines again.

The scene: an alley near the corner of La Brea Avenue and West Adams Boulevard in Los Angeles. Two police officers observe a speeding car with five occupants. They stop the car to write a citation, but while checking the vehicle registration they detect "a strong odor of marijuana" inside the car. Result: Lucius Allen and four other persons, including a coed who is now his wife, are arrested and booked for possession of marijuana. It was Thursday night, May 23, 1968 — a year to the day since Allen's previous arrest.

Allen was charged the next day with two counts of possession of marijuana, and that's when it was learned publicly that he had shot his last eighteen-foot corner jumper for UCLA. He had quietly dropped out of school because of academic troubles and had planned to join the National Guard for six months of active duty. And John Wooden said he was "not counting on him." That left UCLA without a second-team All-American guard and Lucius Allen with a shadow cast across his future.

A few months later, he was placed on one-year probation and fined $300 by a judge who suggested that Allen hereafter "set a good example for the youth of the country."

They were tormenting months for Allen. "I was sitting in jail and I figured that I'd thrown away all that I had worked to gain," he said. "Where do you go from there? I didn't know."

Enter the "man in the shadows" again, Sam Gilbert. The man whom Allen had met while thinking of quitting UCLA with Lew Alcindor a year earlier was ready to help. Gilbert contacted a friend, Sam Schulman, owner of the Seattle Super-Sonics, who signed Allen to a personal services contract, whereupon Allen played in obscurity one year with the AAU Kitchen Fresh Chippers in Los Angeles. All the while, his companions at UCLA were basking in the public glare and merrily winning another NCAA crown.

Today, Allen is reunited with Big Lew on the Milwaukee Bucks after having played briefly for Seattle. He talks of returning to school to pursue his degree in sociology, and his words — as he looks back on all that has happened to him — convey a seemingly genuine maturity now, an honest self-evaluation that does, indeed, "set a good example for the youth of the country."

He tells of a life of ups and downs, mostly ups, while at UCLA: "Everything was done for me. When everyone else had to stand in long lines to get their registration package, I just had to sign my name. The athletic department arranged all my classes and I got the courses I wanted . . . I studied hard my first year, and then I got to know the system and college was just a whole lot of fun. And, the winning in basketball made the social life outta sight."

He tells of peer-pressure socially with regard to marijuana and does so with strong insight: "I was in an ultraliberal situation at the time, and the people I associated with all smoked marijuana. I didn't want to be with the people who didn't. We were all doing the same thing, but I had the misfortune of being caught. Still, what I was doing was definitely against the law — regardless of my personal feelings. You have to abide by the law whether you agree with it or not . . . It could have been a lot worse. I think the maximum sentence could have been five years. But the judge felt that I still had the possibility of making it in society and the punishment would do more harm than good."

A trip across the country and back home to Kansas City reinforced that feeling. "I got a chance to see reactions from many people," he said. "It was a maturing process. Although my friends at home were disappointed in me, they still had hope for me. So I had to have hope for myself."

Lucius Allen, who thought he had ruined his life and once wondered whether he should quit basketball and leave the country, looked back once more and remembered his teen-age friends, the ones who were pimps and hustlers and whose lives seemed to accentuate the positive values in his own life.

"I got to see both sides," he said. "I saw those people who say, 'Man, why did you do this and throw your whole life away?' And I saw the Sam Gilberts, who help you when the chips are down."

News item:

DENVER, Oct. 6, 1972 — Kareem Abdul-Jabbar and Lucius Allen of the Milwaukee Bucks were jailed for five hours after being arrested on suspicion of possession of marijuana. Police had stopped their car for a routine traffic check. Abdul-Jabbar, twenty-five, later was cleared, while Allen, twenty-six, was freed on bail and his case remained under investigation.

*

"And as I watched that crowd I thought of how it was to devote your life to something, something crazy like basketball, and become highly skilled in your performance and love the game, only to have it become a business, at that. But ironically it was even worse to be on the outside, and not a part of it, and have to sit on the bench and watch others play."

— From a short story by an ex-Bruin

The evening began like any victory party anywhere — cocktails and a rising level of conversation as they took effect, pomp and ceremony as befitted a team that had won a record fourth straight NCAA title.

It was UCLA custom to have each senior make a speech — a paean to the alma mater, usually, how much the college basketball experience, playing for the Bruins and the master coach, had meant. That's the sort of speech that John Vallely, one of the two graduating seniors, made. It was not the sort of speech that Bill Seibert, a reserve forward, made.

His nickname was "Funky." He had always been a Bruin in the background — playing rarely, friendly with his teammates but not close to most of them.

John Wooden has always had an edict for his players: no swearing. Freshman coach Gary Cunningham carried out the rule and if his players violated it, he'd send them to the showers. As a rookie, Bill picked up a nickname: "Early Showers Seibert."

Then there was the time in the California game at Berkeley the season when a late shooting spree by Vallely had turned a tense contest into an easy UCLA win. With less than a minute to play, Assistant Coach Denny Crum moved earnestly down the bench to Seibert and said, "Get your jacket off, Bill. You're going in!" Seibert answered, "You've *got* to be kidding."

And now it was May and he was standing before 800 people at the Beverly Hilton Hotel, haltingly but effectively taking the UCLA basketball program apart. As he talked, on and on, shock spread around the room. The crowd whispered at first, things such as, "Isn't that terrible?" Then it booed and finally some people began to shout, "Make him sit down!"

But he said what he had to say, and when he finished, his teammates rose in unison and gave him a standing ovation.

Seibert, a psychology major, insisted his speech was delivered not just because "I didn't get much chance to play. I found a defense for that — a defense I regret. It got so it was very hard to care and to work hard." But most of his displeasure, he said, was based on "unequal treatment of starters and reserves" and "lack of communication between players and coaches."

He charged that the Bruin trainers spent more time helping starters than they did reserves and that starters got preferential consideration in other ways. He said he learned more about life in a water fight on a road trip than at any other time at UCLA. The entire team was involved, he said, but when the coaches found out about it they benched the last four players on the team — for two weeks — as an example. The other eight players, according to Seibert, were not disciplined. And then, he said, on a later road trip, some starting players were discovered with girls in their room and — again — no penalty. The coaches, Seibert said, lacked "sensitivity."

"My point about lack of communication," he said later, "was directed mostly toward Coach Wooden. I had hoped it would be received as constructive. I don't believe the lack of communication was a conscious thing on his part and it was my fault too. I didn't continue to go see him and talk to him the way I should have."

Some people came up to him after the speech and praised him for his "honesty and courage." The large majority of the audience was appalled. One man was "shaking with anger" when he approached him, Seibert said, and could barely articulate his feelings. Another threatened to hit him. His own parents, who were at the banquet, were chagrined at the speech. His mother cried.

Later, another ex-Bruin reserve was to say: "The coach isn't above criticism, but Seibert was way out of line. He thought he should have played more but that was bullshit. Who was he gonna play in front of? Wicks and Rowe?"

"A lot of the criticism I got," Seibert said, "is that while people felt I had the right to speak, they thought it was the wrong time and the wrong place. I hated to destroy a lovely evening but to me it was the *only* time and place."

After Seibert's speech, Wooden gave a short, gracious, and conciliatory response. He was sorry Bill felt the way he did, he said, but he respected his right to express himself so openly. Later, Wooden helped get Seibert a teaching-coaching fellowship in Australia, and the news reached the public.

The coach was deeply upset by the speech — much more than the public knew — perhaps more than by any player incident over all the years. He called three reserves — Terry Schofield, Andy Hill, and John Ecker — into his office in the first days after the Seibert remarks and told them, separately, that if they agreed with Seibert's remarks (and were, in effect, co-conspirators) then he wanted them to leave the team. Patterson promptly said if they left, he'd go with them. The team had a meeting at the home of Sam Gilbert, who planned to rent a hotel conference room and call the coaches in to talk with the players.

But UCLA officials heard of it — and a meeting was arranged in the office of Athletic Director J. D. Morgan. The players and coaches sat around the room informally but the atmosphere was supercharged.

"No one knew what to expect," one player said. "The meeting probably lasted forty-five minutes to an hour. It seemed like a week."

It was a time when it was in vogue for players to give coaches "ultimatums" and Wooden had made it clear before the meeting that he'd accept no such arrangement. He reportedly added he would resign if pressured.

One Bruin said, "The whole thing just got out of hand. The

floor was sort of thrown open to debate. Some of the players were defending themselves. But, mostly, we just told the coach we didn't want to challenge him. We just wanted the right to get up and say something if things were going badly. I told him we came to UCLA because we wanted him to coach basketball, not our private lives. He had been trying to divide and harass us. Wooden had always said we were students first and players second. But he never considered what the ramifications of that are — that, as a basketball coach, he can't control our identities."

The meeting was going nowhere. The feelings were tense. Finally Wicks, the star, one of the favored few, spoke up — for all the Bruins. "You shouldn't feel threatened by this," he told Wooden. "We're here as a team. You're the one who taught us to be a team."

The breach wasn't healed but Wicks's words helped. Schofield, Ecker, and Hill stayed on the team. Seibert, however, was not forgotten. Recently, a UCLA official bristled when asked about him.

"He was the twelfth man on a twelve-man team," the official said of Seibert. "He talked about a double standard. Yet, after the championship win in College Park, John Wooden granted his request to stay in Washington, D.C., and visit the historical sites. We had to take out special insurance for him to fly home alone so this was special treatment. A double standard. He never said anything about that in his speech, did he?"

Meanwhile, Seibert remained Down Under. He had departed for Australia bearing a copy of Coach Wooden's basketball textbook — at his mother's request. By late 1972, he was teaching and coaching in New Guinea.

There has been no Bruin basketball banquet since the year Bill Seibert stood up. Coincidence?

"No," said a former assistant coach, "it's no coincidence."

And Seibert?

"I feel I can understand things much better now," he says, "and my feelings have mellowed. I haven't forgiven anything,

although understanding may be a form of forgiving. While I
am criticizing UCLA — because it is what I know — I am at
the same time criticizing a great many others. The point is
UCLA and Wooden are not perfect . . . and have as far to
go as everyone else, as much as image-makers might try to
show otherwise.

"I do have questions as to whether I did the right thing by
giving that speech. But if I were to give another senior speech
today I would still try to convey my feelings and basic points,
but hopefully in a less 'bitterly attacking' way. I could not
give the usual 'thanks, it's been great' speech that I feel so
many other unhappy players have given.

"If I had the whole four years to do over again, I think the
best thing to do would be to leave basketball after my freshman year and save many of us a lot of wasted time, hurt, and
trouble. My time could have been better spent.

"I should say that my being overseas and the tremendous ex-
periences I have had over the last two years are, in part, due
to Coach Wooden, as he recommended me for the position —
in fact, just days after my speech. Whatever his reasons for
doing so, it was certainly a very generous thing to do and for
that I am very grateful . . ."

"As I sat there next to Bill as I had sat next to him during two
years of games and through waterfights and all the other good
and bad times we endured, I knew I could never in public say
what he had said. He had defied a king in his own court because
he needed to be defied. He was a hero."

— From a short story by an ex-Bruin

Color him red, white, and blue.

No, Bill Walton does not speak at Fourth of July picnics, or
campaign for Orange County politicos or throw punches at
American flag burners. Rather, he is UCLA's Red Baron,
White Hope, and Blue-eyed Soul Brother.

When the red-headed kid from suburban San Diego joined

the varsity, he captivated basketball crowds like a Merriwell folk hero. He was brave and spirited and humble. He spoke compassionately in behalf of the poor and oppressed, a feeling rooted in a home where his father worked as a welfare official. He was sincere about subjugating self to team — and his performance showed it.

And he was extremely good. Highly skilled. Intimidating. All-conquering. UCLA fans who were lulled into boredom by Lew Alcindor's methodical efficiency became deliriously ecstatic over Walton's refreshingly good-natured enthusiasm. "Isn't that nice," said a matronly admirer in Pauley Pavilion, "how that boy just grins and shakes his head 'yes' or 'no' when the referee calls a foul on him?" At last, a "Great White Hope" had arrived to make winning fun again, surely more enjoyable than the restless Alcindor years.

But as the season played on, his public image marched to the sound of a different drum. The young man whom John Wooden had praised for being so mature suddenly became an angry voice that reflected quite the contrary.

He cried "Foul!" to officials when he caught elbows during the NCAA tournament, whereupon rival rooting sections crackled with taunts of "Crybaby!" His surliness toward newsmen and autograph seekers in the wake of the championship game astonished Walton watchers who presumed his humility would be showing all over the place. His displeasure with his own performance — and with the fact that UCLA had beaten Florida State by only five points — seemed to indicate that, well, maybe winning isn't very much fun after all.

As if that weren't enough, Walton soon thrust himself into controversy. His refusal to try out for the Olympic team, depriving the Americans of the world's best amateur center, carried echoes of the Alcindor era. Ostensibly, Walton said no because his tender knees probably could not withstand the punishment of nine games in eleven days. But it is not illogical to assume his political and social views weighed heavily too.

He is close to black teammates and frequently speaks out

against racial injustices in America. "I don't blame the blacks for hating the whites," he says. "They've gotten a raw deal for so long."

His sentiments were mirrored, too, by an incident before the Washington game at Seattle last summer. While the UCLA team was engaging in pregame warm-ups, a color guard marched onto the floor and stood at midcourt. It was too late for the Bruins to make their customary exit to the locker room. As the National Anthem played, only one player did not face the flag: Bill Walton.

Then came several days early last May in which Walton's athletic "image crisis" became more pronounced than ever. He was arrested and subsequently fined fifty dollars and placed on a year's probation for his part in an antiwar demonstration at UCLA.

It all began a few hours after President Nixon went on national television to announce that North Vietnam's harbors would be mined. Walton told friends of an act of protest — his plan to lead a demonstration that would seal off the San Diego Freeway near the campus, thus possibly jamming the entire Los Angeles freeway system.

The next day, Walton and teammates Greg Lee, Keith Wilkes, and Larry Farmer reportedly marched with student demonstrators to a nearby federal building but did not participate in the rally. A day later, he sat down with protesters in the middle of a Westwood street and was one of the last to leave when authorities broke up the demonstration.

One witness told of Walton and Lee interrupting a UCLA class and exhorting students to "shut this school down." The professor countered by saying that those who wished to demonstrate could leave, those wishing to discuss the war could stay. The room exploded into applause for the professor's words. Walton grumbled. "You can't get anything accomplished by just debating the war," he told his schoolmates. "You should be out there demonstrating!"

Then, twenty-four hours later, came another rally in front

of Murphy Hall, where students demanded that the administration close the university. Walton was a highly visible face in the crowd, removing wooden barricades and placing obstacles, including an electric janitor's cart, at the entrance. He was one of dozens of students arrested, and during his arrest, he shouted, "The whole world is watching."

The charges against Walton: failure to disperse, unlawful assembly, rioting, disturbing the peace. Walton was promptly released from jail when his older brother, Bruce, a UCLA football tackle, went to a friend for bail money. The friend's name: Sam Gilbert.

Walton also faced possible disciplinary action from the university, but it was not expected to keep him from sinking jump shots and hurling outlet passes for UCLA. Wooden commented by saying that Walton's actions occurred during the off season, thereby releasing him from possible punishment by the athletic department.

Meanwhile, Walton has changed in other areas, notably his resistance to pro basketball offers. Early last season, he was saying, "Who knows? I might lose interest. Sometimes it doesn't seem that playing pro basketball is all that fun." But later, when the talk of a possible $2 million contract whirled about him, he modified his views by saying this, his junior year, might be his last at UCLA. "I have turned down one pro offer already," he said. "My decision . . . is on a year-to-year basis now."

For the most part, Walton's idealism, his sincerity, and selflessness in basketball cannot be challenged. He talks about money ("Sure it would be nice to have a lot of money, but I know a lot of people with lots of money who are unhappy") and his team-before-self approach ("I wish you wouldn't write about how I match up with other centers," he told a reporter, "because it's not Bill Walton who wins — it's UCLA . . . five guys playing as a team").

But there are those who question Walton's maturity, who

theorize that it may not be what his earlier image suggested. Teammates tell of his Ruthian thirsts for life, while UCLA alums angered by his arrest have reportedly ordered him to "Cool it!"

For the present, however, the Bill Walton case has aroused contrasting responses. Says a friend, "He's too tall to be eligible for the military. Hell, he could just sit back and do nothing more than smile behind his four-F card. But he doesn't. He is only backing up his beliefs with action." A man close to the team counters: "He has the right to protest the war, but when his protest interferes with others' rights, that's immaturity."

Still another view of Walton was offered by Dr. Jack Scott, the athletic revolutionary who heads the Institute for the Study of Sport and Society at Oberlin (Ohio) College: "What Walton's experience shows is that the athletic world is more heterogeneous than before. It used to be that everybody thought of the athlete as somebody who would beat up antiwar demonstrators or would be told he couldn't play if he joined SDS or protested the war. I'm not saying Walton is what a majority of athletes are — or should be — and I'm not encouraging all athletes to participate in sit-ins. But I think the athlete should also represent the feelings of the nonathlete and of society at large. This is what I think Bill Walton is doing."

What Bill Walton also has done, to be sure, is add another gray hair to the scalp of John Wooden.

His suite of offices sprawls luxuriously across the twelfth floor of a high-rise building constructed by his company and overlooking the San Fernando Valley.

The door to his office slides open and shut electronically at the press of a button beside his desk. He communicates with his associates and secretaries via push-button intercom. This is a place where the trappings repose in wood-paneled elegance, where copies of *Ebony* magazine lie in the reception room, where Kareem Abdul-Jabbar used to write papers on an electric typewriter on quiet Sunday nights when he was known as Lew Alcindor, and where the telephone rings frequently with calls from basketball players, mostly those who play — or have played — for UCLA.

"Go see Frank Arnold [UCLA assistant coach] about it and tell me what he says," a UCLA player seeking advice via telephone is told. "But make an appointment with his secretary first . . . Got that? . . . Don't go in there unannounced . . ."

It is the home of the Wilson-Gilbert Construction Company, builder of high-rises and homes. The rotund little man behind the desk is Sam Gilbert, man of vast wealth and influence and very strong opinions. Of the four men who have been forces and counterforces in John Wooden's tenure at UCLA, he is surely the least visible and the least influential, directly, on all those championship banners and shouts of "We're Number One!"

But he holds an almost spellbinding rapport with many of the young men who play for John Wooden, a rapport that transcends any that might be cultivated by Wooden or anybody else in the UCLA basketball family.

To the casual observer, Gilbert is just another face backstage. To players and insiders, his image is that of "father confessor" and "rich uncle," a source of jobs, purchaser of players' tickets to Bruin games, self-appointed tutor, and booster of tottering egos.

He has been characterized as eager to use all his resources to assist UCLA players in any manner he can. But not necessarily *all* players and not exclusively UCLA players. For the most part, his involvement has been limited to blacks, notably the exceptionally skilled. He surfaced publicly four years ago when he negotiated the $1.4 million contract for Alcindor, to whom he had become a confidant. He did likewise for Lucius

Allen, Sidney Wicks, Curtis Rowe, Steve Patterson, Henry Bibby, and ex-California star Ansley Truitt — all without, he says, "taking a single penny in compensation."

Interestingly, Gilbert and Wooden are contemporaries, two years apart. They struggled through the Depression as collegians (Gilbert, the son of a Lithuanian immigrant, quit school briefly to support his wife and family) and they are one-time athletes (Gilbert says he was a middleweight boxer before quitting at age twenty-three).

But there, the similarities end. Both are called "Papa" — but Wooden got the nickname from his grandchildren, Gilbert from UCLA players who gave him a wristwatch inscribed with "Thanks, Papa Sam" (his car bears personalized license plates that read: PAPA G). Moreover, Gilbert is light years apart from Wooden in personality — a tough-talking man whose vocabulary includes four-letter words beyond just "UCLA," who inhales the world of high finance and "big dollars," and who can be unabashedly frank in his attacks on society, higher education, and the United States government and its war policies with regard to Vietnam.

Both Wooden and Gilbert represent parental figures to UCLA players. However, Wooden is the authoritarian parent — the man who has to say no more than yes, while Gilbert is the benevolent patriarch who offers a shoulder rather than a stick.

For those reasons, he has struck responsive chords with many Bruin players — almost to the extent that when players speak out against society and authority, as with Alcindor, Walton, and Seibert, people often question whether those are really UCLA basketball players — or Sam Gilbert — talking.

Thus, given their contrasts in life-style and ideology, Gilbert and Wooden seemingly wage a cold war. They merely coexist amid the UCLA kaleidoscope of winning streaks and NCAA titles and dreams of six-figure contracts.

Their chasm may be deeper, too, than anyone realizes, for

neither is willing to say very much publicly about the other beyond noncombustible platitudes.

Says Gilbert of Wooden: "He's successful because of superb coaching and superb recruiting. One without the other is meaningless. He recruits selectively for positions, where Bob Boyd tries to recruit everybody on the horizon. That's what causes internal problems. He also coaches them properly in fundamentals and spots them in the right positions . . . Now that's all I'm going to say to you about him . . ."

Says Wooden of Gilbert: "I personally hardly know Sam Gilbert . . . I think he's a person who's trying to be helpful in every way that he can. I sometimes feel that in his interest to be helpful it's in direct contrast with what I would like to have him do to be helpful. I think he means very well and, for the most part, he has attached himself to the minority-race players. I really don't want to get involved in saying much about that, to be honest with you."

Privately, however, it is known that both are sharply at odds over relating to players — a delicate issue within the UCLA basketball program. One view is that Gilbert "interferes" (item: trainer Ducky Drake having to tell Gilbert not to knock on players' motel doors during pregame naps on a road trip), while another is that Wooden gets low marks from Gilbert for "ignoring" the players as persons.

Whatever their differences, Gilbert's presence bears no small amount of significance in the world of John Wooden. And Gilbert will be the first to tell others that he is significant.

The scope of his activities — which intensified noticeably during the Wicks-Rowe years — is far ranging. He is viewed as someone who might throw a team party at his Malibu home or Lake Arrowhead retreat, or combine with his wife (a high school teacher) in tutoring players, or assist a player who might have contracted venereal disease or unwedded fatherhood.

He insists, in the face of skeptics, he does not accept reimbursement in any form for negotiating contracts of pros-to-be, as do "agents" who usually command a 10 percent fee ("Hell, I don't need the money and, besides, nobody is worth 10 percent of a man's earnings!"). He argues, too, that he does not "brainwash" players. In one breath, he says, "My generation has deceived the present generation. The gobbledygook we've fed them about our society, our economy, our fight for democracy, has been false." In another, he says, "Of course, the kids challenge things I say!" And he exploded at the Los Angeles *Times* in 1970 for having printed only a paragraph to report that UCLA players had wired the President to protest the Cambodian invasion, rather than print the entire telegram, which he offered to a reporter by telephone.

Gilbert delights in discussing his involvement with UCLA players, particularly the blacks. Why not the black nonathlete? "Oh, he's not exploited. The athlete is."

How is Gilbert assessed by others? The observations vary:

"Sam," said Sidney Wicks, "is the conscience of Sidney Wicks. He broke the age barrier with me by admitting that people his age, and the overthirty generation, have messed things up in the world today. That's how we were able to communicate with him. He's not afraid to sit down and tell you what's wrong — even if people his age are at fault."

Says John Ecker: "He's somebody you can talk to about anything. You can be open with him about your personal problems, about politics, about religion . . . because you know he'll listen."

Another former UCLA player, who is white, says, "He's just a little Jewish man who wants to see his name in print."

One player agreed that Gilbert did not accept remuneration for negotiating contracts, but suspected he might "do it for a tax write-off."

A source close to the team said, "Most players are much closer to Gilbert than Wooden." He adds, "When Henry Bibby had a bad game in nineteen seventy-one, he'd go over and see Sam, who would tell him how great he is . . . He found houses for the players to live in, if they couldn't find something on their own. These are things Wooden would never get involved in. It just doesn't fit the image of college basketball, at least as Wooden sees it."

The same source said Gilbert "got the satisfaction of his ego being fed by being so close to the players . . . You had to feed his ego and let him know how much you liked him and how great you thought he was, or the favors would end . . . I think this 'rich-uncle' relationship upsets Wooden, for in many cases, the players go first to Gilbert before they go to Wooden."

A UCLA spokesman said Gilbert has "no official capacity" with the athletic department. J. D. Morgan labels him a "humanitarian . . . a volunteer advisor . . . someone who is in a unique position of helping the kids after they finish school." A former player adds, "I'm sure there have been times when Sam and the athletic department haven't seen eye to eye. But I also know that they've gone after Sam's help when they've needed it."

Is Sam Gilbert just a middle-aged basketball "groupie"? Or is he an alumnus of enormous power and persuasion?

One thing is certain about his alliance with UCLA basketball: it has endeared some partisans to him, repulsed others, and worried still others. There are those who say Gilbert has seized only a gentle foothold on the athletic department, but others will argue that Gilbert's influence has become a double-fisted stranglehold.

CHAPTER 12

The Man through Six Eyes

THREE PLAYERS look back through different, two-way mirrors . . .

An eccentric forward who needled and tested him, but now reveres him, a star-guard-turned-coach who watched and learned from him, an All-American center who praised him, but now questions him.

The proprietor of Jackson Bowl, a renovated bowling alley in Glendale, California, kept his visitor waiting for about fifteen minutes. He emerged from his office, tucked away behind the cash-register counter, and smiled and admitted he forgot we had an appointment for lunch.

Jack Hirsch was tanned and neatly groomed, casually attired in powder-blue slacks and white shoes, slightly bulkier than he was in his playing days, and thirty. As he strode past the adjoining store fronts and used-car lots to a restaurant a block or so away, he talked, almost boastfully, about how he had "not even touched a basketball in six years," about how he never goes to a professional game, and, oh, maybe catches one UCLA-USC game every year, "the one at the Arena."

He slumped into a booth and lit a cigar — the first of several he would smoke during the next couple of hours — and ordered a vodka tonic and a hamburger. He spoke openly of his cataclysmic private life since the winter of 1964, the year he starred at forward on UCLA's first championship team —

his triumphs and failures in business, his divorce and recent
remarriage, trying to get over the death of a father with whom
he was very close, the four agonizing months last year when
he suffered from strep throat, which developed into mono-
nucleosis, then a siege of pneumonia in which he said he lost
fifty pounds.

"I'd been jogging down at the beach — seven miles a day —
every day, and I was really in shape," he said. "But I was going
out every night and not getting much sleep. I was run down.
I remember lying in that hospital bed every day, too weak to
move or get up, and thinking I was going to die. I know I
felt like dying sometimes. I did a lot of thinking about who I
was and where I was going . . ."

Then his interviewer questioned him about the subject they
had come to talk about: John Robert Wooden.

"A helluva guy," said Hirsch unhaltingly. "We're the best
of buddies."

But it was not always so. Jack Hirsch, again with an air
of pride, describes himself as "the first player who gave him
any crap." Hirsch was given to eccentricity in those days, a
brash, cocky youngster who had been Los Angeles City High
School co-player of the year and starred at Valley Junior College. He smilingly tells about how he needled and tested the
coach, who in turn had called him "immature." He laughs
about wearing a Beatle wig to practice one day ("The coach
called the team over and said, 'If Jack wants to improve his
appearance, that's O.K. with me'") and how, when practice
sessions got too exhausting, he used to scream, "That's enough,
JW!"

"I didn't think of him as an idol like everybody else did," he
said, looking back. "Everybody was scared of him. Hell, I
didn't even want to go to UCLA. I had offers from
other places. But my dad wanted me to go there and play for
Wooden. Well, my dad had this terrible smoking habit — six
or seven packs a day. I wanted him to quit. So I told him, 'O.K.

I'll go if you quit smoking.' He did. But it lasted only a month."

By then, Hirsch had enrolled at UCLA for the 1961-1962 season, but he suffered an ankle injury one afternoon during practice and was red-shirted. His strongest impression of the coach, he said, became very evident as he lay there, twisting in pain. "I remember him telling somebody, 'Get him off the floor and let's get going,'" he said. "My ankle hurt like hell. They just swept me off the court as if nothing had happened. I was expendable then and the coach knew it."

He inhaled contemplatively on his cigar. "That's when I first realized," he said, "that Wooden is only human. He was doing his job, that's all. His job is to win basketball games, right? This is how my dad felt. If a guy didn't do his job, he might not have a job. This is what the kids today should realize when they bad-mouth the coach and the system at UCLA. Remember, nobody's forcing them to play."

Hirsch is a businessman, as was his father, who died shortly before the 1963-1964 season and left him three corporations, including bowling alleys and a trucking business. Upon leaving UCLA, Hirsch made money and lost money — bundles of it — because he was, in his words, "too young and inexperienced . . . I made mistakes and other people took advantage of them. I was too nice to people when I shouldn't have been, and I paid through the nose for it."

His nine years in the hard, impersonal world of private enterprise, he said, have taught him much about life and reality and human interaction. He talks the language of business and applies it to the way Wooden — or any coach, for that matter — should run a team.

"Being in business — and let's face it, college basketball is big business — a man does the best job he can to keep his job," said Hirsch. "They say Wooden doesn't relate to the players? Well, what's he supposed to say, 'Sorry, son, I'm not gonna play you — I wanta win games'? Hell, it's hard for him to put any-

thing ahead of winning. That's his job, isn't it? He's not
gonna say, 'I'm gonna relate to you 'cause you're not happy.'
Pretty soon you've got ten guys playing almost an equal
amount of time and then nobody's happy because they all
think they should be playing more. That's when you've got
real problems."

He talked of "double standards" and "faults" of John
Wooden's — qualities that have come under fire by players in
recent years.

"He's a family man and just because he goes to church
doesn't mean he doesn't have faults," he said. "Hell, we all do.
The double standards? Hell, there are double standards in
life, aren't there? I don't see anything wrong with them.
That's the way our country has been built, the way things are
accomplished. Look at the kids drinking when they're
eighteen and they're underage. What would you do? Turn
them in? No, you look the other way. That's a double standard and it happens every day. Sometimes you've gotta look
the other way. Sure, Wooden does that. But he's only a human
being like everybody else."

One evidence of the "double standard" at UCLA, he said,
was the mood in the training room. "When I was red-shirting
and I was nothing," said Hirsch, "I'd go in there to have my
ankles taped, and Ducky Drake would scowl and hardly have
anything to do with me. But when I was on the starting team
as a senior, it was another story. I'd walk in and Ducky would
say, 'Hi, Jack, come on in.' Taping my ankles was really important to him now because I was more important to the team.
That's a double standard if I ever saw one, but it's no different than anywhere else."

He talked about "personal favors," the incentive money, for
instance, that was paid by alumni to the 1964 Bruins after each
game for rebounds. "This is life, too," he said. "You've done
favors for people to get things done, right? Well, this was no
different. This was like slipping a guy five bucks in Vegas to
get a better seat at a show."

Looking back on his college years, Hirsch said they meant more to him now than they did a decade ago. "I remember Ducky's saying that's posted in the training room — 'A few weeks to work hard, a lifetime to remember,'" he said. "I look back now and see how important those words really were. But the kids who are eighteen and nineteen — what do they do now? They complain about everything. Wait till these smart-ass kids get out on their own and try to work. They've gotta listen to the coach because he's doing what he thinks is right to win games. That's his job. They're babies, that's all. Hell, I was, too, at twenty-one."

Hirsch told of a reunion of former UCLA players a few years ago. "Every guy there thanked Wooden for what he meant to them as far as their lives now were concerned," he said. "Most of the guys he coaches are successful — in business and other areas."

A player's perspective about life, he said, is far narrower during college than the postgraduate years. "As you get older, you look at life and how it's going to be three and four years from now," he said. "I'm thirty and I do that all the time. But when you're eighteen, you don't look past your nose. Sure, Wooden makes mistakes. But they make mistakes too. And I'll say one thing: he's made a lot of guys very wealthy right now. Maybe he doesn't get personally involved with them, but he put a name on our backs."

"Preferential treatment" of star players — a common complaint of UCLA reserves — was described by Hirsch as "human nature": "Sure, Wooden bent for me when I was a starter. He treated me as a personality. It can't be equal treatment for all because each person has a different personality. The question is: Did I treat him fairly for what he was? A star? Or a benchwarmer? The stars got preferential treatment not just by the coach, but the fans too. That's who they care about. And when you get right down to it, *all* basketball players at UCLA get preferential treatment. You got the classes you wanted; you didn't have to wait in registration lines. Everything was taken care of for us and I didn't expect that either. Hell, the peons didn't get treated like that."

Wooden, he said, was "fair" in his treatment of the 1964 players: "He kicked me out of the gym at one practice. I'd been up all night and was playing lousy. He knew I shouldn't have been there. Hell, he kicked us all out at one time or another. But he was fair in my case. I deserved to be kicked out."

Jack Hirsch lit another cigar. He climbed out of the booth and the words rambled on and on as he walked back to work, along the busy boulevard to the sounds of crashing tenpins and automatic pinsetters.

Once inside, he pointed out the modernization of Jackson Bowl, the sleek eighteen lanes, the fresh paint, and other refinements. He also nodded toward a group of youngsters bowling on several lanes. "Mentally retarded kids," he said. "We let 'em come in free one afternoon a week. Gives 'em something to look forward to."

But his thoughts, for the moment, harked back to an earlier time. The roar of sellout crowds at the Sports Arena. The first chants of "We're Number One!" The dramatic, all-conquering march through the NCAA tournament by five little guys who outquicked and outfinessed every team they played.

"Our team put UCLA on the map," he said proudly. "If we hadn't won, UCLA wouldn't have won all those other championships. Do you think Alcindor would have gone there? Walton too? Hell, no. I like to think it wouldn't have happened without us. And looking back, if I knew I didn't have Dad's business to fall back on, I know I could be playing in the pros today. A lot of those same guys I outplayed in college are still in the NBA. A guy like Cazzie Russell, for instance. And Jeff Mullins. Can you believe that? They said I was too small for the pros. Well, I had good court sense. I knew where to be at the right time . . ."

And what of the little man he played for, the man he battled in the 1960s and reveres in the 1970s?

"Maybe I spoke my mind too much then," he said. "Well, I'm still speaking my mind now. But I'm part of a different generation. He's gonna change with the times. I knew what he was all about then. And I respect him even though he's got faults. Hell, we all have faults, don't we?"

His eyes scanned across the hardwood lanes at all the customers — the kids and the elderly kibitzers with nothing else to do, the blue-collar guys and the mascara-caked women talking and laughing in the bar. But he still thought about the old coach who works twenty-five miles away.

"Sure, he comes across as a little too Puritan," he said. "Maybe that's part of the trouble. Sometimes I pick up the papers and I tell my wife, 'Oh, no! They're making him out to be God!' Really, he's just a human being with faults like the rest of us."

Jack Hirsch excused himself and said he had to return to work. He bade good-bye and vanished back into his office — back to an obscurity he seemed to enjoy — another human being.

Freddie Goss, back where it all began, in Compton, a mostly black city on the fringes of Watts. He is there for the summer, working in a youth basketball program.

It's late morning, at Lueders Park gymnasium, and Goss is officiating a game between nine- and ten-year-olds ("and some eight-year-olds," he says, "left here by their mothers as if we were baby-sitters").

Everyone, including Goss, is wearing a white T-shirt stamped with "Compton Model Cities Basketball Camp." Enthusiasm springs from these youngsters, just as it has, Goss says, from other sessions in this, the camp's first year. He signals the end of practice and gathers the kids around him. Some fidget but most are attentive.

"Now what did I tell you?" he asks. "And what did you forget out there today?"

Silence.

"Court balance," he says. "We have to have that."

Freddie Goss is young and he is black and he is the head basketball coach at UC Riverside. But the words might just as well have been coming from an old white man who is the head coach at UCLA. Because they are John Wooden's words.

Goss has seen Wooden from several perspectives. He played under him three seasons, one as the Bruins' captain, and closely observed Wooden a fourth season (1963-1964) when he asked to red-shirt "because I knew who was coming back and I wanted to get myself together a little more." And he is in the still unusual position of being a black coach at a primarily white school. So he is uniquely equipped to judge Wooden. And the marks he gives his former coach are high.

"I practiced all through my red-shirt year," he says, "but I knew I wasn't going to play in games so it was different. I was more an observer. I saw Wooden as being very simple . . . in his approach to techniques, in his dealings with players. Right is right. Wrong is wrong. No shadings. I've learned from all my coaches but he taught me organization and basic, psychological strategy. He knew what our strengths and weaknesses were, and he got the players to realize what they could and could not do. Then he motivated them."

Wooden had a couple of outstanding sophomore guards on the 1962-1963 team — Gail Goodrich and Freddie Goss. Privately, Wooden told a reporter that Goss had slightly more potential and played a little better in early practices. Yet Goodrich started. Why?

"Freddie has a better attitude," he told the reporter. "He'll give me one hundred percent whether I start him or bring him in later. Gail sulks if he doesn't get to start. I'd rather get one hundred percent from both of them by starting Gail than get one hundred percent from Freddie and only sixty percent from Gail by starting Freddie."

"I knew Gail was still immature in those days," says Goss now. "I just wanted to win; I wasn't hung up on not starting.

I'd been taught that the coach made honest decisions for what was best for the team. A lot of players criticized my acceptance of this — but if they were into coaching as I am now, they'd understand it. Wooden and I talked about it. It just wasn't a big thing to me."

Goss had three goals — to become CIF Player of the Year, be on a national championship team, and then coach. He'd made the first two by the time he was a college junior. But the third — becoming a coach — seemed out of reach.

"I decided I had the tools for it my sophomore year," he says, but I never thought I'd get a chance unless it was at Grambling or some black school like that. It was the nature of the coaching fraternity then — there weren't any black coaches except at black schools."

It was a different era for black players' too. "I wasn't looking for things the way players are now. It didn't bother me that there wasn't a certain kind of food on the training table. I wasn't proud or disproud of my heritage. We hadn't come to that yet. I was only interested in playing the game, in traveling, in getting my degree."

It rankles Goss that UCLA still has no black assistant basketball coach. "I don't like the idea of them hiring a black assistant just to go out and get black players," he says, "but I'm at a loss to understand why a black isn't part of that staff. The black athlete has had a very large part in making the program."

But he doesn't question Wooden's rapport — or lack of it — with black players: "I think it's an *age* thing mainly, not a racial thing. Wooden has always told his players all of them are not going to like him. Say ten don't . . . well, ten do too. Every promise that was made to me at UCLA was kept. This isn't true for everyone, I know. It is true for me.

"It would be interesting to catalogue those former Wooden players who are coaches — or pro players—now, and see what *they* think of him. Most of the things he taught me hold true today. You know, at some point, every coach has got to make decisions that certain players think are bad.

"Sure, I've heard he doesn't 'relate' to players. They probably say the same thing of me. I don't want to get too close to my players. I've got a job to do and I'm the one who is responsible for it. If it affects winning or losing, then I will consider changing something but I feel I should relate to my players primarily on basketball issues. I have one assistant coach in charge of classes, another for recruiting. If they can't handle their areas, then I get involved. But I don't want to be close to one or two players. That's asking for trouble.

"And there's the time problem, too, the demands from speaking engagements, clinics, luncheons. I don't want to be a sounding board who has the players running to me with every little thing . . . even if I can help. I want to help them on the really *big* things."

Goss has not won a College Division championship at UC Riverside. He came close a couple of seasons ago, but the next year injuries killed him.

"That's a very crucial factor in UCLA's success," he says. "The lack of serious injuries. What would have happened if they'd lost Sidney Wicks for a lot of games his junior and senior years? I think we could have won a national championship in nineteen sixty-five–sixty-six but I was out a long time and then Edgar Lacey was hurt. We just didn't have the bench to make up for it."

But Goss doesn't think lack of injuries to key players is the only reason for UCLA's triumphs. It is very obvious, as he sits behind glasses that make him look much older than he is and eats lunch in a cafeteria, that he has an enduring regard for John Wooden. Like many other former players, he calls Wooden "Coach."

"Coach paid his dues," says Goss. "If you stay in the game as long as he has, are as dedicated, work as hard, and are as intelligent, you've *got* to hit the right combination eventually. He did. Quick, mobile players. Great defense.

"I'll tell you . . . players are so much different today. We didn't look so deeply into decisions and issues even a few years ago. Players challenge you now. A lot of coaches get out after a few years. Wooden hasn't.

"I don't see him as larger than life. I don't think he wants to be idolized or eulogized either. He'll always be just 'coach' to me."

Freddie Goss, recently divorced and rearing a small son, finished what was only an adequate lunch. He looked at his watch. Time to get back. The day was hot, but the car was air-conditioned. It was just starting to cool off when Leuders Park loomed on the left.

He waved hello to a young secretary on her way to lunch. He then would advise a young black player about where he could and could not get into school. And he would talk, again, to the kids.

The handshake was firm, strong. "You have my phone numbers," he said. "You have any problems, don't hesitate . . . call."

News item — February 25, 1954: "Willie," the coach said, "this is it." Willie Naulls stared back, wide-eyed. "This is your last chance," said John Wooden. "I've been pretty easy on you all year because you started late but I've been waiting for you to come along and show something. So far you haven't. You've let those other centers push you around; you haven't been shooting or rebounding.

"I'm going to start you tonight. But the first time I see you shoved around or not scrapping, you're coming out of there. And you might not get back in the rest of the year."

News item — December 17, 1954: Willie Naulls made his conference debut against the California Bears last season and a couple of critics ventured the opinion that he couldn't have hit the backboard with a handful of gravel. Coach Johnny Wooden benched him so hard his teeth rattled like a sack of castanets.

"I blame myself," said Wooden. "He'd worked out with us for just one practice, so when he came up empty against the Bears I had no one to blame but myself."

But easygoing Willie turned into a panther. He haunted the ball, shot like a demon, and inspired the Bruins to score an 81-63 victory over USC and snap a three-game losing streak.

News item — March 7, 1955: "There are times when I don't know what to do with Willie Naulls," said John Wooden. "He's such a likable kid that it's pretty hard to get sore at him for failing to give it the blood-and-thunder treatment. Exasperated would be more like it.

"Willie isn't reluctant to mix it up. It's just that he loves the game so much and gets such great enjoyment out of playing that he forgets himself now and then. He gets so fascinated watching the action, figures he's got the best seat in the house to see what's going on and just stands there and enjoys himself."

News item — March 1, 1956: As far as Coach John Wooden is concerned, Willie (The Whale) Naulls is the greatest player he's ever had — and Wooden's been in the profession twenty-three years.

"Willie's a better all-around player than Bill Russell," says Wooden. "Willie can do so many more things. He's about as close to having all the various shots as anyone you can find. Certainly better than any I've ever had. He's a very unselfish boy, despite his tremendous scoring. His first thought is of the team, not Willie."

News item — March 1, 1956: "Aren't you going to ask me about the coach?" Naulls said to an interviewer. "John Wooden is the greatest coach in the world."

News item — April 6, 1956: "I cannot possibly see how they could leave Willie Naulls off the Olympic team," said John Wooden.

News item — February 15, 1961: Willie Naulls, soft-spoken, hard-driving star of the New York Knickerbockers, credits

Coach John Wooden of UCLA for his success in pro basketball.

"Wooden never has had a losing season at UCLA," Naulls points out, "and I guess this factor instilled the confidence needed for a lot of kids who played on his teams. It helped me tremendously. That plus the wonderful coaching job Wooden does — his ability to strengthen the weak points of his players, especially me."

News item — April 6, 1966: Willie Naulls, thirty-one-year-old forward for the Boston Celtics, said he will retire after the National Basketball Association play-offs are finished.

"I'm tired of traveling and tired of athletics," he said.

News item — February 13, 1972: Willie Naulls is quietly becoming a force in Los Angeles.

An illustrious career in basketball and the building of a shopping center in Watts are behind him now. But Willie Naulls isn't through yet. On the one hand he is a driving businessman with restaurant and land development operations that are fulfilling dire needs in the Watts-Compton area. And on the other hand are his philanthropic efforts and such things as his help in negotiating contracts for soon-to-be professional athletes.

Today, he estimates his total assets at more than $2.5 million, including the Willie Naulls Shopping Plaza, at 103rd and Avalon Streets, which alone is worth more than $2 million.

An interview with Willie Naulls, July 1972: "John Wooden is the best college basketball coach of all time. Really, he's a professional college coach. He works at it twenty-four hours a day. He does what he gets paid to do — he produces winning teams and he'll always be a winning coach.

"But I don't think he does much to make the college experience more beneficial to his players. His Pyramid of Success and things like that imply that he spends a lot of time in the development of men, not just in basketball and fundamentals. But he doesn't. I certainly needed a lot of help in other directions and I didn't get it."

❖

Willie Naulls's roots are in the black ghetto.

"I used to come home from basketball trips to visit my parents," he said. "They lived near One-hundred-and-twelfth and Central Avenue. My mother used to bug me about taking her to the supermarket, but we had to drive for miles to get good food. That's when I started thinking about building a shopping center.

"I thought, 'Why in hell shouldn't there be a nice shopping center in Watts?' Blacks didn't own anything. It was all owned by absentee landlords. We'd go to stores and buy half-rotten fruit and food in bent cans. We were treated like animals.

"Today, I could take that shopping center of mine and put it in the middle of Beverly Hills and it would still look good."

Willie Naulls's office is in the middle of Beverly Hills — on the eleventh story of the Beverly Hills Financial Center at Canon and Wilshire. The offices are not exorbitantly expensive but tasteful, as is the man who works there — the entrepreneur of Willie Naulls Enterprises.

A friend says of him: "He's extremely bright. Throughout his pro career, he was sharp enough to recognize that he couldn't play basketball forever. He saved his dough and when he quit, he had a sizable amount of capital. One of the keys to Willie's success has been that he knows if he doesn't have the ability, he admits it to himself and seeks the proper information intelligently, then utilizes it to his best advantage."

One of the people from whom Naulls sought help was Sam Gilbert. In Naulls's opinion, Gilbert has filled a "father figure role for the players that Wooden has not.

"He's very close to them," Willie says. "He's stabilized a lot of them. When they really have problems, most of them have either come to me and I've sent them to Sam or they've gone directly to Sam. He has a lot more experience than I do — and more wherewithal to do things."

Behind the scenes, for the most part, Naulls has been close to turbulence on the UCLA scene for years.

He recalls that he "almost quit" his sophomore year, in 1954:

"The story broke in the paper that Bob McKeen, the California center, and I were good friends. Wooden didn't start me in either game against Cal at Berkeley. I barely played and I was tremendously insulted because he never even discussed it with me. I can only guess he didn't think I'd play my normal game if it was against someone I knew and with whom I had a good relationship. This had a helluva lot of bad implications so I decided to quit. But I talked to a lot of people and decided to go back."

Naulls reportedly talked Walt Hazzard out of quitting his sophomore season:

"I felt responsible for him. I'd sent him to UCLA. I first learned of Walt when he was a baby-sitter for a friend of mine in pro ball — Woody Sauldsberry — then saw him play and thought he was tremendous. I told Coach Wooden that if he didn't make the team, I'd pay for his scholarship out of my own salary.

"When I was with the Knicks and Walt was in Los Angeles, he called me a couple of times asking me to loan him the money for a plane ticket to Philadelphia. He wanted to go home . . . but I talked him out of leaving."

Then came Lew Alcindor and Lucius Allen.

The Knicks had finished a workout at a high school gym several years ago and were leaving the building when a squeaky voice said, "Hello, Mr. Naulls, I want to introduce myself . . ."

The voice belonged to a splinter-thin ninth-grader named Lew Alcindor, the 6-11 center of the Power Memorial Academy team.

Naulls helped to polish Lew his freshman year at Westwood (along with assistant Jay Carty) and Willie says, "I had a lot of personal contact with both him and Lucius. I liked and respected both of them very much. We discussed things like personalities, people, different personal problems. They were unhappy and came to see me and I steered them to Sam Gilbert. And they stayed in school too."

Finally, there was Sidney Wicks. "I talked him out of quitting

his sophomore season when he was playing behind Lynn Shackelford. Coach Wooden had told Sidney that whoever did the
best in scrimmages would play in the games. Sidney dominated
the scrimmages but he was a second-stringer. We had many
long talks about this. I know I had a big effect on keeping him
at UCLA."

Naulls will talk of the past — "I maintained a 'B' average but
it was done with a lot of tutors and special treatment. That part
of the deal in which the athlete gets a free ride is detrimental
in the overall picture." But he would rather talk about what
he views as a thread running through all the seasons at UCLA.

"You enter into a contractual agreement," he says. "It's
a business deal. You both perform your part of the bargain,
ideally. The university has offered the boy an educational opportunity. Once that is established, promises are made, many
of them by people outside the athletic department. A lot of
alumni promise things the players never get.

"There is a total lack of describing to the athlete what his
role really is going to be when he gets to UCLA — as it applies
to the coaches and athletic department. When that situation
is rectified, you will have fewer situations that bring complaints
and things will be more stable.

"When a boy leaves home for the first time, his coach becomes a father figure, a guy you should be able to go to with
your problems and your questions. With Wooden, you don't
feel you can do this.

"The players are immature; Wooden has a very strict list of
rules and regulations. I believe the players are often judged
too harshly. And their requirements change. If there was a
basic, direct honesty out front by UCLA, I think you might
lose more players at the start but you'd have fewer frustrated
players later on."

Naulls praises Wooden for "standing by his system — that's
one of his fortes. He's implemented it and stuck by it all these
years." But after the earlier, impassioned words, would Willie
Naulls have his son play for John Wooden?

"I would if he wanted to be a professional player, because I could help guide him," Willie says. "Because I wanted to play professionally, I still think I'm better off having gone to UCLA than I would be if I'd gone to USC or elsewhere."

CHAPTER 13

The Wizard's Crystal Ball

THE CHARGE most heard against John Robert Wooden is that in his drive to win and to perpetuate UCLA's success and his own success he has forgotten how to "relate" to his players.

It is a complaint that he certainly does not bear alone. Nearly every coach at every level in every sport in every city and hamlet in the country has heard it the last few years.

Is it valid in Wooden's case?

Strangely but typically, he is the Man of Contrasts when he discusses this. In one interview, he says: "I think I've always related well to my players. Go back to my early years. Talk to my players at Dayton, South Bend, Terre Haute, and through the years at UCLA. You'll find I've always related well to them — at least, to most of them.

"I've always been honest with my players — to a point where they can't say I was dishonest. I don't think I appease the players either. I may, in some cases, but not to the detriment of the team. Even though they may disagree and question me, I'm sincerely interested in them as individuals. On the floor, I'm not interested in them as individuals but as a team. Off the floor it's different. Some of them may not realize my interest in them as individuals — at the start — but they later will."

In another interview on the same subject a few weeks later, however, Wooden says: "I personally have not made the effort I could have made in trying to relate — because I felt, beginning a few years ago, they resented it. They wanted me to confine my relationship with them to that of coach and basketball players. I have conceded that reluctantly, but I have conceded it nonetheless. Now, I feel close only to those who want to be close."

He adds that because of "peer pressure, the other players might resent one player coming to me — or me going to him. I don't know. The idea seems to be, why go to the coach, he's a square."

Because he never was a substitute as a player, too, he says he's been told, " 'You really don't know what it's like to be a sub. You never had to sit on the bench.' But I *do* know. I've been in coaching long enough to know what it's like."

Wooden, despite the talk about lack of relating, has escaped most of the racial problems that have plagued many other coaches throughout the nation.

He has had black players at South Bend Central, at Indiana State, and almost from the start at UCLA — at a time, in fact, when practically no Pacific Coast Conference teams played blacks.

In *Sports Illustrated* three years ago, Mike Warren, the ex-star black guard of the Bruins, said that Wooden's relationships with blacks "have no meaning. The coaching staff was seriously interested only in us playing, studying, and keeping out of trouble. Our individual progress in terms of maturing as black men was of no concern. It's all superficial, the same kind of dialogue every day."

Warren said in the same report that he was called in by Wooden and confronted about dating a white girl. Wooden told Warren he had received threatening phone calls and that Mike was doing the wrong thing.

"I would discourage anybody from interracial dating," Wooden said. "I imagine whites would have trouble dating in an Oriental society too. It's asking for trouble. But I've never told a player who he could or couldn't date."

"He didn't stop me," said Warren. "But, man, how about telling me my life is in danger? How's that for a hint?"

Wooden said, "I think I've had good discussions with various black members of my teams. I've tried to understand and adapt. I remember when Wilt Chamberlain came out here, he told a reporter he couldn't be 'handled,' that only animals were 'handled.' I had used that term before, but I never have since. I had made a mistake. I learn more every year. But there are some things I have to stand upon."

Fred Slaughter, the black center on the Bruins' first title team and now a member of the UCLA administration, says, "There is no perfect place for the black athlete, but if a black kid wants to get his game together for the pros, this is the best place to come. Coach Wooden is a product of his experience and background and he relates to the blacks as well as his background lets him. That's better than most.

"I don't believe he has ever been openly prejudiced or discriminatory; he just doesn't understand the black man in terms of social values, needs, and moods.

"I believe he matured quite a bit in this area, though, during Kareem Jabbar's years here. Being the intelligent man he is, he became aware of certain things. Off the court, this had a positive effect on his personality. He no longer had obscure minority players like Walt Hazzard and me — at least, players who were obscure to people in California before we got here. As far as his ability to relate to black players during that era, well, he was really green.

"UCLA's basketball fortunes were not being as closely scrutinized in those days either. But once we started winning championships, the fans started watching who was coming to play here. They had this hunger for more. And when Jabbar and Lucius Allen came in, people knew who they were. The coach had to become conversant with the black culture — because he had a very, very good team that was being watched by everybody.

"He's a better person now, socially. It's all a part of how attitudes change. In the midfifties, black people were smarting from discrimination and not saying anything. In the sixties, when blacks began protesting, white people simply said, 'Why do they feel the way they do?' And now it's 'All in the Family' where people laugh at race. You don't know where it'll go next."

Wooden himself says that "As I've gotten older, I have become more tolerant. I'm not as strict but neither is society. But that's good because society can't stand still. Perhaps I've erred in some respects. But who can say, for sure? At least, I'd rather make the mistake of going too far with a boy than not far enough. Today, I'll go further than I did in nineteen thirty-five. Perhaps in nineteen seventy-five, I'll go further yet, if I'm still around. That's not rationalization, that's fact."

To Wooden, it's not a matter of fairness *and* equality. "No two of us are alike," he says. "If I treat any two players alike, that's showing partiality, because you're not being fair with either one.

"If I treated everyone alike, all players would get the same amount of playing time. If I give the players who play most often a better pair of shoes, is that partiality? No! If Bill Walton gets a bigger steak than Andy Hill, is that partiality? Yes! You have to go along with decisions that will affect the betterment of the team. The players who have better shoes are going to need those shoes because they're playing more . . .

"In business, for example, you're not going to draw as much money as a guy who's worked five more years than you have and has seniority and priority. If you treat everyone alike, you're implying they *are* alike. In life, it's going to be the same. I want my players to know I'll treat them fairly, but that doesn't mean they'll be treated equally.

"I must also ask: 'Whom am I being fair to?' My obligation is to develop the best possible team for UCLA. My obligation is not to curry the players. If I can develop a fine team, that will mean I'm doing the best job I can.

"It's like Adolph Rupp once said: 'I'm too busy coachin' 'em to court 'em.' Or Amos Alonzo Stagg, whose philosophy I admired tremendously and who said, in effect, 'I never had a player I did not love. I had many I did not respect or did not like what they did.' But he loved them just the same."

He seeks team unity, but not camaraderie.

"One of the great misconceptions — and I didn't always believe this — is to feel you have to have great camaraderie to have a fine team. For instance, Tinker, Evers, and Chance were probably the greatest double-play combination there ever was in baseball. That may be hard to authenticate but a poem was written about them — they had to be good. But the truth was, they *hated* each other.

"Still, when you get into competition, you want to do well, just as they did. I'm blocking for the other guy in football because it helps the team, not me. I've had players — a couple of forwards — who detested each other, yet we had a fine team that year. I also had two guards who didn't like each other. One of them, in fact, refused to play my way for a long time. But when he did, he played extremely well.

"My teams have to play *my* way. They can't be individuals. They *must* play my way. Eventually, they learn when they can shoot, when they can dribble, and when they can't. I'm not blowing my own horn when I say this, but I think my teams, for the most part, play closer to their level than most teams.

"I don't want teams of great heights and great depths. We generally strive for consistency. That's why I'm very fond of the Curtis Rowes and the Mike Warrens. I don't think either of them had a bad game."

To Wooden, handling players is almost an art form:

"You give them too much rein, and they go every which way. If you're too tight, you smother them. I really liked what Al Campanis [a Dodger vice president] said of Walt Alston [Dodger manager and a close friend of Wooden's]: 'Good managing is like holding a dove in your hand. Squeeze it too tight and it dies, not tight enough and it flies away. Alston has a nice touch with the dove, not too tough, not too soft.'"

Wooden implies that he has the same sort of touch and he'll

tell you that "Players really haven't changed that much. They're more vocal, possibly, and they express themselves more openly. But this is something you must accept."

But at another time he will say: "If I had it to do over again, I probably would have stayed in high school coaching. The youngsters are more impressionable and receptive at that age. They ask you *how* not *why*."

The point appears sound. Two white players who gave Wooden little or no trouble off the Alcindor teams — one a starter, Lynn Shackelford, one a reserve, Neville Saner — are inclined to ask "why?" in retrospect and talk about the things the coach did *not* do as much as the things he did.

"He's older and he's set in his ways," says Shackelford. "He believes there are certain things that are right and certain things that are wrong. He's not willing to *discuss* them with players. He's willing to *tell* them what's right and wrong. I believe a lot of players don't like that. They'd rather have things discussed. That wasn't a conflict with me. I'd rather have him come in and tell me what's right and wrong. I think he's interested in people as individuals, but maybe because he's set in his ways he probably has a lot of trouble communicating with people."

Says Saner: "He's a tough, cold guy — and he should just come out and admit that he is. It's as simple as that. He didn't give me the time of day. For instance, when I was in Jerry Norman's office one time, J. D. Morgan came by and said, 'How are your marks coming?' I was impressed by that. Here's a man who has eight hundred athletes to worry about, and he was concerned. I know Wooden didn't take the time to do this."

Time, the precious factor. There has never seemed to be enough of it since Wooden has been winning. And winning — the scrap to get to the top and then cling there — has become what UCLA basketball is all about in many eyes.

Win one championship, it would seem, and the pressure

builds from that roaring throng in Pauley Pavilion to win another and another. But Wooden says, "No. I don't feel at all
that I have to match what we've already done. I mean that
sincerely. And I try to get that across to the players, although
it may be a little more difficult every year.

"But each year's a new year. Absolutely. One of the things
I said in my annual letter to this year's team is that it was going
to be more difficult for them because they would be *expected*
to win. Some might consider it an unenviable position but I
told them I consider it an enviable position . . . a mark of respect they had earned. I also told them that the past is history
and that nothing that happened in the past can change or affect what they were going to do in the future. What you did
yesterday, that's gone by. You can do something about today,
so you must think in those terms."

Are the terms always winning?

"The easiest path," says Wooden, "is down the middle.
Don't take a stand. Don't go to the left or right. You never accomplish or do much that way but you never have any particular problems either. That's the easy way. I don't want that.
I want to do the best I am capable of doing, even though there's
only one worse thing than losing too much for the majority of
people — and that's winning too much.

"I don't believe the sign on J. D. Morgan's desk — WINNING
SOLVES ALL PROBLEMS. I'm more inclined toward what
Charlie Brown says in the comics: 'Winning ain't everything
but losing is nothin'.'

"I've pretty well been able to adopt the philosophy I've had
— to embrace the Pyramid of Success pretty well. I believe
that we have 'won' — that is, accomplished all we're capable
of accomplishing — when we've *lost* games.

"No, I don't think we've created a monster by winning so
much. Rather than calling what we've achieved a dynasty, I
prefer to think of it as a cycle. And I believe all cycles come
to an end. But certain things can make the cycle extend longer

than normal — little things, such as attentiveness to detail.
Things that don't show up in box scores. Things that help a
player shoot better, rebound better, switch men on defense better. They're only minor things but they mean a great deal.

"I feel I'm a better coach now than I was last year. And I'm
better in nineteen seventy-two than I was in nineteen sixty-
two. I like to think I'll be better next year than I am now. But
I'm not better than the other coaches. *Every* coach is better
than he was in nineteen sixty-two."

But the other coaches have not been around success as players and coaches the way John Robert Wooden has. "Yes, I've
had great success as a player and a coach," he says, "but the
roar of the crowd has never particularly influenced me. I'm
not saying I'm not *aware* of it. I care for others and what they
think but I don't *live* for them — I live for myself, and for my
family."

Obviously, he is far from oblivious to the fact that UCLA's
winning thirty-two straight NCAA games has been called the
greatest sports achievement of all time.

"That pleases me very much," he says. "Why wouldn't I be
proud of it? And, yes, I think there's validity in comments like
that.

"If you would start right now and say some team would win
six national championships in a row and eight out of nine, I'd
say, 'You're crazy! There's no way.' Maybe in pro ball where
you've got the same players to build on and a long season and
you can lose three out of seven in the play-offs. But not in college! If we had lost any time during that streak, we'd have
been through — out. So many things had to fall into place.
I'm not taking credit for it but I am a part of it and I have to
be proud of it.

"When we had Alcindor, one coach told me that if *he'd* had
Lewis he would have won three national championships too.
I said, 'Well, the only thing I can say to you is, "You'll never
know what it's like and I do.'" I'd like to have said, 'I've

watched your material through the years and I believe if I had it I would have won an awful lot more games with it than you won.' But I didn't, I guess, because there is no easy way. It may look easy to the other fella but it isn't — anywhere."

Both Wooden and his wife say that the achievements of the last decade have not changed him.

"Do you really think I've changed?" the coach asks.

Then he adds: "I get letters from old friends and high school classmates — some of whom I honestly don't remember — who say they've perhaps seen me on television or at games and add, 'You're the same as you always were.' That makes me pleased and proud. You hope you're that way. Nellie and I have a saying we use often: 'You meet the same people on the way down that you met on the way up.' "

Other people, however, say Wooden *has* indeed changed, some for the better, some for the worse. If there is a consensus, it is that he has grown more "up-tight" as both national titles and player problems have built up but that he has bent and mellowed toward referees and rival players and coaches as he has aged too.

Officials, particularly, seem to think he has softened.

Walter (Dutch) Thurstin remembers working games when Wooden was at South Bend Central: "He never affected me but I'm sure he affected some of the boys who officiated — influenced them. He never swore but there was not a coach in the United States who could use the English language any better than he could. He was always technically and grammatically correct when he was chewing you out."

"Yes, I yell at officials," Wooden once said. "I want my players to know I'm behind them."

"He was sort of a tiger when he came into the league," says former PCC official Al Lightner. "But that was in the days when he was trying to make his mark. After he started winning national championships he just sat there with that rolled-up program in his hands — I had more trouble with those danged UCLA assistants."

Former assistant coach Ed Powell recalls a "psychological warfare" game Wooden used to play with officials: "Sometimes during the first half, or just before the half ended, if there were a close play, he'd bounce up and chew out the refs up and down. He'd do that so the refs would remember it all through half time. Then, when they'd come out for the second half, he'd walk over to them and smile and say, 'I apologize for saying you missed that call. You didn't do it deliberately, I know. You're doing a job — and it's a tough job.'

"He'd just walk away, but now the refs would *really* start wondering. First, they had seen him as a holy terror and their minds dwelled on it for a long time. Now, they see him do an about-face and they'd say to themselves: 'Hey, he's not such a bad guy after all.'

"You can see John's reasoning behind this. If there's a close play in the second half, a thought is gonna go through the ref's mind: 'Do I take advantage of a nice guy? Or do I remember him as a holy terror?' More than likely, the ref would make the call in our team's favor. And John knew that one or two calls in our favor — in a close game — would often mean the difference between victory and defeat. This is one way he built up for close games — by setting up refs so he could win. The refs would see him act two ways. When it came time to make a close call, a doubt would already have been planted in their minds."

Bill Bussenius, long-time Pacific Coast official, confirmed Powell's story. "Wooden was no saint. He'd mince no words in the old days. And he did have this half-time routine. There were just two doors in the old Westwood gym and he'd wait for you by one and give it to you when you came out. I'd loiter by the scorer's bench, giving the illusion I was checking the scores, but really I was seeing if I could outwait him.

"But he doesn't bring out the beast in most officials anymore. He can be a gracious winner and a fine loser. And in all the years I worked his games, I never heard more than two or three words from any of his players except the captain, and then it would just be something like, 'The coach told me to tell you to watch number thirty-one, he's holding.' "

It is typical of Wooden that his captain — the floor leader of the team — should be the spokesman.

The coach's most gratifying moments in basketball have come, he says, in areas concerning team play. He mentions the poem the South Bend players wrote him in 1943 and the support he got from both Sidney Wicks and Curtis Rowe after the national finals in 1971.

Then he talks about the Purdue team banquet the year he was a sophomore ("Stretch Murphy, who was the star, had a lot of nice things to say about my team ball") and the Purdue banquet when he was a senior ("I'd broken the Big Ten scoring record but Coach Lambert mentioned I had never missed an open man and was the finest defensive man he'd seen. That meant something").

And he recalls 1964, "when a lot of people weren't expecting us to win a national championship. They said we were unbeaten and were very good, we had a tremendous *little* team but Duke was so big and . . . but we won."

There are always things people want to know about too — particularly his involvement, or lack of it, with Olympic basketball, the finest players he's coached and seen, and why he's never become a professional coach. He talks about these things.

On the Olympics: "I think there is a feeling that the spirit of the Games has changed. It has become more political . . . the kids just don't have the desire anymore. When you ask the average person about the Olympics, he'll ask: 'How are we going to do against the Russians?'

"Is that what the Olympics are about? Are we participating against just one team, or are we participating against all countries? I'm just as patriotic as anyone, but I've become disillusioned with the political nature of the Olympics."

The disillusionment started, apparently, in 1956, when Bruin center Willie Naulls was snubbed for the team. Naulls had scored forty-two points in three Olympic trials games. Carl

Cain of Iowa, who made the team in Willie's place, had scored fourteen. Too many Western players had already been selected for the team — including Bill Russell of USF — and that was the reason for Naulls's rejection, one source said.

Then came 1964, when Walt Hazzard was chosen (and went to the Games — the last Bruin to do so) but when Wooden strongly thought Gail Goodrich should have been picked too.

In 1968 three Bruins — Alcindor, Allen, and Warren — rejected Olympic bids in what some said was part of a black power protest. And Bill Walton and Keith Wilkes both spurned invitations to try out for the 1972 team. Walton's back-up man, Swen Nater, went to the trials and played well — making the team. But then he left camp after a minor disagreement with crusty coach Henry Iba. Nater said he had lost twenty pounds because his hunger pangs and the team's eating schedule did not coincide.

A UCLA spokesman says he thinks Wooden's pronounced aversion for Olympic competition and other international basketball stems mainly from the fact that "He doesn't want to be away from his family as long as he'd have to be to coach one of these teams."

On the finest players he's coached and seen: Wooden has never picked an all-time UCLA top five. He probably never will because he does not see players as individual examples of talent and proficiency but as members of a team, complementing each other.

"And I would not," he says, "want to leave someone off an all-time team. If I picked Sidney Wicks and Curtis Rowe as my forwards," he says, "where would that leave Keith Erickson? If I ran a press, I'd *have* to have Keith. He was the best number five man in the press I ever had. And if I picked Walt Hazzard and Gail Goodrich as the other guards, where would that leave Mike Warren? I'd have to start with Lewis Alcindor as my center, but is that fair to Willie Naulls, who played in a different era, or Bill Walton?"

Wooden thinks that players are better now, generally, and

so are coaches. He will name a couple of names. "I've never seen a better player than Robert (Fuzzy) Vandiver," says Wooden. "He was awfully good." Vandiver, a 6-foot guard-forward, led the Franklin High School "Wonder Five" to a record three straight Indiana state prep championships in the early 1920s, then guided the whole bunch, intact, on to stardom at Franklin College, a small Baptist school that defeated Notre Dame and Purdue. "I was very impressionable then," says Wooden. "Vandiver was my idol."

Among the modern players, the name Wooden often mentions first is Oscar Robertson, "who, in his prime, could do more things and was the finest all-around player I've seen. Not the most valuable, by any means [Wooden leans toward Alcindor in this regard], but could do more things. Score, play good defense when he wanted to, and pass well without dribbling behind his back or throwing it behind his back. He looked for the pass first, too, rather than the shot. Some think he loafs — to me he just doesn't waste energy. He doesn't *run* down the floor if there's no point in getting there that fast.

"On occasions, people have made the comment on one of my players that 'Boy, he's a real hustler, diving for loose balls, all over the floor!' I say, 'Yes, he hustles all the time but he never gets anything done.'"

Assuming shoes, basketballs, coaching techniques, and such were equal for both, how would Wooden, the intense competitor of the 1920s and 1930s, match up against Oscar Robertson, the superstar of the 1950s, 60s, and 70s? Wooden smiles.

"I could never compare myself with Robertson," he says. "At my height [5-10] I'm not even sure I could play today. But I am pleased that when Tony Hinkle, who's been around Indiana basketball for many, many years, named his all-time state high school team, he said, 'Well, you start with Johnny Wooden, then Oscar Robertson, then Fuzzy Vandiver.'"

On why he's never coached a professional team: "I enjoyed high school teaching and coaching as much as anything I've ever done. I enjoy college coaching and I'd like the *challenge* of pro coaching. But the type of men you deal with in the pros, the traveling, this is a different kind of life and I know I'd have trouble adjusting."

He's turned down many professional opportunities and one question will never be answered: How could the master college coach do in a different game?

CHAPTER 14

Loneliness of the Long-Distance Coach

WHEN THE STAR MEMBERS of his current team — the Bill Waltons and the Keith Wilkeses — were freshmen, John Wooden made a promise. He would stay to coach them until they finished their college careers.

That would be after next season, 1973-1974. He would be sixty-three years old. Retirement age at UCLA is sixty-five, but he could be allowed to go on coaching there until he's sixty-seven.

Nell Wooden says that his children — Jim and Nan — would just as soon he got out of it as soon as he can — even right now.

"These last few years haven't been the happiest of our lives," Nell says. "Fans are so greedy. They're dissatisfied if we win a championship game by only five points. That's why his children want him to get out. If he loses, then a lot of fans are going to say he's too old and has lost his touch. You learn to condition yourself to critics — if he hadn't, he would have broken sometime during the last eight or nine years. But they do have an effect.

"I've never asked him to get out of coaching but I think he's about ready. He's been in it thirty-seven years, twenty-four of them at UCLA. I don't know if he'll ever really retire in the truest sense — leave basketball entirely, I mean.

"I'll see him after one season ends, sitting in a chair and jotting down on a newspaper his line-ups for the next year. He doesn't feel he'll miss the excitement, but I don't know . . ."

Wooden himself is much more reserved when he talks about retirement. He doesn't go much past, "Yes, I'll miss basketball. Everything I have in life is directly or indirectly related to basketball. But my health is good and there are other things I'd enjoy."

What things? Well, he talks about his basketball camps, which he runs along with another powerful, behind-the-scenes figure in UCLA athletics, Max Shapiro, and the "joy" he gets working with youngsters. And he's thought of television work, as a sports commentator.

"We could never just close ourselves off," says Nell. "We've been around too many people too long. And if you just stand in one place, it gets boring."

It would be more than a little ironic if Wooden turned TV reporter because he has "used" the press and the media in many, mostly subtle, ways over the years. He has employed an effective brand of psychology with writers and broadcasters, just as he has with players.

After each game — while his players are sealed off in the quiet of the locker room — Wooden briefly "holds court" for reporters. Someone will ask about a player who'd scored twenty-five points, taken down eighteen rebounds, and blocked seven shots, and Wooden might answer, "Well, fellows, he was good, but he did look a little lazy out there tonight . . . and he wasn't hitting the open man the way he should have been. Now who we *really* should talk about is . . ."

And he'll pick a name, maybe an obscure name of a player who needs to have his ego boosted at this particular point in the season.

Many of the writers will downgrade the star — just as Wooden has done — and praise the sub, and the coach will have accomplished two valuable objectives.

"I caught on to his tricks early," says a newspaper writer who once covered UCLA basketball games. "And I quickly developed my own approach. I'd leave the press table the last minute or so before the game ended and be waiting for Wooden at the bench. I'd conduct *my* interview as he walked from the bench to the dressing room . . . and then stand there in the background and listen to him tell reporters from bigger papers just the opposite of what he told me. Often, from behind his rolled-up program, he'd smile at me as he talked. I should add that he was honest with me. He is not, by nature, a devious man, and I had already made clear both my knowledge of basketball and my unwillingness to play his game."

John Wooden is a man who has been enormously successful employing the tricks of — and, to an extent, speaking the language of — one generation, while he would appear to be more comfortable in another.

His major victories, as a coach, have come in his later years, in the twentieth century. But he might be more at home in the nineteenth century, running a white, frame, one-room school as principal and teacher, and maybe serving one night a week as unpaid village mayor.

He has existed and bent in the world of ban the bombs, the bras, and the bullshit, but if you had to place him it would be in a time capsule of a different world — horse-drawn buggies, gas lamps, and Sunday afternoon picnics, after church, down on the banks of the Wabash. Occasionally, he'd crane his neck and look out into the next century but then he'd withdraw into the time capsule again.

Success has not spoiled him, but, in a way, it has consumed him. Once you win a national championship — despite what he sometimes says — there is nothing left to do but win another and another and another.

John Wooden was an artist in his playing days, a man who used to fly into the bleachers game after game to prove himself. Now he's asking young men to do roughly the same things. It has been, so it shall be.

How will history judge him?

Like Lombardi? No, Wooden is revered by many but few fear him except rival coaches.

Like Stengel? No. Wooden's words are precise, incisive, and grammatical.

Like Rupp? No. Wooden has courted some players while he has coached them.

So, what is he, then? Selfless, yes, if sometimes with a purpose. Prideful, with a touch of vanity, certainly. Looking for the Edge, the Extra Edge, always.

All of this is part of his legacy. He grew up in the Depression and for him like so many others molded in that time work is nearly everything. He saw his father lose crops, lose hogs through improper use of a serum, eventually lose his farm and have to move into town and take a demeaning job. Wooden has forgotten none of this, just as others have not forgotten fleeing the Dust Bowl of the prairies or picking head lettuce in the Northwest from dawn to dusk, just to live. His credo is hard work. If you work hard, work better than the next man, then you will beat him — and you will provide well for yourself and your family. It is Wooden's Game Plan for Life.

The dominance that goes along with that standard, perhaps, is the ultimate difference between men, particularly Midwestern men who grew to maturity when the country was lying on its back and being counted out in the early 1930s.

The determination creates winners and this is still a nation that enshrines its winners. Wooden already has been enshrined and will be more so. As one UCLA official says: "Won't it be something, in the years to come, just to say you knew him — and knew him well enough to call him 'John'?"

And it is as Lombardi said: "The will to excel and the will to win; they endure. They are more important than any of the events that occasion them."

And, ah, yes, the team. Five men, working as one, subjugating their own identities for the good of the whole. A player passes the ball to another player who passes it to a player who scores. By the numbers. One, two, three, push-pull, click-click. Beautiful to behold. And the coach, standing off to one side, smiling ever so slightly and looking very pleased.

Los Angeles *Times* columnist Jim Murray, taking a look at the scene one day, wondered where Johnny Wooden had put his coveralls and pitchfork. "He looks like something that escaped from that painting of American Gothic," wrote Murray. "He is so square, he's divisible by four."

But the square little man has fit a lot of his players into the right slots — a remarkable number, probably, considering his background and theirs, and the vast personal and generational differences.

A recent player can say of him, "He has this gigantic ego. He is sold on John Wooden. He has this thing about becoming the greatest basketball coach of all time." Yet, even feeling this way, the same player will remain at UCLA, play for John Wooden, and help him win national championships.

A couple of years ago, the players from Wooden's first twenty-two teams held a reunion. "We just thought it was about time to get together," said Jerry Norman, the 1951-1952 co-captain and former assistant coach. "We're not honoring anybody or anything in particular. Just ourselves. We wanted to see what we had been up to."

And what had they been up to? Well, some were coaches, some pro players, some teachers, some attorneys, some dentists, some actors, one a doctor, one a minister, many business executives. Success, obviously, had followed success.

What's more, Wooden has done several other things. He has turned college basketball into almost an obsession for many people. He has given kicks — and a sense of being part of a winner — to fans throughout the nation. More than a few people use the pronoun "we" when they talk about UCLA now. John Wooden and Bruin basketball are the reasons.

Most, if they recognize the name John Wooden, probably equate it with success.

That is not an unfair appraisal but it is incomplete. The facet of the man that has been the least explored, perhaps, is the loneliness that seems to surround him, that forces him to keep moving and punching and looking over his shoulder to make sure that nobody is gaining on him — aware of how fragile any "achievement," even one as majestic as his, really is.

It does not seem by accident that he usually takes pains to say, after making a controversial statement: "Of course, this is just my belief. Others might think different."

This is part of his image-building that appears to mask an enduring insecurity. That farm — his father's farm back in Indiana — is figuratively safe from the creditors. Bought and paid for, many times over. But it does not seem that, behind the often tough exterior and the championship luster, John Wooden will really admit it to himself.

The room overflows with inane cocktail-party gabble that is so typical of college sports booster club gatherings: "So very nice to meet you but didn't you used to write *for* USC?" a fan asks a sportswriter . . . "Tell me, do you like the coaches at UCLA better than the coaches at USC?" . . . "Dammit, why does that John Hall *always* write about USC? He's a Stanford grad, isn't he?" . . . "Tell me, who's better, Alcindor or Walton?" . . . "You know, it sure is nice to have *you* with us this year instead of that *other* guy. Why, he's negative, not with our program" . . . "What do you think? Can we go all the way again? Guards a little weak? What's wrong with the zone press this year? Got the greatest coach, though, haven't we?"

They break up into knots of men at tables, the jabbering rising as each round of martinis arrives and is consumed, and you wonder if their sons are in more private places, smoking grass or blowing hash.

Sitting at the head table with a writer, drinking coffee, is John Robert Wooden. It's his world and welcome to it. He's the featured speaker, hero, Saint John, as long as he keeps on winning, condemned behind his back to hellfire and damnation if he loses. But he's alone in the crowd — always and still alone.

Not so far removed from that day a quarter century ago when a writer thrust a drink in his face and said, "You gotta have one with me." Not so far removed from the prepositional phrases and dangling participles and misplaced modifiers in a South Bend Central classroom.

He turns to the writer — who has become a friend — and for the moment all the sham and half-truths and manipulations and subtle image-building and maintaining are gone.

Here is an exceedingly bright man and brilliant coach who has brought vicarious pleasure to millions and riches to his school looking out on a room full of half-drunk men and leveling, really leveling. For the moment, he is forgetting the thunderclap cheers of Kansas City and Portland and Louisville and College Park and Houston and Los Angeles. He is not tossing in qualifying phrases like, "Oh, but that's the way it really is, I guess; I don't like it, but I have to live with it."

What he is saying, looking out on that raucous group of middle-aged men in conservative gray and brown and blue business suits, is: "The place wasn't this full in the old days. I wonder how many of my friends would still be out there if we were losing?"

No answer came. He knew the question was enough.